There Are So Many Reasons to Celebrate

Flip through your datebook or calendar, and you'll be reminded of the many occasions throughout the year that call for a memorable meal: holiday dinners, kids parties, special luncheons, game-day gatherings, brunch buffets, backyard barbecues and other moments worth celebrating. This year's *Taste of Home Holiday & Celebrations* cookbook serves up 23 events and 248 impressive dishes, all guaranteed to have guests piling their plates high and begging for the recipe. More than just a collection of great menu ideas, the book you're holding features hundreds of gorgeous photos, a handy guide for setting the perfect table, timelines to help you get everything done, quick and easy decorating ideas, and clever kitchen tips and how-to's for making the most of your culinary creations. Let the celebration begin!

SUBMIT YOUR RECIPE!

Would you like to see one of your family recipes featured in a *Taste of Home* collection?

Visit **tasteofhome.com/submit** to share your story and recipes.

ON THE COVER

ON THE FRONT COVER
Gingerbread Snow Globe (p. 71)

ON THE BACK COVER
Crown Roast with Apricot Dressing (p. 32); Strawberry Watermelon Lemonade (p. 219); Chicken & Cheddar Biscuit Casserole (p. 190); Gender Reveal Cake (p. 214)

PAGE 62

PAGE 161

PAGE 204

PAGE 103

PAGE 172

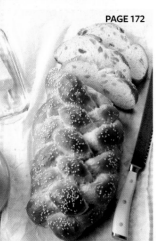

PAGE 244

Taste of Home
Holiday
& CELEBRATIONS

EDITORIAL

Editor-in-Chief **Catherine Cassidy**

Vice President, Content Operations **Kerri Balliet**
Creative Director **Howard Greenberg**

Managing Editor/Print & Digital Books **Mark Hagen**
Associate Creative Director **Edwin Robles Jr.**

Editor **Amy Glander**
Associate Editor **Julie Kuczynski**
Art Director **Raeann Sundholm**
Layout Designer **Courtney Lovetere**
Editorial Production Manager **Dena Ahlers**
Editorial Production Coordinator **Jill Banks**
Copy Chief **Deb Warlaumont Mulvey**
Copy Editors **Chris McLaughlin, Ellie Piper, Dulcie Shoener**
Contributing Copy Editors **Michael Juley, Valerie Phillips, Kristin Sutter**
Editorial Intern **Maddie Rashid**

Content Director **Julie Blume Benedict**
Food Editor **Peggy Woodward, RDN**
Recipe Editors **Sue Ryon (lead), Mary King, Irene Yeh**
Business Architect, Publishing Technologies **Amanda Harmatys**
Solutions Architect, Publishing Technologies **John Mosey**
Business Analyst, Publishing Technologies **Kate Unger**
Junior Business Analyst, Publishing Technologies **Shannon Stroud**
Editorial Services Administrator **Marie Brannon**

Test Kitchen & Food Styling Manager **Sarah Thompson**
Test Cooks **Nicholas Iverson (lead), Matthew Hass, Lauren Knoelke**
Food Stylists **Kathryn Conrad (lead), Shannon Roum, Leah Rekau**
Prep Cooks **Bethany Van Jacobson (lead), Melissa Hansen, Aria C. Thornton**
Culinary Team Assistant **Megan Behr**

Photography Director **Stephanie Marchese**
Photographers **Dan Roberts, Jim Wieland**
Photographer/Set Stylist **Grace Natoli Sheldon**
Set Stylists **Melissa Franco (lead), Stacey Genaw, Dee Dee Jacq**
Set Stylist Assistant **Stephanie Chojnacki**

Editorial Business Manager **Kristy Martin**
Rights & Permissions Associate **Samantha Lea Stoeger**
Editorial Business Associate **Andrea Heeg Polzin**

Editor, *Taste of Home* **Emily Betz Tyra**
Associate Creative Director, *Taste of Home* **Erin Timmons**
Art Director, *Taste of Home* **Kristin Bowker**

BUSINESS

Vice President, Group Publisher **Kirsten Marchioli**
Publisher, *Taste of Home* **Donna Lindskog**
Business Development Director, Taste of Home Live **Laurel Osman**
Promotional Partnerships Manager, Taste of Home Live **Jamie Piette Andrzejewski**

TRUSTED MEDIA BRANDS, INC.

President & Chief Executive Officer **Bonnie Kintzer**

Chief Financial Officer **Dean Durbin**
Chief Marketing Officer **C. Alec Casey**
Chief Revenue Officer **Richard Sutton**
Chief Digital Officer **Vince Errico**
Senior Vice President, Global HR & Communications
Phyllis E. Gebhardt, SPHR; SHRM-SCP
General Counsel **Mark Sirota**
Vice President, Magazine Marketing **Christopher Gaydos**
Vice President, Operations **Michael Garzone**
Vice President, Consumer Marketing Planning **Jim Woods**
Vice President, Digital Product & Technology **Nick Contardo**
Vice President, Digital Content & Audience Development **Diane Dragan**
Vice President, Financial Planning & Analysis **William Houston**
Publishing Director, Books **Debra Polansky**

FRONT COVER PHOTOGRAPHY

Photographer **Dan Roberts**
Food Stylist **Leah Rekau**
Set Stylist **Melissa Franco**

© 2016 RDA Enthusiast Brands, LLC.
1610 N. 2nd St., Suite 102, Milwaukee WI 53212-3906

International Standard Book Number: 978-1-61765-555-5
International Standard Serial Number: 1535-2781
Component Number: 118000046H
All Rights Reserved.

Printed in USA.
1 3 5 7 9 10 8 6 4 2

Table of Contents

'Tis the Season

Giving Thanks

Easter Gatherings

Special Celebrations

'Tis the Season

Twinkling lights, the aroma of warm cookies, stockings hung by the chimney with joyful anticipation...Christmas is steeped in tradition and in the making of cherished memories. Capture the magic and merriment with an impressive lineup of foods. From tantalizing appetizers and fun finger foods to hearty pasta dishes and showstopping cakes, here's how to make this year's celebration unforgettable.

Holiday Appetizers

It's the most wonderful time of the year...the season of good food, good cheer and a "more is merrier" frame of mind. From large to small, casual to formal, impromptu to planned, happy holiday parties abound. **And nothing kicks off a festive celebration like cheesy dips, creamy spreads and nibbles of all kinds.**

Introduce guests to fun, new flavors with Warm Feta Cheese Dip, Mushroom Bundles, Mini Mac & Cheese Bites and other tantalizing seasonal starters.

With this lineup of special occasion finger foods and a few easy party-planning tips (p. 15) in your arsenal, **you're in for a celebration that's nothing short of impressive.**

Festive Holiday Sliders (p. 15) **Antipasto Cups** (p. 10) **Warm Feta Cheese Dip** (p. 10)

CURRIED CRAB SPREAD

CURRIED CRAB SPREAD

Keep ingredients on hand for this easy and elegant crab spread, and drop-in holiday guests will get a special snack.

—**JENNIFER PHILLIPS** GOFFSTOWN, NH

START TO FINISH: 30 MIN. • **MAKES:** 24 SERVINGS

- 1 **package (8 ounces) cream cheese, softened**
- 1 **teaspoon grated lemon peel**
- ¾ **teaspoon curry powder**
- ¼ **teaspoon salt**
- 1 **to 2 teaspoons Sriracha Asian hot chili sauce, optional**
- 1 **can (6 ounces) lump crabmeat, drained**
- 1 **tablespoon canola oil**
- ½ **cup panko (Japanese) bread crumbs**
- ¾ **cup mango chutney**
- 1 **tablespoon minced fresh cilantro or chives**
  Assorted crackers

1. In a small bowl, beat cream cheese, lemon peel, curry powder, salt and, if desired, chili sauce; gently fold in crab. Shape into a disk; wrap in plastic wrap. Refrigerate 15 minutes.
2. Meanwhile, in a large skillet, heat oil over medium heat. Add bread crumbs; cook and stir for 2-3 minutes or until golden brown. Transfer bread crumbs to a shallow bowl.
3. Unwrap disk and press all sides into bread crumbs; place on a serving plate. Spoon chutney over top; sprinkle with cilantro. Serve with crackers.

DID YOU KNOW?

Curry 101

Curry powder is a blend of many different ground spices used to replicate the individual spices combined in the cuisine of India. It imparts a distinctive flavor and rich golden color to recipes and can be found in both mild and hot versions. Season dishes lightly with curry powder and add more as desired to reach an acceptable spice level.

MUSHROOM BUNDLES

MUSHROOM BUNDLES

Guests always count on me to invent fun starters and drinks. I made up this recipe for a holiday party. After these bundles, everyone was fed, happy and wanting to come back for more.

—**TINA COOPMAN** TORONTO, ON

PREP: 30 MIN. • **BAKE:** 15 MIN. • **MAKES:** 1 DOZEN

- 1 **tablespoon olive oil**
- 1 **cup chopped fresh mushrooms**
- 1 **cup chopped baby portobello mushrooms**
- ¼ **cup finely chopped red onion**
- 2 **garlic cloves, minced**
- ¼ **teaspoon dried rosemary, crushed**
- ⅛ **teaspoon pepper**
- 4 **sheets phyllo dough (14x9-inch size)**
- 3 **tablespoons butter, melted**
- 2 **tablespoons crumbled feta cheese**

1. Preheat oven to 375°. In a large skillet, heat the oil over medium-high heat. Add mushrooms and onion; cook and stir 4-5 minutes or until tender. Add garlic, rosemary and pepper; cook 2 minutes longer. Remove from heat.
2. Place one sheet of phyllo dough on a work surface; brush with butter. (Keep remaining phyllo covered with plastic wrap and a damp towel to prevent it from drying out.) Layer with three additional phyllo sheets, brushing each layer. Using a sharp knife, cut layered sheets into twelve 3-in. squares. Carefully press each stack into ungreased mini-muffin cup.
3. Stir feta into mushroom mixture; spoon 1 tablespoon into each phyllo cup. Form into bundles by gathering edges of phyllo squares and twisting centers to close. Brush the tops with remaining butter. Bake 12-15 minutes or until golden brown. Serve warm.
FREEZE OPTION *Freeze cooled pastries in resealable plastic freezer bags. To use, reheat pastries on a greased baking sheet in a preheated 375° oven until crisp and heated through.*

ANTIPASTO CUPS

These cups are easier to fill than the stockings hung by the chimney. Use different veggies and cheese to make them exactly how you'd like them. See photo on page 7.

—MELISSA OBERNESSER UTICA, NY

PREP: 20 MIN. • **BAKE:** 10 MIN./BATCH
MAKES: 2 DOZEN

- 24 slices Genoa salami (3½ inches)
- 1 can (14 ounces) water-packed artichoke hearts
- 1 jar (8 ounces) marinated whole mushrooms
- 1 jar (8 ounces) roasted sweet red peppers
- ½ pound fresh mozzarella cheese, cut into ½-inch cubes
- 3 tablespoons olive oil
- 2 tablespoons red wine vinegar
- ½ teaspoon garlic salt
- ⅛ teaspoon pepper

1. Preheat oven to 400°. Press half of the salami into twelve muffin cups. Loosely crumple aluminum foil to form twelve 2-in. balls; place in cups to keep salami from sliding. Bake 6-8 minutes or until edges begin to brown. Using tongs, remove from pans and invert onto paper towels to drain. Wipe muffin cups clean. Repeat with remaining salami, reusing foil balls.

2. Meanwhile, drain and coarsely chop artichoke hearts, mushrooms and red peppers; transfer to a small bowl. Stir in cheese. In another bowl, whisk oil, vinegar, garlic salt and pepper until blended. Drizzle over vegetable mixture; toss to coat. Using a slotted spoon, fill salami cups with vegetable mixture.

MINI MAC & CHEESE BITES

I made these for a Christmas gathering because I wanted something fun for my young nephews and niece to eat. As it turns out, the adults also loved them. The poor kids only got to have a few!

—KATE MAINIERO POUGHKEEPSIE, NY

PREP: 35 MIN. • **BAKE:** 10 MIN. • **MAKES:** 3 DOZEN

- 2 cups uncooked elbow macaroni
- 1 cup seasoned bread crumbs, divided
- 2 tablespoons butter
- 2 tablespoons all-purpose flour
- ½ teaspoon onion powder
- ½ teaspoon garlic powder
- ½ teaspoon seasoned salt
- 1¾ cups 2% milk
- 2 cups (8 ounces) shredded sharp cheddar cheese, divided
- 1 cup (4 ounces) shredded Swiss cheese
- ¾ cup biscuit/baking mix
- 2 large eggs, lightly beaten

1. Preheat oven to 425°. Cook macaroni according to package directions; drain.

2. Meanwhile, sprinkle ¼ cup bread crumbs into 36 greased mini-muffin cups. In a large saucepan, melt butter over medium heat. Stir in flour and seasonings until smooth; gradually whisk in milk. Bring mixture to a boil, stirring constantly; cook and stir 1-2 minutes or until thickened. Stir in 1 cup cheddar cheese and Swiss cheese until melted.

3. Remove from heat; stir in biscuit mix, eggs and ½ cup bread crumbs. Add macaroni; toss to coat. Spoon about 2 tablespoons of the macaroni mixture into prepared mini-muffin cups; sprinkle with remaining cheddar cheese and bread crumbs.

4. Bake 8-10 minutes or until golden brown. Cool in pans 5 minutes before serving.

WARM FETA CHEESE DIP

—ASHLEY LECKER GREEN BAY, WI

START TO FINISH: 30 MIN. • **MAKES:** 2 CUPS

- 1 package (8 ounces) cream cheese, softened
- 1½ cups (6 ounces) crumbled feta cheese
- ½ cup chopped roasted sweet red peppers
- 3 tablespoons minced fresh basil or 2 teaspoons dried basil
  Sliced French bread baguette or tortilla chips

Preheat oven to 400°. In a small bowl, beat cream cheese, feta cheese, peppers and basil until blended. Transfer to a greased 3-cup baking dish. Bake 25-30 minutes or until bubbly. Serve with baguette slices or chips.

SPICED NUTS

These seasoned mixed nuts make a great gift for a party host or you could tuck some in with a Christmas present for a yummy touch. We like cardamom so I often add another teaspoon to this recipe.

—JUDI OUDEKERK BUFFALO, MN

PREP: 20 MIN. + COOLING • **MAKES:** 3½ CUPS

- ¼ cup butter, cubed
- ½ cup plus 3 tablespoons sugar, divided
- 2 teaspoons ground cardamom
- 1 cup salted cashews
- 1 cup salted peanuts
- 1 cup pecan halves

1. In a large heavy skillet, melt butter. Add ½ cup sugar; cook and stir over high heat until sugar is dissolved. Meanwhile, place cardamom and remaining sugar in a large bowl; set aside.

2. Reduce heat to medium; add the cashews, peanuts and pecans to butter mixture. Cook and stir until nuts are toasted, about 3 minutes. Add hot nuts to reserved cardamom mixture; toss to coat. Spread on foil to cool.

WARM FETA CHEESE DIP

"We're big on eating appetizers at our house. This cheesy dip is a mash-up of some of our favorite ingredients—basil, sweet peppers and feta."

—ASHLEY LECKER, GREEN BAY, WI

BEST-EVER STUFFED MUSHROOMS

I make these small delights every Christmas Eve. If you don't have mushrooms on hand, spread the filling on baguette slices or crackers. It's a good veggie dip, too.

—DEBBY BEARD EAGLE, CO

PREP: 20 MIN. • **BAKE:** 15 MIN.
MAKES: 2½ DOZEN

- **1 pound bulk pork sausage**
- **¼ cup finely chopped onion**
- **1 garlic clove, minced**
- **1 package (8 ounces) reduced-fat cream cheese**
- **¼ cup shredded Parmesan cheese**
- **⅓ cup seasoned bread crumbs**
- **3 teaspoons dried basil**
- **1½ teaspoons dried parsley flakes**
- **30 large fresh mushrooms (about 1½ pounds), stems removed**
- **3 tablespoons butter, melted**

1. Preheat oven to 400°. In a large skillet, cook sausage, onion and garlic over medium heat 6-8 minutes or until sausage is no longer pink and onion is tender, breaking up sausage into crumbles; drain. Add cream cheese and Parmesan cheese; cook and stir until melted. Stir in bread crumbs, basil and parsley.

2. Meanwhile, place mushroom caps in a greased 15x10x1-in. baking pan, stem side up. Brush with butter. Spoon the sausage mixture into mushroom caps. Bake, uncovered, 12-15 minutes or until mushrooms are tender.

TOP TIP

Preparing Mushrooms

Mushrooms can be eaten raw, marinated, sauteed, stir-fried, baked, broiled or grilled. To clean mushrooms, gently remove dirt by rubbing with a mushroom brush or a damp paper towel. Do not peel. To remove the stems, hold mushroom cap in one hand and grab the stem with the other hand. Twist to snap off the stem. Proceed as recipe directs.

BEST-EVER STUFFED MUSHROOMS

GINGER PORK LETTUCE WRAPS

These snack wraps provide a wonderful taste and texture combination. The first time I served them, we ate so many that we were too full for supper. I've also used ground chicken in them.
—**MARY KISINGER** MEDICINE HAT, AB

START TO FINISH: 30 MIN. • **MAKES:** 2 DOZEN

- 1 **pound lean ground pork**
- 1 **medium onion, chopped**
- ¼ **cup hoisin sauce**
- 4 **garlic cloves, minced**
- 1 **tablespoon minced fresh gingerroot**
- 1 **tablespoon red wine vinegar**
- 1 **tablespoon reduced-sodium soy sauce**
- 2 **teaspoons Thai chili sauce**
- 1 **can (8 ounces) sliced water chestnuts, drained and finely chopped**
- 4 **green onions, chopped**
- 1 **tablespoon sesame oil**
- 24 **Bibb or Boston lettuce leaves**

1. In a large skillet, cook pork and onion over medium heat 6-8 minutes or until pork is no longer pink and onion is tender, breaking up pork into crumbles.

2. Stir in hoisin sauce, garlic, ginger, vinegar, soy sauce and chili sauce until blended. Add water chestnuts, green onions and oil; heat through. To serve, place pork mixture in lettuce leaves; fold lettuce over filling.

FREEZE OPTION *Freeze cooled meat mixture in freezer containers. To use, partially thaw in refrigerator overnight. Heat through in a saucepan, stirring occasionally and adding a little water if necessary.*

GINGER PORK LETTUCE WRAPS

GORGONZOLA POLENTA BITES

Here's a cozy appetizer for a cold day. The flavors blend so well, and prepared polenta makes the prep super fast.
—**MARGEE BERRY** WHITE SALMON, WA

START TO FINISH: 25 MIN.
MAKES: 16 APPETIZERS

- ⅓ **cup balsamic vinegar**
- 1 **tablespoon orange marmalade**
- ½ **cup panko (Japanese) bread crumbs**
- 1 **tube (18 ounces) polenta, cut into 16 slices**
- 2 **tablespoons olive oil**
- ½ **cup crumbled Gorgonzola cheese**
- 3 **tablespoons dried currants, optional**

1. In a small saucepan, combine vinegar and marmalade. Bring to a boil; cook 5-7 minutes or until liquid is reduced to 2 tablespoons.

2. Meanwhile, place bread crumbs in a shallow bowl. Press both sides of polenta slices in bread crumbs. In a large skillet, heat oil over medium-high heat. Add polenta in batches; cook 2-4 minutes on each side or until golden brown.

3. Arrange polenta on a serving platter; spoon cheese over top. Sprinkle with currants if desired; drizzle with vinegar mixture. Serve warm or at room temperature.

SWEET & SPICY ASIAN
CHICKEN PETITES

SWEET & SPICY ASIAN CHICKEN PETITES

My family loves Asian flavors and finger food, which inspired me to create this appetizer. It's super quick and fun to make. And seconds are a must! Freeze a batch to reheat when guests stop by.
—**JEANETTE NELSON** BRIDGEPORT, WV

PREP: 25 MIN. • **BAKE:** 10 MIN.
MAKES: 16 APPETIZERS

- 4 teaspoons olive oil, divided
- ⅓ cup finely chopped sweet red pepper
- 3 green onions, finely chopped
- 2 garlic cloves, minced
- 1 cup finely chopped cooked chicken breast
- 2 tablespoons island teriyaki sauce
- 1 tablespoon white grapefruit juice or water
- 1 tablespoon sesame oil
- 1 teaspoon Sriracha Asian hot chili sauce
- 1 tube (8 ounces) refrigerated crescent rolls
- 2 teaspoons sesame seeds
  Sweet chili sauce

1. Preheat oven to 375°. In a large skillet, heat 2 teaspoons olive oil over medium-high heat. Add red pepper, green onions and garlic; cook and stir 3-5 minutes or until vegetables are tender. Stir in the chicken, teriyaki sauce, grapefruit juice, sesame oil and hot chili sauce. Remove from the heat; cool slightly.
2. Unroll the crescent dough into one long rectangle; press perforations to seal. Roll the dough into a 12-in. square; cut into sixteen 3-in. squares. Place 1 tablespoon chicken mixture in center of each square. Bring edges of dough over filling, pinching seams to seal; shape into a ball.
3. Place on ungreased baking sheets, seam side down. Brush tops with remaining olive oil; sprinkle with sesame seeds. Bake 10-12 minutes or until golden brown. Serve warm with sweet chili sauce.
FREEZE OPTION *Freeze cooled appetizers in resealable plastic freezer bags. To use, reheat the appetizers on a baking sheet in a preheated 375° oven until heated through.*

GARLIC-ONION APPETIZER ROUNDS

I think this recipe is the perfect way to showcase Hawaii's famous, local Maui sweet onions. They thrive in our balmy tropical climate and rich, volcanic soil. The appetizer is a beautiful addition to any holiday spread.
—**KRISTINE SNYDER** KIHEI, HI

PREP: 30 MIN. + COOLING • **BAKE:** 15 MIN.
MAKES: 16 APPETIZERS

- 2 large sweet onions, chopped (about 4 cups)
- 2 tablespoons butter
- 2 garlic cloves, minced
- 1 sheet frozen puff pastry, thawed
- 1 large egg
- 1 tablespoon water
- ⅓ cup shredded Swiss cheese
- ¼ cup grated Parmesan cheese
- 2 tablespoons minced fresh basil

1. In a large skillet over medium-low heat, cook onions in butter until golden brown, stirring frequently. Add garlic; cook 1 minute longer. Remove from the heat; cool to room temperature.
2. Unfold puff pastry. In a small bowl, whisk egg and water; brush over pastry. Spread onion mixture to within ½ in. of edges. Sprinkle with cheeses and basil; roll up jelly-roll style. Cut into 16 slices.
3. Place 2 in. apart on greased baking sheets. Bake at 425° for 12-14 minutes or until puffed and golden brown. Serve warm.

FESTIVE HOLIDAY SLIDERS

I almost called these S'more Holiday Sliders because whenever I make them my friends ask, "Do you have s'more?" These stand up well in the fridge, so I make them in advance for get-togethers when we bake or wrap presents. See photo on page 7.
—**PAMELA MILLER** BIG RAPIDS, MI

START TO FINISH: 30 MIN. • **MAKES:** 2 DOZEN

- 1 package (8 ounces) cream cheese, softened
- ½ cup mayonnaise
- ¼ cup Creole mustard
- 2 tablespoons minced fresh gingerroot
- 1 tablespoon grated orange peel
- 1½ teaspoons prepared horseradish
- 1 cup whole-berry cranberry sauce
- 4 green onions, sliced
- 2 packages (12 ounces each) Hawaiian sweet rolls or 24 dinner rolls
- 1½ pounds thinly sliced cooked turkey

1. In a small bowl, beat cream cheese and mayonnaise until smooth. Beat in mustard, ginger, orange peel and the horseradish. In another bowl, mix cranberry sauce and green onions.
2. Spread cream cheese mixture on roll bottoms. Top with cranberry mixture and turkey; replace tops.

TOP TIP

Party Planning Made Easy

Whether simple or fancy, savory or sweet, hot or cold, appetizers offer versatility and variety when entertaining. And as an added benefit, many appetizers can be made ahead of time—some even weeks in advance and then frozen—so you can be ready for guests at a moment's notice or relaxed when party time arrives.

When planning which appetizers to serve, don't overdo it. It's better to prepare a few good choices than to stress over making a lot of items. Start with one spectacular appetizer and then complete your menu with additional easy but delicious foods and beverages.

Choose from an assortment of hot, cold and room temperature foods. Select recipes that offer a variety of colors, textures (soft and crunchy) and flavors (sour, salty, savory, sweet, spicy or subtle). Mix in one or two lighter options to cater to guests concerned about calories or fat. Look for appetizers that make a nice presentation with no last-minute fussing.

Holiday Pasta Party

Happiness is a steaming hot meal on a cold winter's night. Enter pasta. A big platter filled with oodles of noodles brings as much comfort and joy as the seasonal standbys served at more formal affairs, while the laid-back vibe still lets you pull out all the stops.

Escape the ordinary with gooey Alfredo-style lasagna that bakes to bubbly perfection. **Put a tasty twist** on stuffed manicotti that boasts a zesty Southwestern appeal. As for My Best Spaghetti and Meatballs? You'll agree this classic lives up to its name.

The enticing flavors in each of these pasta specialties will have you and your guests shouting "Mangia!" **Let the celebration begin!**

My Best Spaghetti & Meatballs (p. 23)

BOW TIES WITH
GORGONZOLA SAUCE

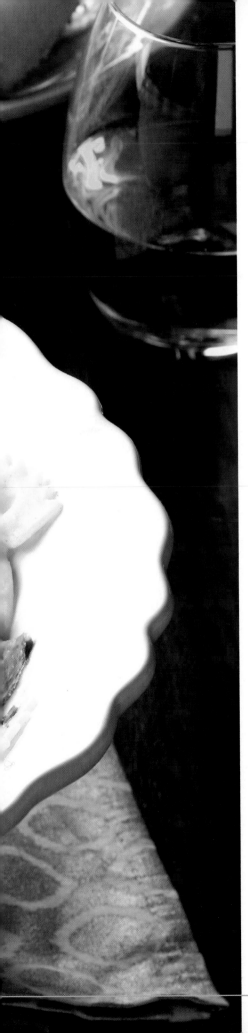

BOW TIES WITH GORGONZOLA SAUCE

No need to wear bow ties, this pasta dish is comforting and simple to prepare. Add a mixed green salad to make it a complete meal for any occasion.

—**NADINE MESCH** MOUNT HEALTHY, OH

START TO FINISH: 30 MIN. • **MAKES:** 8 SERVINGS

- 1 **package (16 ounces) bow tie pasta**
- 1 **package (16 ounces) bulk pork sausage**
- 2 **tablespoons butter**
- 2 **tablespoons all-purpose flour**
- 1½ **cups half-and-half cream**
- ¾ **cup crumbled Gorgonzola cheese**
- ¾ **teaspoon salt**
- ½ **teaspoon lemon-pepper seasoning**
- 4 **cups fresh spinach, lightly packed**
- 3 **tablespoons minced fresh basil**

1. Cook pasta according to package directions. Drain; return to pan. Meanwhile, in a large skillet, cook sausage over medium heat 4-6 minutes or until no longer pink, breaking into crumbles; drain.
2. In a small saucepan, melt butter over medium heat. Stir in flour until smooth; gradually whisk in cream. Bring to a boil, stirring constantly; cook and stir 1-2 minutes or until thickened. Remove from heat. Stir in cheese, salt and lemon pepper. Add cheese sauce, sausage and spinach to hot pasta; toss to combine. Sprinkle with basil.

CREAMY PUMPKIN TORTELLINI

My kids love the creamy, rich sauce on these tortellinis so much that they don't even know pumpkin is inside. Use freshly grated Parmesan cheese for the best, nutty and delicious flavor.

—**TRISHA KRUSE** EAGLE, ID

START TO FINISH: 30 MIN.
MAKES: 6 SERVINGS

- 2 **packages (9 ounces each) refrigerated cheese tortellini**
- 1 **tablespoon butter**
- 3 **tablespoons finely chopped onion**
- 1 **cup solid-pack pumpkin**
  Pinch ground nutmeg
- 1 **cup half-and-half cream**
- ¼ **cup grated Parmesan cheese**
- ½ **teaspoon salt**
- ¼ **teaspoon pepper**
- 1 **tablespoon minced fresh parsley**
  Additional grated Parmesan cheese, optional

1. Cook the tortellini according to package directions; drain, reserving ½ cup cooking liquid. Meanwhile, in a large nonstick skillet, heat butter over medium heat. Add onion; cook and stir 1-2 minutes or until tender. Add pumpkin and nutmeg; cook and stir 1 minute. Stir in cream; bring to a boil. Reduce heat to medium-low; simmer, uncovered, for 4-5 minutes or until thickened, stirring mixture occasionally. Remove from heat; stir in cheese, salt and pepper.
2. Add tortellini; toss with sauce, adding enough reserved pasta water to coat pasta. Sprinkle with parsley and, if desired, additional cheese.

TOP TIP

Clever Pasta Storage

I store all my pastas in canning jars rather than the opened boxes. The pasta stays fresh, and the jars stack nicely, too, conserving pantry space. When I'm preparing my grocery list, I can see what I need at a glance.
—**LAURIE S.** GETTYSBURG, PA

SEAFOOD IN SPICY TOMATO CREAM SAUCE

My fettuccine specialty combines my love of seafood and Italian cuisine. It may look and taste upscale, but it's easy to prepare.

—GEORGE TAYLOR SPRINGFIELD, IL

PREP: 20 MIN. • **COOK:** 30 MIN.
MAKES: 8 SERVINGS

- 1 package (16 ounces) fettuccine
- 3 tablespoons butter
- 2 cups sliced fresh mushrooms
- 2 tablespoons minced fresh basil or 1½ teaspoons dried basil
- 1 teaspoon dried oregano
- ½ teaspoon dried thyme
- ¼ to ½ teaspoon cayenne pepper
- 6 garlic cloves, minced
- 1 can (14½ ounces) Italian diced tomatoes, undrained
- 1 can (10 ounces) diced tomatoes and green chilies, undrained
- 3 cups heavy whipping cream
- 2 tablespoons shredded Romano cheese
- 2 tablespoons tomato paste
- ½ teaspoon salt
- ¼ teaspoon pepper
- ¾ pound uncooked shrimp (26-30 per pound), peeled and deveined
- ¾ pound bay scallops
- ¾ pound fresh or frozen clam meat, thawed
    Additional Romano cheese and fresh basil, optional

1. Cook fettuccine according to package directions; drain.
2. Meanwhile, in a 6-qt. stockpot, heat butter over medium heat. Add mushrooms, basil, oregano, thyme and cayenne; cook and stir 1-2 minutes or until mushrooms are tender. Add garlic; cook 1 minute longer. Add both cans diced tomatoes; bring to a boil. Reduce heat; simmer, uncovered, 6-8 minutes or until liquid is almost evaporated, stirring occasionally.
3. Add the cream; bring to a boil. Reduce heat; simmer, uncovered, 10-15 minutes or until thickened. Stir in cheese, tomato paste, salt and pepper until cheese is melted. Add shrimp; cook 2 minutes. Add scallops and clam meat; cook 3 minutes longer or until shrimp turn pink. Add fettuccine; toss to coat. If desired, sprinkle with more cheese and basil.

NOTE *Two cans (6½ ounces each) chopped clams, drained, may be substituted for fresh clam meat; stir into sauce while cooking scallops.*

MEDITERRANEAN CHICKEN AND ORZO

This mouthwatering Mediterranean dish is the perfect recipe for large dinner parties. I get rave reviews every time I serve it.

—ALLYSON FERTIG AUSTIN, TX

PREP: 15 MIN. • **COOK:** 20 MIN.
MAKES: 6 SERVINGS

- 4 boneless skinless chicken breast halves (6 ounces each)
- 2 teaspoons dried basil, divided
- 2 teaspoons dried rosemary, crushed, divided
- 1½ teaspoons garlic salt, divided
- 1½ cups uncooked orzo pasta
- 6½ ounces fresh baby spinach (about 8 cups)
- ¼ cup olive oil
- 2 teaspoons ground mustard
- ½ teaspoon dried oregano
- 2 large tomatoes, seeded and chopped
- 1¼ cups shredded Asiago cheese, divided
- 1 cup (4 ounces) crumbled feta cheese
- ⅓ cup pine nuts

1. Preheat oven to 350°. Pound chicken breasts with a meat mallet to ½-in. thickness. Place chicken in a greased 15x10x1-in. baking pan. Mix 1 teaspoon basil, 1 teaspoon rosemary and ½ teaspoon garlic salt; sprinkle over chicken. Bake, uncovered, 18-20 minutes or until a thermometer reads 165°. Cut chicken into thin strips.
2. Meanwhile, in a 6-qt. stockpot, cook orzo according to package directions, adding spinach during the last minute of cooking. Drain and return to pan. In a small bowl, whisk oil, mustard, oregano and remaining basil, rosemary and garlic salt; add to orzo. Add tomatoes, 1 cup Asiago cheese, feta cheese, pine nuts and chicken; toss to combine. Sprinkle with remaining Asiago cheese.

EASY CHICKEN ALFREDO LASAGNA

My family was growing tired of traditional red sauce lasagna, so I created this fun twist using a creamy homemade Alfredo sauce. Store-bought rotisserie chicken keeps prep simple and fast.

—CAITLIN MACNEILLY UNCASVILLE, CT

PREP: 35 MIN. • **BAKE:** 45 MIN. + STANDING
MAKES: 12 SERVINGS

- 4 ounces thinly sliced pancetta, cut into strips
- 3 ounces thinly sliced prosciutto or deli ham, cut into strips
- 3 cups shredded rotisserie chicken
- 5 tablespoons unsalted butter, cubed
- ¼ cup all-purpose flour
- 4 cups whole milk
- 2 cups shredded Asiago cheese, divided
- 2 tablespoons minced fresh parsley, divided
- ¼ teaspoon coarsely ground pepper
    Pinch ground nutmeg
- 9 no-cook lasagna noodles
- 1½ cups (6 ounces) shredded part-skim mozzarella cheese
- 1½ cups shredded Parmesan cheese

1. In a large skillet, cook pancetta and prosciutto over medium heat until browned. Drain on paper towels. Transfer to a large bowl; add chicken and toss to combine.
2. For sauce, in a large saucepan, melt butter over medium heat. Stir in flour until smooth; gradually whisk in milk. Bring to a boil, stirring constantly; cook and stir 1-2 minutes or until thickened. Remove from heat; stir in ½ cup Asiago cheese, 1 tablespoon parsley, pepper and nutmeg.
3. Preheat oven to 375°. Spread ½ cup sauce into a greased 13x9-in. baking dish. Layer with a third of each of the following: lasagna noodles, sauce, meat mixture, Asiago, mozzarella and Parmesan cheeses. Repeat the layers twice.
4. Bake, covered, 30 minutes. Uncover; bake 15 minutes longer or until bubbly. Sprinkle with remaining parsley. Let lasagna stand 10 minutes before serving.

EASY CHICKEN
ALFREDO LASAGNA

LEMONY SHRIMP
& MUSHROOM
LINGUINE

LEMONY SHRIMP & MUSHROOM LINGUINE

My husband made this for me shortly before we married. I made some slight tweaks to the recipe over the years, and he says it's even better now. The lemons are a refreshing addition.

—**ANN BAKER** TEXARKANA, TX

PREP: 30 MIN. • **COOK:** 20 MIN.
MAKES: 8 SERVINGS

- 12 **ounces uncooked linguine**
- 2 **medium lemons**
- ¼ **cup butter, cubed**
- ¼ **cup olive oil**
- 8 **ounces sliced fresh cremini mushrooms**
- 1 **medium onion, chopped**
- 6 **garlic cloves, minced**
- ¼ **cup sun-dried tomatoes (not packed in oil), julienned**
- ⅔ **cup chardonnay**
- ½ **teaspoon salt**
- ¼ **teaspoon pepper**
- ¼ **teaspoon crushed red pepper flakes**
- 1½ **pounds uncooked shrimp (26-30 per pound), peeled and deveined**
- ¼ **cup chopped fresh parsley Grated Parmesan cheese, optional**

1. Cook linguine according to package directions. Meanwhile, halve and thinly slice one lemon. Finely grate peel from remaining lemon; place in small bowl. Cut lemon crosswise in half; squeeze juice into bowl; set aside.

2. In a 6-qt. stockpot, heat butter and oil over medium-high heat. Add mushrooms, onion and garlic; cook and stir 5 minutes. Add tomatoes, lemon slices, lemon peel and juice; cook 5 minutes longer, stirring occasionally.

3. Stir in chardonnay, salt, pepper and pepper flakes; cook 3-5 minutes, stirring occasionally until wine is evaporated. Add shrimp; cook and stir 4-6 minutes or until the shrimp just turn pink.

4. Reduce heat to medium-low. Drain linguine, reserving 1 cup pasta water. Stir linguine into shrimp mixture, adding enough reserved pasta water to moisten. Heat through. Serve with parsley and, if desired, cheese.

MY BEST SPAGHETTI & MEATBALLS

MY BEST SPAGHETTI & MEATBALLS

One of my favorite childhood memories is going to the Old Spaghetti Factory with my family and ordering a big plate of cheesy spaghetti, meatballs and garlic bread. My homemade recipe reminds me of those fun times and satisfies everyone's craving for good Italian food.

—**ERIKA MONROE-WILLIAMS** SCOTTSDALE, AZ

PREP: 1 HOUR • **COOK:** 50 MIN.
MAKES: 2½ QUARTS

- ¾ **cup soft bread crumbs**
- ½ **cup grated Parmesan cheese**
- ¼ **cup 2% milk**
- 1 **large egg, beaten**
- 3 **tablespoons minced fresh Italian flat-leaf parsley**
- 3 **garlic cloves, minced**
- ¾ **teaspoon salt**
- ½ **teaspoon coarsely ground pepper**
- ½ **pound ground beef**
- ½ **pound ground pork**
- ½ **pound ground veal or additional ground beef**
- 2 **tablespoons canola oil**

SAUCE

- 2 **tablespoons canola oil**
- 1 **medium onion, finely chopped**
- 2 **garlic cloves, minced**
- 1 **can (6 ounces) tomato paste**
- ¾ **cup dry red wine or beef broth**
- 2 **cans (28 ounces each) crushed tomatoes**
- ¼ **cup minced fresh parsley**
- 2 **teaspoons sugar**
- 1½ **teaspoons salt**
- ¼ **teaspoon coarsely ground pepper**
- ¼ **teaspoon crushed red pepper flakes**
- 4 **fresh basil leaves, torn into small pieces**
   Hot cooked spaghetti
   Additional grated Parmesan cheese

1. In a large bowl, combine the first eight ingredients. Add beef, pork and veal; mix lightly but thoroughly. Shape into 1-in. balls. In a large skillet, heat oil over medium heat. Brown meatballs in batches; drain.

2. In a 6-qt. stockpot, heat oil over medium heat. Add onion; cook and stir 3-5 minutes or until tender. Add garlic; cook and stir 2 minutes. Add tomato paste; cook, stir 3-5 minutes or until paste darkens. Add wine; cook and stir 2 minutes to dissolve any browned tomato paste.

3. Stir in tomatoes, parsley, sugar, salt, pepper and pepper flakes. Bring to a boil. Reduce heat; simmer, uncovered, 15-20 minutes or until thickened, stirring occasionally. Add the basil and meatballs; cook 20-25 minutes longer or until meatballs are cooked through, stirring occasionally. Serve meatballs and sauce with spaghetti. Sprinkle with additional cheese.

CHEESE & SAUSAGE STUFFED SHELLS

I make this meal for special occasions, and everyone who has tried these jumbo stuffed shells has left satisfied. I suggest making a double batch and freezing one for future dinners.

—TIFFANY CARLSON COLFAX, ND

PREP: 55 MIN. • **BAKE:** 45 MIN.
MAKES: 10 SERVINGS

- 30 uncooked jumbo pasta shells
- 1 pound bulk Italian sausage
- 1 large onion, chopped
- 1 package (8 ounces) cream cheese, softened
- 1 package (10) frozen chopped spinach, thawed and squeezed dry
- 1 large egg, beaten
- 3 cups (12 ounces) shredded part-skim mozzarella cheese, divided
- 2 cups (8 ounces) shredded cheddar cheese
- 1 cup (8 ounces) 2% cottage cheese
- ¼ cup grated Parmesan cheese
- ¼ teaspoon salt
- ¼ teaspoon pepper

SAUCE
- 3 cans (15 ounces each) tomato sauce
- 4 teaspoons dried minced onion
- 3 garlic cloves, minced
- 2 teaspoons dried basil
- 2 teaspoons dried parsley flakes
- 1½ teaspoons dried oregano
- 1½ teaspoons sugar
- ¾ teaspoon salt
- ½ teaspoon pepper

1. Preheat oven to 350°. Cook pasta shells according to package directions for al dente; drain and rinse with cold water. Meanwhile, in a large skillet, cook sausage and onion over medium heat 6-8 minutes or until sausage is no longer pink, breaking up sausage into crumbles; drain and return to pan. Add the cream cheese; cook and stir until melted.
2. Transfer to a large bowl; cool slightly. Stir in spinach and egg. Add 1 cup mozzarella, cheddar cheese, cottage cheese, Parmesan cheese, salt and pepper; mix well. In a small bowl, combine the sauce ingredients. Spread 1⅓ cups sauce onto bottom of a greased 13x9-in. baking dish and ⅔ cup sauce over the bottom of a greased 8-in.-square baking dish. Fill pasta shells with sausage mixture; arrange over sauce. Top with remaining sauce.
3. Bake, covered, 45 minutes or until pasta is tender. Sprinkle with remaining mozzarella cheese. Bake, uncovered, 5-10 minutes longer or until cheese is melted.

BAKED CHEESY MOSTACCIOLI

My friends and family often request this family favorite. Because the sauce works well with several Italian meals, I make a large batch to use for weekday dinners or last-minute company.

—DAYNA BROHM GOLD CANYON, AZ

PREP: 35 MIN. • **BAKE:** 25 MIN.
MAKES: 6 SERVINGS

- 3 cups uncooked mostaccioli
- 1 pound ground beef
- 2 Italian sausage links, casings removed
- 1 small onion, chopped
- ½ cup chopped green pepper
- ½ cup chopped sweet red pepper
- ½ cup chopped fresh mushrooms
- 1 garlic clove, minced
- 1 can (15 ounces) crushed tomatoes
- 2 cans (8 ounces each) tomato sauce
- 1 tablespoon Italian seasoning
- ½ teaspoon sugar
- 2 cups (8 ounces) shredded cheddar cheese, divided

1. Preheat oven to 350°. Cook mostaccioli according to package directions for al dente; drain.
2. Meanwhile, in a 6-qt. stockpot, cook beef, sausage, onion, peppers, mushrooms and garlic over medium-high heat 6-8 minutes or until meat is no longer pink and vegetables are tender, breaking up meat into crumbles; drain.
3. Stir in tomatoes, tomato sauce, Italian seasoning and sugar. Bring to a boil. Reduce heat; simmer, uncovered, 8-10 minutes to allow flavors to blend.
4. Stir in 1½ cups cheese and the mostaccioli. Transfer to a greased 13x9-in. baking dish. Bake, covered, 20 minutes. Sprinkle with remaining cheese. Bake, uncovered, 5-10 minutes longer or until cheese is melted.

CHIPOTLE MANICOTTI BAKE

PREP: 30 MIN. • **BAKE:** 30 MIN. + STANDING
MAKES: 8 SERVINGS

- 14 uncooked manicotti shells
- 2 cartons (15 ounces each) part-skim ricotta cheese
- 2 cups (8 ounces) shredded part-skim mozzarella cheese
- 4 green onions, chopped
- 2 large eggs, lightly beaten
- ¼ cup chopped fresh cilantro
- 2 cups chipotle salsa
- 2 cups (8 ounces) shredded pepper jack cheese

1. Preheat oven to 350°. Cook manicotti according to package directions for al dente. Drain.
2. In a large bowl, mix ricotta cheese, mozzarella cheese, green onions, eggs and cilantro. Spoon into manicotti. Spread ½ cup salsa into a greased 13x9-in. baking dish. Top with stuffed manicotti. Pour remaining salsa over top. Bake, uncovered, 20 minutes.
3. Sprinkle with pepper jack cheese. Bake, uncovered, 10 minutes longer or until the cheese is melted. Let stand 10 minutes before serving.

TOP TIP

Manicotti in Minutes

To stuff manicotti in a snap, use a disposable pastry bag (or a resealable plastic bag with one corner cut off) to pipe the mixture inside the shells. This method is quicker and gives much more control than a spoon.

—BRENDA H. QUINCY, IL

"I found this recipe while searching for a vegetarian dish that I could serve as a main course. This rich manicotti has the added spiciness that I love in Mexican cuisine."

—JULIE PETERSON, CROFTON, MD

CHIPOTLE
MANICOTTI BAKE

An Elegant Christmas Dinner

Family and friends will sing your praises when they're greeted with a spectacular Christmas Day dinner—this **dazzling lineup that boasts all the trimmings.**

Your spread will look special when it's decked out with a **classically elegant pork crown roast, baked slowly to perfection**. Sharing the table with this impressive entree is a host of savory side dishes and tantalizing appetizers. Then let them **feast their eyes on a torte that is one stunner of a finale.**

Use the timeline on page 28 as your road map for a stress-free holiday dinner. And setting a stunning table is easy when you look to our formal place setting guide on page 37 for inspiration.

Crown Roast with Apricot Dressing (p. 32)

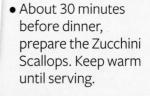

Countdown to Christmas Dinner

Hang the wreath, bring out your finest china and **whip up a batch of cheer. Invite loved ones over for an elegant Christmas they won't soon forget.** There's enough sweet potatoes, buttery dinner rolls and creamy or coconutty desserts for everyone. You'll be the toast of the town!

A FEW WEEKS BEFORE

- Prepare two grocery lists— one for nonperishable items to buy now and one for perishable items to buy a few days before Christmas.

TWO DAYS BEFORE

- Buy remaining grocery items.

- Bake the brownie layer for the Cherry-Coconut Chocolate Torte. Store in an airtight container.

THE DAY BEFORE

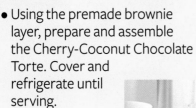

- Prepare the dough for Homemade Golden Crescent Rolls, letting it rise according to the recipe directions. Bake rolls. Cover or store in an airtight container.

- Using the premade brownie layer, prepare and assemble the Cherry-Coconut Chocolate Torte. Cover and refrigerate until serving.

- Prepare the mushroom topping for the Mushroom Pastry Tarts. Cover and refrigerate.

- Bake the puffs for the Eggnog Cream Puffs; do not cut or dust with sugar. Store in an airtight container.

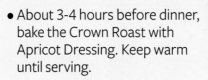

- Set the table. See page 37 for a guide.

CHRISTMAS DAY

- About 3-4 hours before guests arrive, place the ingredients for the Warm Cider Cranberry Punch in the slow cooker.

- About 3-4 hours before dinner, bake the Crown Roast with Apricot Dressing. Keep warm until serving.

- About 2 hours before dinner, prepare the Rum-Raisin Sweet Potatoes. Keep warm until serving.

- About 1 hour before dinner, prepare the Au Gratin Turnips. Keep warm until serving.

- About 45 minutes before dinner, prepare the Balsamic Orzo with Broccoli. Keep warm until serving.

- About 30 minutes before dinner, prepare the Zucchini Scallops. Keep warm until serving.

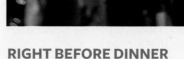

RIGHT BEFORE DINNER

- As guests arrive, assemble and bake the Mushroom Pastry Tarts.

- Warm the crescent rolls in the oven just before serving.

- After dinner but before dessert, whip Eggnog Cream Puff filling. Cut the puffs according to the recipe directions, fill with whipped cream and dust with sugar.

HOMEMADE GOLDEN CRESCENT ROLLS

My family prefers homemade crescent rolls to the typical store-bought kind. They bake up warm and tender.

—MARCY SAVOIE EDWARDSVILLE, IL

PREP: 30 MIN. + RISING • **BAKE:** 10 MIN.
MAKES: 2 DOZEN

- 1 package (¼ ounce) active dry yeast
- ¼ cup warm water (110° to 115°)
- 1 cup warm 2% milk (110° to 115°)
- 1 large egg, beaten
- 2 tablespoons sugar
- 2 tablespoons butter, melted
- 1 teaspoon salt
- 3½ to 4 cups all-purpose flour

1. In a small bowl, dissolve yeast in warm water. In a large bowl, combine milk, egg, sugar, butter, salt, yeast mixture and 1½ cups flour; beat on medium speed for 3 minutes. Stir in enough remaining flour to form a soft dough (dough will be sticky).

2. Turn dough onto a floured surface; knead until smooth and elastic, about 6-8 minutes. Place in a greased bowl, turning once to grease the top. Cover with plastic wrap; let rise in a warm place until doubled, about 1 hour.

3. Punch down dough. Turn onto a lightly floured surface; divide in half. Let rest 10 minutes. Roll each portion into a 12-in. circle; cut each circle into 12 wedges. Roll up wedges from the wide ends. Place rolls 2 in. apart on ungreased baking sheets, point side down; curve to form crescents. Cover with kitchen towels; let rise in a warm place until rolls are almost doubled, about 30 minutes.

4. Preheat the oven to 375°. Bake for 8-10 minutes or until golden brown. Remove to wire racks; serve warm.

BALSAMIC ORZO WITH BROCCOLI

What would a meal be without a tasty and colorful veggie side dish? This one, packed with nutrients and flavor, goes perfectly alongside a Christmas entree.

—GAIL ZIMCOSKY STRONGSVILLE, OH

PREP: 15 MIN. • **COOK:** 25 MIN.
MAKES: 12 SERVINGS (¾ CUP EACH)

- 6 cups fresh broccoli florets
- 4 tablespoons olive oil, divided
- 2 teaspoons garlic-herb seasoning blend
- 3 cans (14½ ounces each) reduced-sodium chicken broth
- 3 cups uncooked whole wheat orzo pasta
- 1 cup chopped sweet onion
- 1 medium sweet red pepper, chopped
- ⅓ cup balsamic vinegar
- ½ teaspoon salt
- ¼ teaspoon pepper

1. Preheat oven to 425°. Place broccoli in a foil-lined 15x10x1-in. baking pan. Drizzle with 2 tablespoons of the oil; sprinkle with seasoning blend. Toss to coat. Roast 12-14 minutes or until broccoli is tender and begins to brown, stirring occasionally. Remove from oven; keep warm.

2. Meanwhile, in a 6-qt. stockpot, bring broth to a boil. Add orzo. Reduce heat; simmer, covered, for 8-9 minutes or until the orzo is al dente, stirring occasionally. Remove and reserve ⅓ cup cooking liquid.

3. In a large nonstick skillet, heat remaining oil over medium-high heat. Add onion; cook and stir 3-5 minutes or until tender. Add red pepper; cook and stir 2-3 minutes longer or until crisp-tender. Add vinegar and reserved cooking liquid; cook until it begins to bubble. Remove from the heat. Add broccoli; stir to coat. Stir in orzo; toss mixture to combine. Season with salt and pepper.

ZUCCHINI SCALLOPS

Here's a healthier alternative to scallops wrapped with bacon. They look elegant and fresh, but they're also simple to make on the stove or grill. Serve warm or make ahead and serve at room temperature.

—ELIZABETH TRUESDELL PETALUMA, CA

START TO FINISH: 30 MIN. • **MAKES:** 1 DOZEN

- 12 sea scallops (about 1½ pounds)
- 1 tablespoon lemon juice
- ¼ teaspoon salt
- ¼ teaspoon pepper
- 1 medium zucchini (8-inches long and 1½-inch diameter)
- 4 teaspoons olive oil, divided
- 2 teaspoons minced fresh parsley Lemon wedges, optional

1. In a small bowl, toss scallops with lemon juice, salt and pepper.

2. Using a vegetable peeler or metal cheese slicer, cut zucchini into very thin lengthwise strips. Wrap one zucchini strip around each scallop, overlapping edges slightly. Secure with a toothpick.

3. In a large nonstick skillet, heat 2 teaspoons oil over medium heat. Add six scallops; cook, uncovered, for 2-3 minutes on each side or until the scallops are golden brown and the zucchini is tender. Repeat with remaining oil and scallops. Sprinkle with parsley. If desired, serve with lemon wedges.

HOW-TO
How To Wrap Scallops

CUT zucchini into very thin lengthwise strips using a vegetable peeler or metal cheese slicer. Wrap a zucchini strip around each scallop. Secure where the zucchini ends overlap by piercing with a toothpick (if pan searing) or a wooden skewer (if grilling).

MUSHROOM PASTRY TARTS

MUSHROOM PASTRY TARTS

Putting anything on a puff pastry crust makes it special, but these mushrooms taste so good that combining the two makes an unforgettable dish.

—SUSAN SCARBOROUGH
FERNANDINA BEACH, FL

PREP: 20 MIN. • **BAKE:** 15 MIN. • **MAKES:** 1 DOZEN

- ¼ cup chopped walnuts or hazelnuts
- 3 tablespoons olive oil, divided
- 2 medium sweet onions, thinly sliced
- 1 garlic clove, minced
- 1 teaspoon brown sugar
- ½ teaspoon sea salt
- ¼ teaspoon coarsely ground pepper
- ⅓ cup dry red wine
- 10 ounces sliced fresh shiitake mushrooms
- ½ pound sliced baby portobello mushrooms
- 2 teaspoons minced fresh thyme, divided
- 1 sheet frozen puff pastry, thawed
- 1 package (4 ounces) fresh goat cheese

1. In a small dry skillet, toast walnuts over low heat for 5-7 minutes or until lightly browned, stirring occasionally. Remove and set aside.

2. In a large skillet, heat 2 tablespoons of oil over medium heat. Add onions, cook and stir 6-8 minutes or until the onions are softened. Reduce the heat to medium-low; cook 20-22 minutes or until deep golden brown, stirring occasionally. Add garlic, brown sugar, salt and pepper; cook 1 minute longer. Transfer to a small bowl.

3. Add wine to pan, stirring to loosen browned bits from pan. Bring to a boil. Cook and stir 1 minute; pour over the onions. In same skillet, heat remaining oil over medium-high heat. Add the mushrooms and 1 teaspoon thyme; cook and stir 8-10 minutes or until the liquid is almost absorbed. Stir in onions. Remove from heat; cover and set aside.

4. Preheat oven to 400°. Unfold puff pastry. On a lightly floured surface, roll pastry into a 12-in. square. Cut into two 12x6-in. rectangles. Transfer to baking sheet. Using a sharp knife, score ½ in. from edges of each pastry (do not cut through). Using a fork, poke holes in the pastry. Bake 10-12 minutes or until puffed and lightly browned. Remove from oven. Press down center with a spoon if necessary. Reduce oven setting to 350°.

5. Spoon the mushroom mixture over tarts. Sprinkle with walnuts; top with cheese. Sprinkle with the remaining thyme. Bake 5 minutes longer or until the cheese is melted. Cut each tart into six pieces.

AU GRATIN TURNIPS

My father's favorite food was turnips—either cooked or raw. This cheesy dish always reminds me of his many second helpings of turnips at our dinner table.

—JANIE COLLE HUTCHINSON, KS

PREP: 30 MIN. • **BAKE:** 20 MIN.
MAKES: 12 SERVINGS (⅔ CUP EACH)

- 3 pounds medium turnips (about 6), peeled and cubed
- ½ cup butter, cubed
- 4 green onions, chopped, divided
- ⅓ cup all-purpose flour
- ¾ teaspoon salt
- ¼ teaspoon pepper
- 3 cups half-and-half cream
- 2 cups (8 ounces) shredded cheddar cheese, divided

1. Preheat oven to 350°. Place turnips in a 6-qt. stockpot; add water to cover. Bring to a boil. Cook, uncovered, for 12-15 minutes or until tender. Drain and return to pan.

2. In a large saucepan, melt butter over medium heat. Add half of the green onions. Cook and stir for 2-3 minutes or until tender. Stir in flour, salt and pepper until blended; gradually whisk in cream. Bring to a boil, stirring constantly; cook and stir 2-3 minutes or until thickened. Stir in ¾ cup cheese until melted. Pour sauce over turnips; toss to coat.

3. Transfer to a greased 3-qt. baking dish. Top with remaining cheese. Bake, uncovered, 20-25 minutes or until bubbly and cheese is melted. Sprinkle with remaining onions.

CROWN ROAST WITH APRICOT DRESSING

RUM-RAISIN SWEET POTATOES

My family and I have traded in baked potatoes for sweet potatoes with a spicy twist. The Chinese five-spice powder gives the spuds an added tasty kick.

—PAMELA WEATHERFORD SAN ANTONIO, TX

PREP: 20 MIN. • **COOK:** 1 HOUR + COOLING
MAKES: 16 SERVINGS (¾ CUP)

- 8 **large sweet potatoes (about 6½ pounds)**
- 1 **cup raisins**
- ⅔ **cup dark rum**
- 1 **cup half-and-half cream**
- ½ **cup butter, cubed**
- 3 **tablespoons brown sugar**
- 1 **tablespoon Chinese five-spice powder**
- 1¼ **teaspoons salt**
- ½ **teaspoon pepper**
- ½ **cup chopped walnuts, toasted**

1. Place potatoes in a stockpot; add water to cover. Bring to a boil. Reduce heat; cook, uncovered, 40-45 minutes or until tender. Meanwhile, in a microwave-safe bowl, combine raisins and rum. Microwave, uncovered, on high for 30 seconds; set aside. In a small saucepan, heat cream and butter until butter is melted. Drain potatoes. When cool enough to handle, peel potatoes; return to stockpot.
2. Mash potatoes, gradually adding brown sugar, five-spice powder, salt, pepper and butter mixture. Stir in raisin mixture. If necessary, warm potatoes over low heat, stirring occasionally. Transfer to a serving bowl. Sprinkle with walnuts.

CROWN ROAST WITH APRICOT DRESSING

I've been making crown roasts for many years, but combining a few recipes finally led to this guest-pleasing version that also satisfied me. Beautifully roasted with an apricot glaze and nicely browned stuffing, it's truly the crown dish for a celebration.

—ISABELL COOPER CAMBRIDGE, NS

PREP: 20 MIN. • **BAKE:** 2½ HOURS + STANDING
MAKES: 12 SERVINGS

- 1 **pork crown roast (12 ribs and about 8 pounds)**
- ½ **teaspoon seasoned salt**
- ⅓ **cup apricot preserves**

APRICOT DRESSING

- ¼ **cup butter, cubed**
- 1 **cup sliced fresh mushrooms**
- 1 **medium onion, finely chopped**
- 1 **celery rib, finely chopped**
- 1 **cup chopped dried apricots**
- ½ **teaspoon dried savory**
- ½ **teaspoon dried thyme**
- ¼ **teaspoon salt**
- ¼ **teaspoon pepper**
- 3 **cups soft bread crumbs**

1. Preheat oven to 350°. Place roast on a rack in a shallow roasting pan. Sprinkle with seasoned salt. Bake, uncovered, 1 hour.
2. Brush sides of roast with preserves. Bake 1½-2 hours longer or until the meat reaches desired doneness (for medium-rare, a thermometer should read 145°; medium, 160°). Transfer roast to a serving platter. Let stand 20 minutes before carving.
3. For dressing, in a large skillet, heat butter over medium-high heat. Add mushrooms, onion and celery; cook and stir 6-8 minutes or until tender. Stir in apricots and seasonings. Add bread crumbs; toss to coat. Transfer to a greased 8-in. square baking dish. Bake 15-20 minutes or until lightly browned. Carve roast between ribs; serve with dressing.

TOP TIP

Citrus Twist on Spuds

I've always added grated orange peel to my mashed sweet potatoes for an extra burst of flavor. Now to save time and avoid a mess, I simply cut a 2- to 3-inch strip of orange peel and add it to the boiling water with the potatoes. Later, I mash the softened peel with the spuds for a fresh and wonderful citrus flavor.

—PAT W. NEW BLOOMFIELD, MO

**RUM-RAISIN
SWEET POTATOES**

**CHERRY-COCONUT
CHOCOLATE TORTE**

CHERRY-COCONUT CHOCOLATE TORTE

This torte reminds me of two favorite treats—chocolate covered cherries and old-fashioned Cherry Mash candy.

—**DIAN HICKS CARLSON** OMAHA, NE

PREP: 30 MIN. • **BAKE:** 20 MIN. + CHILLING
MAKES: 12 SERVINGS

- 1 **cup sugar**
- 2 **large eggs**
- ½ **teaspoon vanilla extract**
- ½ **cup butter, melted**
- ½ **cup all-purpose flour**
- ⅓ **cup baking cocoa**
- ¼ **teaspoon salt**
- ¼ **teaspoon baking powder**

CHERRY LAYER
- 4 **jars (10 ounces each) maraschino cherries**
- 4 **cups confectioners' sugar**
- ¼ **cup butter, softened**

COCONUT LAYER
- 1 **package (14 ounces) flaked coconut**
- ¼ **cup sweetened condensed milk**

CHOCOLATE GANACHE
- 12 **ounces semisweet chocolate, chopped**
- 1 **cup heavy whipping cream**
- 1 **cup chopped walnuts, toasted**

1. Preheat oven to 350°. In a large bowl, beat the sugar, eggs and vanilla until blended. Beat in melted butter. In a small bowl, whisk the flour, cocoa, salt and baking powder; gradually add to batter and mix well.

2. Spread brownie mixture into a greased 9-in. springform pan. Bake for 18-20 minutes or until a toothpick inserted in center comes out clean. Cool completely in pan on a wire rack.

3. Drain cherries, reserving ½ cup juice. Arrange cherries evenly around top edge of brownie; place remaining cherries over top. In a large bowl, beat the confectioners' sugar, butter and reserved cherry juice until creamy. Spread evenly over cherries.

4. In a bowl, combine the coconut and condensed milk. Sprinkle over cherry layer, smoothing down near edges and pressing gently to form an even layer.

5. Place the chocolate in a large bowl. In a small saucepan, bring cream just to a boil. Pour over chocolate. Let stand for 5 minutes; whisk until smooth.

Pour over coconut layer. Refrigerate until set. Loosen sides of pan with a knife. Remove rim from pan. Sprinkle with walnuts.

NOTE *To toast nuts, bake in a shallow pan in a 350° oven for 5-10 minutes or cook in a skillet over low heat until lightly browned, stirring occasionally.*

WARM CIDER CRANBERRY PUNCH

I first made this at an instructional cooking camp. My kids loved it so much that, for a time, they insisted we make it every day. Serve it hot in the winter or with ice during the summer.

—**CAROL GEHRINGER** RALEIGH, NC

PREP: 10 MIN. • **COOK:** 3 HOURS
MAKES: 20 SERVINGS (¾ CUP EACH)

- 1 **bottle (64 ounces) cranberry juice**
- 6 **cups apple cider or juice**
- 2 **cans (12 ounces each) frozen lemonade concentrate, thawed**
- 1 **medium lemon, cut into wedges**
- 4 **cinnamon sticks (3 inches)**
- 2 **teaspoons whole cloves**
- 1 **teaspoon whole allspice**

In a 6-qt. slow cooker, combine the cranberry juice, apple cider, lemonade concentrate and lemon. Place the cinnamon sticks, cloves and allspice on a double thickness of cheesecloth. Gather corners of the cloth to enclose seasonings; tie securely with string. Place in slow cooker. Cook, covered, on low 3-4 hours or until heated through. Discard spice bag and lemon.

DID YOU KNOW?

Ganache 101

Ganache is a French term for a smooth mixture of chocolate and cream used as cake fillings or glazes and in candy making. Traditionally, ganache is made by pouring hot cream over chopped chocolate and stirring until the mixture is velvety smooth. You can add flavorings, and adding corn syrup gives poured ganache a shiny finish. The proportions of cream to chocolate vary depending on the use.

**EGGNOG
CREAM PUFFS**

EGGNOG CREAM PUFFS

If you want to receive rave reviews and recipe requests, combine two Christmas classics—eggnog and cream puffs. When it comes to Santa, I think this recipe goes on his "nice" list!

—**KRISTEN HEIGL** STATEN ISLAND, NY

PREP: 40 MIN. • **BAKE:** 30 MIN. + COOLING
MAKES: ABOUT 2 DOZEN

- 1 **cup water**
- ½ **cup butter, cubed**
- ⅛ **teaspoon salt**
- 1 **cup all-purpose flour**
- ¾ **teaspoon ground nutmeg**
- 4 **large eggs**

WHIPPED CREAM
- 1½ **cups heavy whipping cream**
- 1½ **cups confectioners' sugar**
- ¼ **cup eggnog**
- 1 **teaspoon vanilla extract**
- ⅛ **teaspoon ground nutmeg**
    Additional confectioners' sugar

1. Preheat oven to 400°. In a large saucepan, bring water, butter and salt to a rolling boil. Add flour all at once; add nutmeg and stir until blended. Cook over medium heat, stirring vigorously until mixture pulls away from sides of pan. Remove from heat; let stand 5 minutes.

2. Add the eggs, one at a time, beating well after each addition until smooth. Continue beating until the mixture is smooth and shiny. Drop the dough by rounded tablespoonfuls 1 in. apart onto greased baking sheets. Bake for 30-35 minutes or until puffed, very firm and golden brown. Pierce sides of each puff with tip of a knife. Cool on wire racks. Cut top third off each puff.

3. In a large bowl, beat cream until it begins to thicken. Add confectioners' sugar, eggnog, vanilla and nutmeg; beat until soft peaks form. Fill cream puffs with whipped cream just before serving; replace tops. Dust tops with additional confectioners' sugar. Serve cream puffs immediately.

Table Etiquette 101

Looking to brush up on the basic rules of etiquette for a perfectly set formal table? Refer to this handy guide and the photo above. Set the table and arrange any centerpieces, place cards or decorations the night before so you have more time to attend to other details the day of the party.

DINNER PLATE Put this large plate in the center of the place setting. Then set out your utensils (cutlery).

CUTLERY For most meals, you start using cutlery from the outside and work your way in. When finished with a utensil, place it on your plate, never the table or tablecloth.

DINNER FORK Set the large dinner fork directly left of the dinner plate.

SALAD FORK Salad usually is eaten before the main course, so place the salad fork on the outside to the left of the dinner fork.

DINNER KNIFE The dinner knife goes to the immediate right of the dinner plate, with the blade facing the plate.

TEASPOON Place the teaspoon to the right of the dinner knife, facing up.

SOUP SPOON If you're serving soup, place the large soup spoon to the right of the teaspoon.

SOUP BOWL If you're serving soup, place the bowl directly on top of the dinner plate.

CUP AND SAUCER The cup and saucer go directly above the knife and spoons.

STEMWARE Place the water glass above the dinner plate, within easy reach. Place additional stemware (champagne flutes and wine glasses) to the right of the water glass just above the cup and saucer.

BREAD DISH AND BUTTER KNIFE This small plate goes directly above the forks to the left of the dinner plate. Place the butter knife across the dish at an angle, handle to the right and blade facing down.

NAPKINS Dinner napkins usually are folded and placed to the left of the salad fork, fold side to the plate. For a decorative touch, place the napkin between the dinner plate and soup bowl (or directly on the plate if you're not serving soup.) When everyone is seated one of the hosts unfolds their napkin first and guests follow, unfolding the napkins gently onto their laps. Napkins are never tucked into the shirt or belt. At the end of the meal, fold the napkin loosely and return it to the table near where you found it.

Christmas Classics with a Twist

Food plays an important role in the time-honored traditions of the season. The enchanting aroma of a roasted turkey or baked sweet potatoes will elicit **happy memories of Christmases past.**

As much as we cherish these festive flavors, every now and again it's nice to **spice up the traditional with something fun and different**. Put the spark back in Christmas with a swoon-worthy herb-infused prime rib. Freshen up classic cranberry sauce with a chipotle twist, and **watch guests savor** an Italian spin on green bean casserole.

Turn the page for **a merry mix of entrees and sides** that puts a delicious variation on all your old favorites.

Restaurant-Style Prime Rib (p. 45)

POMEGRANATE-
HAZELNUT ROASTED
BRUSSELS SPROUTS

POMEGRANATE-HAZELNUT ROASTED BRUSSELS SPROUTS

I converted many people to Brussels sprouts with this recipe, and it has since become my most requested dish. The richness of the hazelnuts and the sweetness of pomegranate and orange elevate the sprouts to a new level.
—**MELANIE STEVENSON** READING, PA

START TO FINISH: 25 MIN.
MAKES: 8 SERVINGS

- 2 **pounds fresh Brussels sprouts, trimmed and halved**
- ¼ **cup olive oil**
- 1½ **teaspoons kosher salt**
- 1 **teaspoon coarsely ground pepper**
- 6 **tablespoons butter, cubed**
- ⅔ **cup chopped hazelnuts, toasted**
- 1 **tablespoon grated orange peel**
- ½ **cup pomegranate seeds**

1. Preheat oven to 400°. Place Brussels sprouts in a foil-lined 15x10x1-in. baking pan. Drizzle with oil; sprinkle with salt and pepper. Toss to coat. Roast for 15-20 minutes or until tender, stirring occasionally. Remove from oven.
2. Meanwhile, in a small heavy saucepan, melt butter over medium heat. Heat 5-7 minutes or until golden brown, stirring constantly. Remove from the heat; drizzle over Brussels sprouts. Add hazelnuts and orange peel; gently toss to coat. Transfer to a serving bowl. Just before serving, sprinkle with pomegranate seeds.

WALDORF STUFFED HAM

It's fun to make something new for Christmas dinner. I created this unique take on baked ham and tested it on my willing husband. He thinks it's a keeper!
—**COLLEEN VROOMAN** WAUKESHA, WI

PREP: 35 MIN. • **BAKE:** 1¼ HOURS + STANDING
MAKES: 16 SERVINGS

- 1½ **cups unsweetened apple juice**
- ¼ **cup butter, cubed**
- 1 **package (6 ounces) pork stuffing mix**
- 1 **medium tart apple, finely chopped**
- ¼ **cup chopped sweet onion**
- ¼ **cup chopped celery**
- ¼ **cup chopped walnuts**
- 1 **bone-in fully cooked spiral-sliced ham (8 pounds)**
- 1 **can (21 ounces) apple pie filling**
- ¼ **teaspoon ground cinnamon**

1. Preheat oven to 325°. In a large saucepan, bring apple juice and butter to a boil. Remove from heat; stir in stuffing mix, apple, onion, celery and walnuts.
2. Place ham on a rack in a roasting pan. Spoon stuffing by tablespoonfuls between ham slices. Spoon pie filling over ham; sprinkle with cinnamon.
3. Bake, uncovered, 1¼-1¾ hours or until a meat thermometer reads 140°. Let stand 10 minutes before serving.

ORANGE-PISTACHIO QUINOA SALAD

Add this fresh and healthy salad to your holiday spread. Its citrus and nutty taste is simply delicious.
—**JEAN GREENFIELD** SAN ANSELMO, CA

PREP: 15 MIN. • **COOK:** 15 MIN. + COOLING
MAKES: 8 SERVINGS

- 1⅓ **cups water**
- ⅔ **cup quinoa, rinsed**
- 2 **cups chopped romaine**
- 1 **can (15 ounces) garbanzo beans or chickpeas, rinsed and drained**
- 1 **can (15 ounces) mandarin oranges, drained**
- 1 **medium cucumber, halved and sliced**
- 1 **cup shelled pistachios, toasted**
- ½ **cup finely chopped red onion**
- 1 **medium navel orange**
- 2 **tablespoons olive oil**
- ½ **teaspoon salt**
  Pinch pepper

1. In a large saucepan, bring water to a boil. Add quinoa. Reduce heat; simmer, covered, 12-14 minutes or until liquid is absorbed. Remove from heat; fluff with a fork. Cool.
2. In a large bowl, combine romaine, beans, mandarin oranges, cucumber, pistachios, onion and cooled quinoa. In a small bowl, finely grate peel from orange. Cut orange crosswise in half; squeeze juice from orange and add to peel. Whisk in oil, salt and pepper. Drizzle over salad; toss to coat.

DID YOU KNOW?

The Power of Quinoa

Quinoa, pronounced keen-wah, is a popular health food because it is rich in nutrients. It's a good source of protein and fiber as well as trace minerals—specifically manganese and copper—that are important in turning carbohydrates into energy. Quinoa is one of the only plant foods that has all of the essential amino acids the human body requires. It's also gluten-free, making it easy to digest. Cook quinoa with gluten-free vegetable stock for a meatless meal that's also gluten-free.

APPLE STUFFING BALLS

I served these fun appetizers for the first time on Thanksgiving. My family asked me to make them several times after that, so the tasty little bites made an appearance on my Christmas spread that year, too. We love them so much they've become a holiday tradition.

—TRACY BURDO BURLINGTON, VT

PREP: 15 MIN. • **BAKE:** 30 MIN.
MAKES: 18 STUFFING BALLS

- ¼ cup butter, cubed
- 1 large onion, finely chopped
- 2 celery ribs, finely chopped
- 3 large eggs, beaten
- ¼ cup minced fresh parsley
- ¾ teaspoon salt
- ½ teaspoon dried thyme
- ¼ teaspoon pepper
- 9 cups soft bread crumbs
- 2 medium apples, peeled and finely chopped

1. Preheat oven to 350°. In a large skillet, heat butter over medium heat. Add onion and celery; cook and stir 4-6 minutes or just until tender.

2. In a large bowl, mix eggs, parsley, salt, thyme and pepper. Stir in bread crumbs, apples, onion mixture. Shape into 2-in. balls. Place in a foil-lined 15x10x1-in. baking pan. Bake for 30-35 minutes or until golden brown.

SLOW COOKER HERBED TURKEY BREAST

A holiday meal warrants an elegant and satisfying entree. This one promises to deliver. The turkey comes out of the slow cooker moist and tender, and the herbs make a flavorful gravy.

—LORIE MINER KAMAS, UT

PREP: 15 MIN. • **COOK:** 6 HOURS + STANDING
MAKES: 12 SERVINGS

- 1 bone-in turkey breast (6 to 7 pounds), thawed and skin removed
- ½ cup water
- ⅔ cup spreadable garden vegetable cream cheese
- ¼ cup butter, softened
- ¼ cup soy sauce
- 2 tablespoons minced fresh parsley
- 1 teaspoon dried basil
- 1 teaspoon rubbed sage
- 1 teaspoon dried thyme
- ½ teaspoon pepper

1. Place turkey breast and water in a 6-qt. slow cooker. In a small bowl, mix remaining ingredients; rub over turkey. Cook, covered, on low for 5-6 hours or until turkey is tender.

2. Remove turkey from slow cooker; tent with foil. Let stand 15 minutes before slicing.

SLOW COOKER HERBED TURKEY BREAST

TOP TIP

Leftover Turkey Makes Terrific Soup

To use up leftover turkey, I make a simple and satisfying soup. First I saute onion and green pepper in oil, then add chicken broth. I puree leftover mashed potatoes and vegetables, then stir that into the broth along with the cooked chopped turkey.

—MARION S. CHICAGO, IL

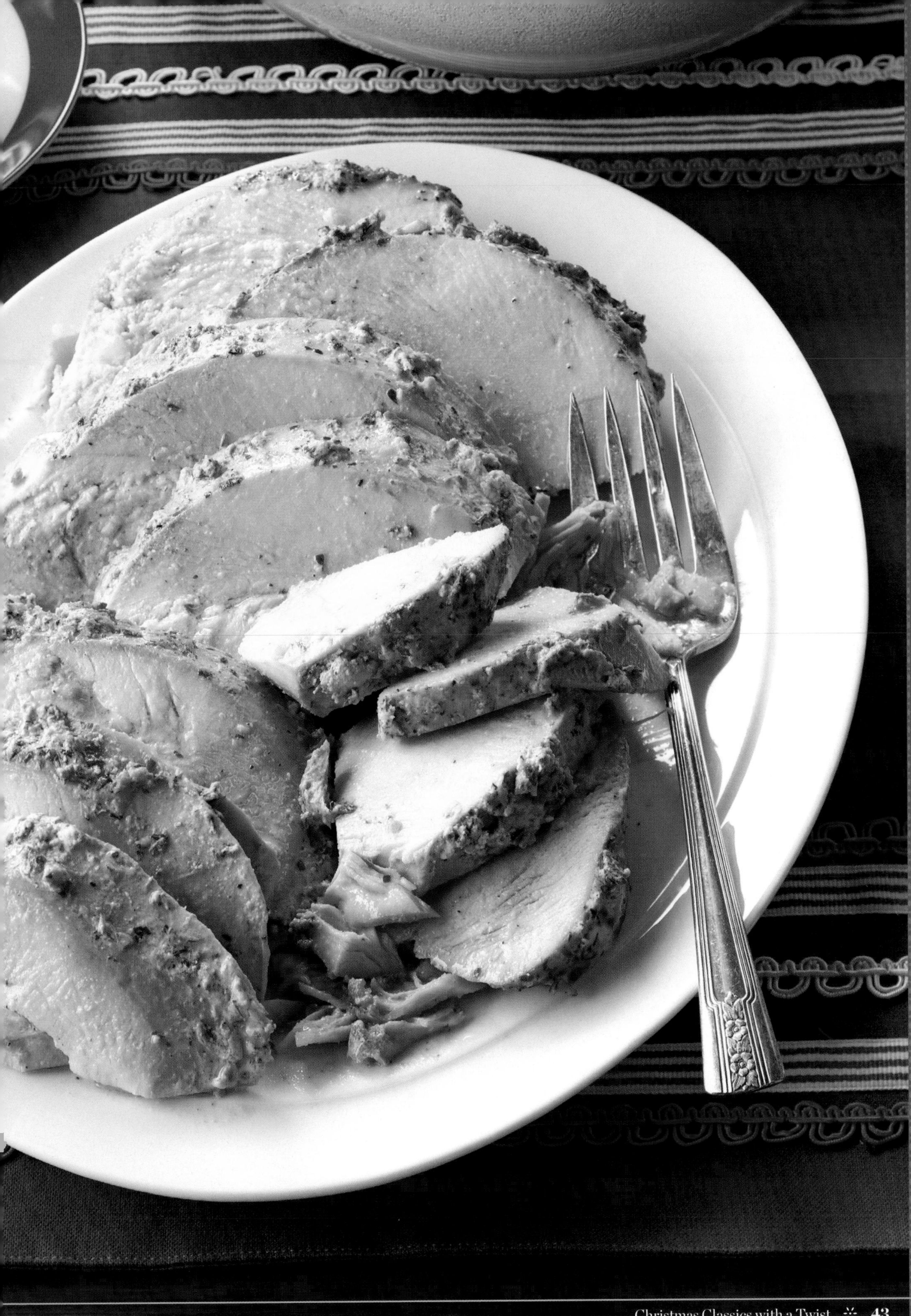

TWICE-BAKED
RUTABAGAS

TWICE-BAKED RUTABAGAS

Mix it up for dinner by substituting your go-to spuds dish with rutabagas. This recipe boasts bacon, cheese and whipping cream—even the skeptics won't be able to resist a bite!

—**LISA BYNUM** BRANDON, MS

PREP: 30 MIN. • **BAKE:** 20 MIN.
MAKES: 8 SERVINGS

- 4 **small rutabagas, peeled and cut into 1-in. cubes**
- 3 **tablespoons water**
- 8 **cooked bacon strips, chopped**
- 1 **cup heavy whipping cream**
- ¼ **cup butter, cubed**
- 2 **teaspoons garlic powder**
- ½ **teaspoon salt**
- ¼ **teaspoon pepper**
- 2 **cups (8 ounces) shredded cheddar cheese, divided**
- 3 **green onions, sliced, divided**

1. Preheat the oven to 350°. In a microwave-safe bowl, combine rutabagas and water. Microwave, covered, on high 16-20 minutes or until tender, stirring halfway. Mash rutabagas; add bacon, cream, butter, garlic powder, salt and pepper. Stir in 1 cup cheese and ¼ cup green onions.
2. Spoon mixture into eight greased 6-ounce ramekins or custard cups. Sprinkle with remaining cheese. Place ramekins on a baking sheet. Bake 18-22 minutes or until bubbly and cheese is melted. Sprinkle with remaining green onions.

MANGO-GLAZED SWEET POTATOES

These sweet potatoes remind me of my grandmother's baked sweet potato gratin. The mango nectar adds a sweet citrus twist. To add a little heat, add a dash of cayenne pepper.

—**KATHI JONES-DELMONTE** ROCHESTER, NY

PREP: 45 MIN. • **BAKE:** 50 MIN. + STANDING
MAKES: 8 SERVINGS

- 2 **cans (11.3 ounces each) mango nectar**
- 2 **teaspoons grated orange peel**
- ¾ **teaspoon sea salt**
- ½ **teaspoon coarsely ground pepper**
- ¼ **teaspoon ground nutmeg**
- 4 **large sweet potatoes (about 2½ pounds), peeled and cut into ¼-inch slices**
- ½ **cup dried cranberries**
- ¼ **cup heavy whipping cream**
- 1 **tablespoon butter**

1. Preheat oven to 375°. In a 6-qt. stockpot, combine the first five ingredients over medium-high heat. Add sweet potatoes; stir to coat. Bring to a boil. Reduce heat to medium-low; simmer, covered, for 8-10 minutes or until potatoes just begin to soften. Remove from heat. Using a slotted spoon, layer a fourth of the potatoes in a greased 8-in. square baking dish, leaving sauce in the pan. Top with a third of the cranberries. Repeat layers twice. Top with potatoes.
2. Bring the sauce to a boil over medium-high heat. Whisk in the cream. Reduce the heat; simmer, uncovered, 12-15 minutes or until sauce is reduced by a third, stirring occasionally. Pour over potatoes; dot with butter.
3. Bake, covered, 30 minutes. Bake, uncovered, 20-30 minutes longer or until potatoes are tender and top is lightly browned. Let stand 15 minutes before serving.

RESTAURANT-STYLE PRIME RIB

I've served this recipe to vistors to the U.S. from all over the world as well as to dear friends, family and neighbors. It is enjoyed and raved about by all. It makes a perfect main dish for a Christmas feast.

—**KELLY WILLIAMS** FORKED RIVER, NJ

PREP: 10 MIN. • **COOK:** 2 HOURS + STANDING
MAKES: 8 SERVINGS

- 1 **bone-in beef rib roast (4 to 5 pounds)**
- ¼ **cup kosher salt**
- 2 **tablespoons garlic powder**
- 2 **tablespoons dried rosemary, crushed**
- 2 **tablespoons wasabi powder**
- 2 **tablespoons butter, softened**
- 1 **tablespoon coarsely ground pepper**
- 1 **teaspoon herbes de Provence**

1. Preheat oven to 350°. Place roast, fat side up, on a rack in a foil-lined roasting pan. In a small bowl, mix salt, garlic powder, rosemary, wasabi powder, butter, pepper and herbes de Provence; pat onto all sides of roast.
2. Roast for 2 to 2½ hours or until meat reaches desired doneness (for medium-rare, a thermometer should read 145°; medium, 160°; well-done, 170°). Remove roast from oven; tent with foil. Let stand 15 minutes before carving.

CHIPOTLE-ORANGE CRANBERRY SAUCE

ITALIAN ARTICHOKE-GREEN BEAN CASSEROLE

My mother and I made a few small changes to a recipe we found in a cookbook to create this comforting side dish. We increased the vegetable count and tossed in some seasonings to take the flavor up a notch. It's definitely not your average green bean casserole.
—**DENISE KLIBERT** SHREVEPORT, LA

PREP: 25 MIN. • **BAKE:** 25 MIN.
MAKES: 10 SERVINGS

- 6 **cups cut fresh green beans (about 1½ pounds)**
- ⅓ **cup olive oil**
- 1 **medium onion, chopped**
- 2 **garlic cloves, minced**
- 3 **cans (14 ounces each) water-packed artichoke hearts, drained and chopped**
- ½ **cup minced fresh parsley**
  Pinch cayenne pepper
  Pinch pepper
- 1 **cup seasoned bread crumbs**
- 1 **cup grated Parmesan cheese, divided**

1. Preheat oven to 350°. In a large saucepan, bring 6 cups water to a boil. Add green beans; cook, uncovered, 3-4 minutes or just until crisp-tender. Drain and set aside.
2. In a 6-qt. stockpot, heat oil over medium heat. Add onion; cook and stir 3-4 minutes or until tender. Add garlic; cook 1 minute longer. Add beans, artichoke hearts, parsley, cayenne and pepper. Stir in bread crumbs and ¾ cup cheese.
3. Transfer to a greased 11x7-in. baking dish. Sprinkle with remaining cheese. Bake 25-30 minutes or until lightly browned.

CHIPOTLE-ORANGE CRANBERRY SAUCE

My family prefers traditional dishes on Christmas, but I like to add in a few of my own unique creations. With brown sugar, cinnamon and some chipotle powder for a little kick, this cranberry sauce will earn a permanent spot in the holiday lineup.
—**CHRIS MICHALOWSKI** DALLAS, TX

PREP: 15 MIN. + CHILLING • **MAKES:** 1¾ CUPS

- 1 **medium orange**
- 1 **package (12 ounces) fresh or frozen cranberries**
- ½ **cup packed brown sugar**
- 1 **cinnamon stick (3 inches)**
- ¼ to ¾ **teaspoon ground chipotle pepper**
- ¼ **teaspoon pepper**

1. Finely grate peel from orange. Cut orange crosswise in half; squeeze juice from orange. Place peel and orange juice in a large saucepan. Add the remaining ingredients.
2. Bring to a boil, stirring to dissolve sugar. Reduce heat to a simmer; cook, uncovered, for 5-7 minutes or until berries pop, stirring occasionally. Remove from heat.
3. Transfer to a small bowl; cool slightly. Refrigerate, covered, until sauce is cold.

CREAMY CAULIFLOWER RICE

What began as a quick-fix dish has become a staple in our house. It's a delicious way to add veggies to a meal, and it's a nice change from traditional cauliflower.
—**CARESSE CATON** GERMANTOWN, MD

START TO FINISH: 30 MIN. • **MAKES:** 10 SERVINGS

- 3 **cups uncooked long grain rice**
- 3 **cups frozen cauliflower, thawed**
- 6 **cups reduced-sodium chicken broth**
- 6 **ounces cream cheese, cubed**
- ¾ **teaspoon salt**
- ¼ **teaspoon pepper**

In a large saucepan, combine the rice, cauliflower and broth; bring to a boil. Reduce heat; simmer, covered, for 15-20 minutes or until liquid is absorbed and rice is tender. Remove from heat. Add cream cheese, salt and pepper; stir until melted.

TOP TIP

Green Beans Basics

When buying fresh green beans from the grocery store or farmers market, select those with slender green pods that are free of bruises or brown spots. Store unwashed fresh green beans in a resealable plastic bag for up to 4 days. Wash just before using, removing strings and ends if necessary. If you plan on freezing green beans just pulled from the garden, use a lettuce spinner to remove any moisture.

ITALIAN ARTICHOKE-GREEN BEAN CASSEROLE

Winter Warm-Up

Brr! Baby, it sure is cold outside. **Chase away chills on a bleak winter day** with a crackling fire, the company of good friends and some **serious comfort food.**

A winter warm-up party is the perfect excuse to **cozy up to a steamy bowlful of chili, soup or stew.** From-scratch muffins, sinfully sweet cookies and bars, and other goodies lend a warm touch to a snowy celebration. Don't forget the hot chocolate! Ours boasts a hint of pumpkin and is served in cheery, hand-decorated mugs.

No matter how far the mercury drops or how fierce the wind blows, **each piping hot bite will elicit all the *oohs*, *aahs* and *mmms*** that make simple, down-home cooking so worthwhile.

Slow-Cooked Pork Stew (p. 52)

THREE-BEAN
VEGGIE CHILI

THREE-BEAN VEGGIE CHILI

I adapted a recipe that my sister gave me to suit my family's tastes. The bulgur has a nice texture, making it a great substitute for meat. Because I find that this chili is even better the next day, I recommend making it a day ahead.

—**TARI AMBLER** SHOREWOOD, IL

PREP: 20 MIN. • **COOK:** 30 MIN.
MAKES: 8 SERVINGS (3½ QUARTS)

- 2 tablespoons olive oil
- 2 medium onions, chopped
- 2 celery ribs, chopped
- 1 medium green pepper, chopped
- ⅓ cup tomato paste
- 4 garlic cloves, minced
- 4½ teaspoons chili powder
- 1½ teaspoons salt
- 1 teaspoon dried oregano
- ½ teaspoon ground cumin
- ½ teaspoon pepper
- ⅛ teaspoon ground cinnamon
- ⅛ teaspoon ground allspice
- 3 cans (14½ ounces each) vegetable broth
- 2 cans (14½ ounces each) no-salt-added diced tomatoes, undrained
- 1 can (16 ounces) kidney beans, rinsed and drained
- 1 can (15 ounces) pinto beans, rinsed and drained
- 1 can (15 ounces) black beans, rinsed and drained
- 1 can (14½ ounces) fire-roasted crushed tomatoes
- 1 cup bulgur
- 1 large carrot, finely shredded

1. In a 6-qt. stockpot, heat oil over medium-high heat. Add the onions, celery and green pepper; cook and stir 6-8 minutes or until crisp-tender. Add tomato paste, garlic and seasonings; cook 2 minutes longer.
2. Stir in the remaining ingredients. Bring to a boil. Reduce heat; simmer, uncovered, 20-25 minutes or until thickened and bulgur is tender, stirring occasionally.

SESAME CHEESE CRACKERS

These tasty homemade crackers are irresistible! Enjoy them with soups, or munch on them by themselves. The cayenne pepper adds a bit of a kick, so add as much or as little as you like.

—**MARGARET INLOW** JOLIET, IL

PREP: 25 MIN. + CHILLING • **BAKE:** 15 MIN.
MAKES: 77 CRACKERS

- 1 cup all-purpose flour
- ½ teaspoon salt
- ⅛ to ¼ teaspoon cayenne pepper
- 6 tablespoons cold butter
- 1 cup (4 ounces) finely shredded cheddar cheese
- ¼ cup sesame seeds, toasted
- 6 to 7½ teaspoons ice water, divided
- ½ teaspoon soy sauce

1. In a small bowl, whisk flour, salt, cayenne; cut in butter until mixture resembles coarse crumbs. Stir in cheese and sesame seeds. Combine 3 teaspoons water and soy sauce; stir into dry ingredients with a fork. Stir in enough remaining water until dough forms a ball. Wrap in plastic wrap; refrigerate 1 hour or until firm.
2. Preheat oven to 400°. On a floured surface, roll the dough into a 14x11-in. rectangle. Cut into 2x1-in. strips. Place on lightly greased baking sheets. Bake 12-15 minutes or until golden brown. Remove to wire racks to cool.

PRETZEL SNACKERS

I first served this snack when my husband's aunt came to visit. She quickly asked for the recipe—even though she's in her 80s and lives in a convent. She has reported that all her fellow nuns enjoy it as much as we do!

—**ELISSA ARMBRUSTER** MEDFORD, NJ

START TO FINISH: 30 MIN. • **MAKES:** 2½ QUARTS

- 2 packages (16 ounces each) sourdough pretzel nuggets
- 1 envelope ranch salad dressing mix
- 1½ teaspoons dried oregano
- 1 teaspoon lemon-pepper seasoning
- 1 teaspoon dill weed
- ½ teaspoon onion powder
- ½ teaspoon garlic powder
- ¼ cup olive oil

1. Preheat oven to 350°. Place the pretzels in a large bowl. In a small bowl, mix dressing mix, oregano, lemon-pepper, dill weed, onion powder and garlic powder. Drizzle the pretzels with oil; sprinkle with ranch mixture. Toss to coat.
2. Spread mixture in a 15x10x1-in. baking pan coated with cooking spray. Bake 10 minutes. Stir; bake 5 minutes longer. Cool completely. Store in an airtight container.

TOP TIP

Chili Redux

If you have leftover chili, freeze small portions in muffin cups. Later, heat a portion (or a few depending upon your number of servings) and serve it over a cooked hot dog for an easy chili dog. You also can stir it into prepared mac and cheese or over a dollop of mashed potatoes sprinkled with cheddar cheese and bacon bits. The possibilities are endless!

SLOW-COOKED PORK STEW

TOFFEE PECAN BARS

Curl up with a hot cup of coffee and one of these oh-so-sweet treats. The golden topping and flaky crust give way to the heartwarming taste of classic pecan pie.

—**DIANNA CROSKEY** GIBSONIA, PA

PREP: 15 MIN. • **BAKE:** 40 MIN. + CHILLING
MAKES: 3 DOZEN

- 2 **cups all-purpose flour**
- ½ **cup confectioners' sugar**
- 1 **cup cold butter, cubed**
- 1 **large egg**
- 1 **can (14 ounces) sweetened condensed milk**
- 1 **teaspoon vanilla extract**
- 1 **package English toffee bits (10 ounces) or almond brickle chips (7½ ounces)**
- 1 **cup chopped pecans**

1. Preheat oven to 350°. In a large bowl, mix flour and confectioners' sugar; cut in butter until mixture is crumbly.
2. Press into a greased 13x9-in. baking pan. Bake 15 minutes. Meanwhile, in a small bowl, mix egg, milk and vanilla. Fold in toffee bits and pecans. Spoon over the crust. Bake 24-26 minutes or until golden brown. Refrigerate until firm. Cut into bars.

TOP TIP

Tips for Cutting Bars

- With a knife, use a gentle sawing motion. Remove the corner piece first. Then the rest will be easier to remove.
- For perfectly sized bars, lay a clean ruler on top of the bars and make cut marks with the point of a knife. Use the edge of the ruler as a cutting guide.
- For basic bars (those without soft fillings or toppings), line the pan with foil before baking. When cool, lift the foil from the pan. Trim the edges of the bars, then cut into bars, squares or diamonds. Scraps can be crumbled and used as a topping for ice cream or pudding.

SLOW-COOKED PORK STEW

Try this comforting stew that's easy to put together, but tastes like you've been working hard in the kitchen all day. It's even better served over polenta, egg noodles or mashed potatoes.

—**NANCY ELLIOTT** HOUSTON, TX

PREP: 15 MIN. • **COOK:** 5 HOURS
MAKES: 8 SERVINGS

- 2 **pork tenderloins (1 pound each), cut into 2-inch pieces**
- 1 **teaspoon salt**
- ½ **teaspoon pepper**
- 2 **large carrots, cut into ½-inch slices**
- 2 **celery ribs, coarsely chopped**
- 1 **medium onion, coarsely chopped**
- 3 **cups beef broth**
- 2 **tablespoons tomato paste**
- ⅓ **cup pitted dried plums, chopped**
- 4 **garlic cloves, minced**
- 2 **bay leaves**
- 1 **fresh rosemary sprig**
- 1 **fresh thyme sprig**
- ⅓ **cup Greek olives, optional**
  Chopped fresh parsley, optional
  Hot cooked mashed potatoes, optional

1. Sprinkle pork with salt and pepper; transfer to a 4-qt. slow cooker. Add carrots, celery and onion. In a small bowl, whisk broth and tomato paste; pour over vegetables. Add plums, garlic, bay leaves, rosemary, thyme and, if desired, olives. Cook, covered, on low 5-6 hours or until meat and vegetables are tender.
2. Discard bay leaves, rosemary and thyme. If desired, sprinkle stew with parsley and serve with potatoes.

CHEDDAR
MUFFINS

CHEDDAR MUFFINS

A moisty, cheesy muffin studded with sweet red pepper and green onions is so satisfying during the winter months. I recommend making a double batch because these disappear in a flash!

—MARIA MORELLI KELOWNA, BC

PREP: 20 MIN. • **BAKE:** 15 MIN.
MAKES: ABOUT 1 DOZEN

- 2½ cups all-purpose flour
- 2 tablespoons sugar
- 2 teaspoons baking powder
- 1 teaspoon Italian seasoning
- ½ teaspoon baking soda
- ½ teaspoon salt
- 1 large egg
- 1½ cups buttermilk
- ⅓ cup canola oil
- 2 garlic cloves, minced
- 2 cups (8 ounces) shredded cheddar cheese
- 4 green onions, sliced
- ½ cup finely chopped sweet red pepper
- 2 tablespoons finely chopped oil-packed sun-dried tomatoes, patted dry
- ⅓ cup shredded Parmesan cheese

1. Preheat oven to 400°. In a large bowl, whisk flour, sugar, baking powder, Italian seasoning, baking soda and salt. In another bowl, whisk egg, buttermilk, oil and garlic until blended. Add to flour mixture; stir just until moistened. Fold in cheddar cheese, onions, pepper and sun-dried tomatoes.

2. Fill greased muffin cups up to three-fourths full. Sprinkle with the Parmesan cheese. Bake 15-18 minutes or until a toothpick inserted in center comes out clean. Cool 5 minutes before removing from the pans to wire racks. Serve warm.

BROWNIE COOKIES

My son is a chocoholic and this is his favorite cookie. Melt the chocolate in a heatproof bowl over simmering water, or melt it in the microwave, stirring often.

—JEANIE NEWTON MILNER, GA

PREP: 15 MIN. • **BAKE:** 10 MIN./BATCH
MAKES: 16 COOKIES

- ½ cup butter, softened
- 1 cup packed brown sugar
- 3 large eggs
- 8 ounces semisweet chocolate, melted and slightly cooled
- 1 teaspoon vanilla extract
- 1¼ cups all-purpose flour
- ¼ cup baking cocoa
- ½ teaspoon baking powder
  Dash salt
- 1 cup semisweet chocolate chunks

1. Preheat oven to 350°. In a large bowl, cream the butter and brown sugar until light and fluffy. Beat in eggs, one at a time, beating well after each addition. Beat in chocolate and vanilla. In a small bowl, whisk the flour, cocoa, baking powder and salt. Stir into the creamed mixture. Fold in chocolate chunks.

2. Drop the dough by quarter cupfuls 3 in. apart onto lightly greased baking sheets. Spread each to about 3-in. diameter. Bake 9-11 minutes or until tops are cracked and cookies are just set. Cool on pans 2 minutes. Remove to wire racks to cool.

MUSHROOM & WILD RICE SOUP

There's no better way to warm up after a day spent skiing or ice skating than with this comforting soup. It calls for four kinds of mushrooms, and the rice mix makes it a snap to prepare.

—MARY MCVEY COLFAX, NC

PREP: 25 MIN. + STANDING • **COOK:** 45 MIN.
MAKES: 12 SERVINGS (2¼ QUARTS)

- 2½ cups water
- 1 ounce dried porcini mushrooms
- 1 ounce dried shiitake mushrooms
- 3 tablespoons butter
- 1 small onion, finely chopped
- ½ pound sliced fresh mushrooms
- ½ pound sliced baby portobello mushrooms
- 3 garlic cloves, minced
- 4 cups chicken broth
- 1 package (6 ounces) long grain and wild rice mix
- ½ teaspoon salt
- ¼ teaspoon white pepper
- ½ cup cold water
- 4 teaspoons cornstarch
- 1 cup heavy whipping cream

1. In a small saucepan, bring water to a boil; add dried mushrooms. Remove from heat; let stand for 25-30 minutes or until softened.

2. Using a slotted spoon, remove mushrooms; rinse. Trim, discard stems from shiitake mushrooms. Chop mushrooms. Strain soaking liquid through a fine-mesh strainer. Reserve mushrooms and soaking liquid.

3. In a Dutch oven, heat butter over medium-high heat. Add onion; cook and stir until tender. Add fresh and baby portobello mushrooms; cook and stir until tender. Add garlic; cook 1 minute longer.

4. Stir in broth, rice mix with contents of seasoning packet, reserved dried mushrooms and soaking liquid, salt and pepper. Bring to a boil. Reduce heat; simmer, covered, 20-25 minutes or until rice is tender. In a small bowl, mix the water and cornstarch until smooth; stir into the soup. Bring to a boil; cook and stir 2 minutes or until thickened. Stir in cream; heat through.

SLOW-COOKER CHAI TEA

The sweet and spicy aroma that wafts from the slow cooker as this pleasantly flavored chai tea cooks will warm you from head to toe.
—CRYSTAL JO BRUNS ILIFF, CO

PREP: 20 MIN. • **COOK:** 8 HOURS
MAKES: 12 SERVINGS (3 QUARTS)

    3½ ounces fresh gingerroot, peeled
        and thinly sliced
    25 whole cloves
    15 cardamom pods, crushed
     3 cinnamon sticks (3 inches)
     3 whole peppercorns
    3½ quarts water
     8 individual black tea bags
     1 can (14 ounces) sweetened
        condensed milk

1. Place the first five ingredients on a double thickness of cheesecloth. Gather corners of cloth to enclose seasonings; tie securely with string. Add spice bag and water to 5- or 6-qt. slow cooker. Cook, covered, on low 8 hours.
2. Add tea bags; cover and steep 3-5 minutes. Discard tea bags and spice bag. Stir in milk; heat through. Serve warm.

KALE ROMAINE SALAD

Kale can be both good for you and tasty! This hearty salad packs a flavor punch thanks to dried cranberries, feta and bacon. It makes a fine side dish or a light meal on its own. I enjoy it with poppy seed salad dressing.
—SHARON REHM NEW BLAINE, AR

START TO FINISH: 15 MIN. • **MAKES:** 8 SERVINGS

     4 cups torn romaine
     4 cups torn fresh kale
     1 cup grape tomatoes, halved
     1 cup sliced almonds, toasted
     8 bacon strips, cooked and
        crumbled
     ½ cup dried cranberries
     ½ cup crumbled feta cheese
     4 green onions, sliced
        Salad dressing of your choice

In a large bowl, combine the first eight ingredients. Serve with dressing.

PUMPKIN-SPICED HOT CHOCOLATE

As soon as there's a cool breeze in the air, I think of my mother. She served pumpkin pie with homemade hot chocolate. This recipe brings those two amazing scents, and her, back to life for me. To turn your hot chocolate into creamy pumpkin mocha, stir 2 teaspoons of instant coffee into the hot chocolate before adding whipped cream.
—J. MORAND MAITLAND, ON

START TO FINISH: 25 MIN.
MAKES: 8 SERVINGS (1 CUP EACH)

     5 cups 2% milk
     1 package (10 to 12 ounces) white
        baking chips
     1 cup heavy whipping cream
     ½ cup solid-pack pumpkin
    1½ teaspoons ground cinnamon
     1 teaspoon vanilla extract
     ¼ teaspoon ground ginger
TOPPING
     ½ cup heavy whipping cream
     2 tablespoons confectioners'
        sugar
     ¼ teaspoon vanilla extract
     ⅛ teaspoon ground cinnamon

1. In a large saucepan, whisk milk, baking chips and cream over medium heat until mixture is smooth and creamy (do not boil). Remove from heat. Whisk in pumpkin, cinnamon, vanilla and ginger.
2. Meanwhile, in a small bowl, beat cream until it begins to thicken. Add confectioners' sugar and vanilla; beat until soft peaks form. Top servings with whipped cream; sprinkle with cinnamon.

DECORATED MUGS

Embrace your inner artist! You don't need to be a professional calligrapher to handwrite pretty words and designs. Oil-based Sharpie markers—available at craft and art supply stores—make it easy to add a personal touch to plain white ceramic mugs. If you're hosting a winter warm-up party, get guests (kids, too!) involved in the fun of creating the designs. Or decorate and bake the mugs ahead of time to give as a cheery take-home gift.

MATERIALS

White ceramic mugs
**Medium-point oil-based
  Sharpie markers (see Note)**
Rubbing alcohol
Cotton balls
Aluminum foil
Baking sheet

DIRECTIONS

1. Remove any labels or stickers on mugs. Clean mugs if needed, using a cotton ball dipped in rubbing alcohol to wipe surfaces where design will be drawn.
2. If desired, use a pencil to lightly draw the desired design as a guide on each mug. Trace over pencil lines on mugs, using desired markers, or draw desired designs freehand. Let mugs dry for 8 hours or overnight.
3. Place the mugs on foil-lined baking sheet and place in a cold oven. Preheat oven to 350°. When oven reaches 350°, bake mugs for 30 minutes. Without removing mugs, turn off oven, leaving mugs in oven to cool completely.
NOTE *When baked, the Sharpie paint may change color slightly. Decorated mugs must be hand-washed.*

DECORATED MUGS,
WITH PUMPKIN-SPICED
HOT CHOCOLATE

Breakfast at Midnight

Midnight bells have rung in the New Year, but the party is still going strong. Keep all your champagne-sipping friends full and happy with this selection of **impressive breakfast favorites that are just as fabulous after dark.**

Your party will shine when you set a chorizo-stuffed crescent ring on the table. Sparkling **Cranberry Kiss is worthy of a midnight smooch**, while French toast waffles will be enjoyed down to the very last frilled toothpick. As for croque madame? Let's just say **Julia Child would be proud** of this ham and cheese.

New Year's is all about living in the moment, so grab one of these extra-special finger foods and **raise your glass to the year ahead!**

Scrambled Egg Hash Brown Cups (p. 65) **Holiday Peppermint Mocha** (p. 60) **French Toast Waffles** (p. 62)

HOLIDAY PEPPERMINT MOCHA

APPLE 'N' PEAR KABOBS

Instead of scooping chunks of fruit on a platter, be adventurous and go kabob-style. Drizzled with a butter pecan sauce, these are irresistible.

—ROBIN BOYNTON HARBOR BEACH, MI

START TO FINISH: 30 MIN. • **MAKES:** 12 SERVINGS

- 5 **medium apples, cut into 1-inch chunks**
- 4 **medium pears, cut into 1-inch chunks**
- 1 **tablespoon lemon juice**
- BUTTER PECAN SAUCE
- ⅓ **cup packed brown sugar**
- 2 **tablespoons sugar**
- 4 **teaspoons cornstarch**
- ¾ **cup heavy whipping cream**
- 1 **tablespoon butter**
- ½ **cup chopped pecans**

1. Toss apples and pears with lemon juice. Thread fruit chunks alternately onto 12 metal or soaked wooden skewers; place on an ungreased baking sheet. Bake at 350° for 15-20 minutes or until tender.
2. Meanwhile, in a small saucepan, combine the sugars and cornstarch. Gradually stir in cream until smooth. Bring to a boil, stirring constantly; cook and stir for 2-3 minutes or until slightly thickened.
3. Remove from the heat; stir in butter until smooth. Add pecans. Serve warm with kabobs.

HOLIDAY PEPPERMINT MOCHA

The classic flavors of mint, chocolate and coffee unite in this tempting hot beverage. Coffee liqueur in place of the peppermint schnapps also will yield fantastic results. For extra fun, slip a mini doughnut over the rim of the mug (see previous page). Dunk away!

—LAUREN BRIEN-WOOSTER SOUTH LAKE TAHOE, CA

START TO FINISH: 10 MIN.
MAKES: 8 SERVINGS

- 4 **cups 2% milk**
- 8 **packets instant hot cocoa mix**
- 1½ **cups brewed espresso or double-strength dark roast coffee**
- ¾ **cup peppermint schnapps liqueur or 1 teaspoon peppermint extract plus ¾ cup additional brewed espresso**
  Whipped cream, optional

1. In a large saucepan, heat milk over medium heat until bubbles form around sides of pan. Add cocoa mix; whisk until blended. Add espresso and heat through.
2. Remove from heat; stir in liqueur. If desired, serve with whipped cream.

HAM AND CHEDDAR SCONES

Flecks of cheese, ham and green onions add great color to these tasty scones. I first got the recipe from a friend, and I now prepare it often.

—FELICITY LA RUE PALMDALE, CA

PREP: 25 MIN. • **BAKE:** 20 MIN.
MAKES: 1 DOZEN

- 3 **cups all-purpose flour**
- ½ **cup sugar**
- 2 **tablespoons baking powder**
- ½ **teaspoon salt**
- 2 **cups heavy whipping cream**
- 1 **cup diced fully cooked ham**
- ½ **cup diced cheddar cheese**
- 4 **green onions, thinly sliced**

1. Preheat oven to 400°. In a large bowl, combine flour, sugar, baking powder and salt. Stir in cream just until moistened. Stir in ham, cheese and onions. Turn onto a floured surface; knead 10 times.
2. Transfer dough to a greased baking sheet. Pat into a 9-in. circle. Cut into 12 wedges, but do not separate. Bake 20-25 minutes or until golden brown. Serve warm.

TOP TIP

More Fun with Fruit

Looking for more easy and delicious ways to use up apples and pears? Try one of these simple desserts.

- To make baked apples or pears, core fruit and stuff with brown sugar, cinnamon and butter. Place in a baking dish with a little water and bake until tender.
- Fry apple or pear slices in a greased skillet until tender. Sprinkle with cinnamon-sugar. Serve warm with vanilla ice cream.
- Blend a package of cream cheese with brown sugar and vanilla to taste. Serve as a dip with apple or pear slices.

PIGS IN A POOL

If you love pancakes and sausage, this recipe is for you. My homemade version of pigs in a blanket is a great alternative to the packaged kind, and the muffins freeze like a dream.

—LISA DODD GREENVILLE, SC

PREP: 45 MIN. • **BAKE:** 20 MIN. • **MAKES:** 4 DOZEN

- 1 **pound reduced-fat bulk pork sausage**
- 2 **cups all-purpose flour**
- ¼ **cup sugar**
- 1 **tablespoon baking powder**
- 1 **teaspoon salt**
- ½ **teaspoon ground cinnamon**
- ¼ **teaspoon ground nutmeg**
- 1 **large egg, lightly beaten**
- 2 **cups fat-free milk**
- 2 **tablespoons canola oil**
- 2 **tablespoons honey**
  Maple syrup, optional

1. Preheat oven to 350°. Coat the mini-muffin cups with cooking spray.

2. Shape sausage into forty-eight ¾-in. balls. Place meatballs on a rack coated with cooking spray in a shallow baking pan. Bake 15-20 minutes or until cooked through. Drain on paper towels. In a large bowl, whisk flour, sugar, baking powder, salt and spices. In another bowl, whisk egg, milk, oil and honey until blended. Add to the flour mixture; stir just until moistened.

3. Place a sausage ball into each mini-muffin cup; cover with batter. Bake 20-25 minutes or until lightly browned. Cool 5 minutes before removing from pans to wire racks. Serve warm with syrup if desired.

FREEZE OPTION *Freeze cooled muffins in resealable plastic freezer bags. To use, microwave each muffin on high for 20-30 seconds or until heated through.*

PIGS IN A POOL

FRENCH TOAST WAFFLES

Sometimes you just can't decide if you want French toast or waffles, so have both! I'm a from-scratch cook but also like shortcuts. I use a waffle iron to make this hybrid French toast.

—LINDA MARTINDALE ELKHORN, WI

PREP: 15 MIN. • **COOK:** 5 MIN./BATCH
MAKES: 16 WAFFLES

- 8 **large eggs**
- 2 **cups 2% milk**
- ½ **cup sugar**
- 1 **teaspoon vanilla extract**
- ½ **teaspoon ground cinnamon**
- ½ **teaspoon ground nutmeg**
- 16 **slices Texas toast**
  Maple syrup

In a large bowl, whisk the first six ingredients until blended. Dip both sides of bread in egg mixture. Place in a preheated waffle iron; bake 4-5 minutes or until golden brown. If desired, cut waffles into thirds. Serve with syrup.

FREEZE OPTION *Cool waffles on wire racks. Freeze between layers of waxed paper in resealable plastic freezer bags. Reheat frozen waffles in a toaster on medium setting.*

SPARKLING CRANBERRY KISS

Cranberry and orange juices pair terrifically with ginger ale in this party punch. I use cranberry juice cocktail, but other blends like cranberry-apple also sparkle. The recipe is easily doubled, tripled or even quadrupled.

—SHANNON COPLEY PICKERINGTON, OH

START TO FINISH: 5 MIN.
MAKES: 14 SERVINGS (¾ CUP EACH)

- 6 **cups cranberry juice**
- 1½ **cups orange juice**
- 3 **cups ginger ale**
  Ice cubes
  Orange slices, optional

In a pitcher, combine cranberry juice and orange juice. Just before serving, stir in ginger ale; serve over ice. If desired, serve with orange slices.

BREADED BRUNCH BACON

Make bacon even more delicious with this recipe. It earned a permanent spot in my tried-and-true recipe collection after just one bite! Guests can't resist it.

—REBECCA NOVAKOVICH DALLAS, TX

PREP: 15 MIN. • **BAKE:** 30 MIN.
MAKES: 10 SERVINGS

- 2 **large eggs**
- 2 **tablespoons white vinegar**
- 1 **teaspoon prepared mustard**
- ½ **teaspoon cayenne pepper**
- 1½ **cups finely crushed reduced-sodium saltines (about 45 crackers)**
- 10 **thick-sliced bacon strips, halved widthwise**

1. In a shallow dish, whisk the eggs, vinegar, mustard and cayenne. Place cracker crumbs in another shallow dish. Dip bacon in egg mixture, then roll in crumbs.

2. Arrange in a single layer on two foil-lined 15x10x1-in. baking pans. Bake at 350° for 15 minutes; turn. Bake 15-20 minutes longer or until golden brown. Remove to paper towels to drain. Serve warm.

CROQUE MADAME

Croque madame is a variation of the classic croque monsieur, a French-style grilled ham and cheese sandwich similar to a Monte Cristo. My son and I both love the madame version, which calls for a fried sunny-side egg on top. Who would have guessed that French cooking could be so easy and so fun?

—CAROLYN TURNER RENO, NV

START TO FINISH: 30 MIN. • **MAKES:** 8 SERVINGS

- 1 **pound thinly sliced Gruyere cheese, divided**
- 16 **slices sourdough bread**
- 1½ **pounds thinly sliced deli ham**
- ½ **cup butter, softened**
- 4 **to 6 tablespoons mayonnaise**

EGGS

- 2 **tablespoons butter**
- 8 **large eggs**
- ½ **teaspoon salt**
- ½ **teaspoon pepper**

1. Preheat oven to 400°. Place half of the cheese on eight bread slices; top with ham and remaining bread. Spread outsides of sandwiches with softened butter.

2. On a griddle, toast sandwiches over medium heat 2-3 minutes on each side or until golden brown. Spread tops with mayonnaise; top with remaining cheese. Transfer to an ungreased baking sheet; bake 4-5 minutes or until cheese is melted.

3. Meanwhile, for eggs, heat 1 tablespoon butter on griddle over medium-high heat. Break four eggs, one at a time, onto griddle. Reduce the heat to low. Cook until desired doneness, turning after whites are set if desired. Sprinkle with salt and pepper. Place eggs over sandwiches. Repeat with remaining ingredients.

CROQUE
MADAME

CHORIZO & EGG
BREAKFAST RING

CHORIZO & EGG BREAKFAST RING

People go crazy when I bring this loaded crescent ring to parties. I bake it at home the night before. Of course, everyone's happy when we have it for dinner, too!

—FRANCES BLACKWELDER
GRAND JUNCTION, CO

PREP: 25 MIN. • **BAKE:** 15 MIN.
MAKES: 8 SERVINGS

- 2 tubes (8 ounces each) refrigerated crescent rolls
- ½ pound uncooked chorizo, casings removed, or bulk spicy pork sausage
- 8 large eggs
- ¼ teaspoon salt
- ¼ teaspoon pepper
- 1 tablespoon butter
- 1 cup (4 ounces) shredded pepper jack cheese
- 1 cup salsa

1. Preheat oven to 375°. Unroll crescent dough and separate into triangles. On an ungreased 12-in. pizza pan, arrange the triangles in a ring with points toward the outside and wide ends overlapping. Press overlapping dough to seal.
2. In a large skillet, cook chorizo over medium heat 6-8 minutes or until cooked through, breaking into crumbles. Remove with a slotted spoon; drain on paper towels. Discard drippings, wiping skillet clean.
3. In a small bowl, whisk eggs, salt and pepper until blended. In same skillet, heat butter over medium heat. Pour in the egg mixture; cook and stir until eggs are thickened and no liquid egg remains.
4. Spoon egg mixture, chorizo and cheese across wide end of triangles. Fold pointed end of triangles over filling, tucking points under to form a ring (filling will be visible).
5. Bake 15-20 minutes or until golden brown. Serve with salsa.

SCRAMBLED EGG HASH BROWN CUPS

These cuties pack favorite breakfast foods—eggs, hash browns and bacon—in one single-serving-size cup (see page 59). Grab one and get mingling.

—TALON DIMARE BULLHEAD CITY, AZ

PREP: 10 MIN. • **BAKE:** 25 MIN.
MAKES: 1 DOZEN

- 1 package (20 ounces) refrigerated Southwest-style shredded hash brown potatoes
- 6 large eggs
- ½ cup 2% milk
- ⅛ teaspoon salt
- 1 tablespoon butter
- 10 thick-sliced bacon strips, cooked and crumbled
- 1¼ cups (5 ounces) shredded cheddar-Monterey Jack cheese, divided

1. Preheat oven to 400°. Divide the potatoes among 12 greased muffin cups; press onto bottoms and up sides to form cups. Bake 18-20 minutes or until light golden brown.
2. Meanwhile, in a small bowl, whisk eggs, milk and salt. In a large nonstick skillet, heat butter over medium heat. Pour in egg mixture; cook, stir until eggs are thickened and no liquid egg remains. Stir in bacon and ¾ cup cheese. Spoon into cups; sprinkle with remaining ½ cup cheese.
3. Bake 3-5 minutes or until cheese is melted. Cool 5 minutes before removing from pan.

BANANA BEIGNET BITES

When I was a little girl, my grandmother taught me how to make her famous banana beignets. Although we made them during the holidays, they're fantastic any time of the year.

—AMY DOWNING SOUTH RIDING, VA

START TO FINISH: 30 MIN.
MAKES: ABOUT 3 DOZEN

- ¾ cup sugar
- ¼ cup packed brown sugar
- 1½ teaspoons ground cinnamon

BEIGNETS

- 2 cups cake flour
- ¾ cup sugar
- 2½ teaspoons baking powder
- ½ teaspoon ground cinnamon
- 1 teaspoon salt
- 1 large egg
- 1 cup mashed ripe bananas (about 3 medium)
- ½ cup whole milk
- 2 tablespoons canola oil
  Oil for deep-fat frying

1. In a small bowl, mix sugars and cinnamon until blended. In a large bowl, whisk the first five beignet ingredients. In another bowl, whisk egg, bananas, milk and 2 tablespoons oil until blended. Add to flour mixture; stir just until moistened.
2. In an electric skillet or deep fryer, heat oil to 375°. Drop tablespoonfuls of batter, a few at a time, into hot oil. Fry about 45-60 seconds on each side or until golden brown. Drain on paper towels. Roll warm beignets in sugar mixture.

HOW-TO

MAKE A BREAKFAST RING
Carefully pull the points of the crescent dough triangles straight over the filling to the inside of the ring. Tuck the points under the base, and bake away.

Secret Santa Cookies

For any Christmas celebration, there's nothing like a warm, freshly baked cookie to make the moment memorable. From gem tassies to classic gingerbreads, these **melt-in-your-mouth cookie creations make it easy and fun** to indulge in the sweetness of the season.

Not only are cookies a joy to bake, but they also are a joy to give. If you're part of a Secret Santa group this year—or just want to **surprise a loved one** with an anonymous gift—let our recipes and packaging ideas be your inspiration. And turn to page 76 for a photo gift tag project that will make your delivery even merrier.

It's time to **break out the mixing bowls.** Let the baking begin!

Gingerbread Snow Globe (p. 71)

**COCONUT
RUM BALLS**

COCONUT RUM BALLS

My mom has made rum balls for as long as I can remember. They look beautiful on a dessert spread and can be packaged in a decorative tin as a gift. I swapped coconut rum for the traditional rum and added shredded coconut.

—**JANA WALKER** MACOMB, MI

PREP: 25 MIN. + STANDING
MAKES: 4½ DOZEN

- 1 **package (12 ounces) vanilla wafers, finely crushed**
- 1 **cup confectioners' sugar**
- 2 **tablespoons baking cocoa**
- 1 **cup flaked coconut**
- 1 **cup chopped pecans**
- ½ **cup light corn syrup**
- ¼ **cup coconut rum**
  Additional confectioners' sugar

1. In a large bowl, whisk the crushed wafers, confectioners' sugar and cocoa. Stir in coconut and pecans. In a small bowl, whisk corn syrup and rum; stir into wafer mixture. Shape into 1-in. balls; let stand 1 hour.
2. Roll in additional confectioners' sugar. Store in an airtight container.

GINGERBREAD SNOW GLOBE

I make a big batch of these gingerbreads every Christmas to give to co-workers and family. For a festive decoration, arrange cookies in a large clear jar to look like a snow globe.

—**KELLY KIRBY** VICTORIA, BC

PREP: 1¼ HOURS + CHILLING
BAKE: 10 MIN./BATCH + COOLING
MAKES: ABOUT 6 DOZEN (4-IN. COOKIES)

- ½ **cup warm water**
- 2 **tablespoons white vinegar**
- 1 **cup shortening**
- 1 **cup sugar**
- 1 **cup molasses**
- 6 **cups all-purpose flour**
- 3 **teaspoons ground cinnamon**
- 3 **teaspoons ground ginger**
- 2 **teaspoons baking soda**
- 1 **teaspoon salt**
- ½ **teaspoon ground cloves**
  Light corn syrup
  Coarse sugar
  Assorted sprinkles

1. Mix water and vinegar. In a large bowl, cream shortening and sugar

GINGERBREAD SNOW GLOBE

until light and fluffy. Beat in molasses. In another bowl, whisk the flour, cinnamon, ginger, baking soda, salt and cloves; add to creamed mixture alternately with water mixture, beating well after each addition.
2. Divide the dough into six portions. Shape each into a disk; wrap in plastic wrap. Refrigerate 2 hours or until firm enough to roll.
3. Preheat oven to 350°. On a lightly floured surface, roll each portion of dough to ¼-in. thickness. Cut dough with assorted holiday cookie cutters. Place 2 in. apart on ungreased baking sheets. Bake 10-12 minutes or until set. Cool on pans 1 minute. Remove to wire racks to cool completely.
4. Using a new paintbrush, brush corn syrup onto edges of cookies; dip into coarse sugar. Decorate with sprinkles. Let stand until set.
5. For snow globe, place coarse sugar in a large decorative glass jar. Arrange cookies in sugar so they stand upright. Decorate jar with ribbon.

NOTE *To decorate cookies like those on the cover, frost or pipe cookies with plain or tinted frosting. Decorate with sprinkles. Let stand until set.*

TOP TIP

Frost it Up!

We love the simplicity of these plain gingerbreads decorated with just a touch of whimsy, but you can go all out and decorate with frosting, too. For a very simple look, pipe the frosting on as an outline around the edge of the cookies. Or sponge some thinned frosting on the cookies with a trimmed piece from a new, clean sponge. If you're not concerned about calories, spread frosting over the cookies and decorate as desired. Put the frosting in clean, empty squeeze bottles like those used for ketchup and mustard. They are easier to fill than decorating bags and also quick to clean.

CHOCOLATE-DIPPED LEMON COOKIES

I make these light and tasty cookies every holiday season, and everybody finds them irresistible. I dip the ends into melted chocolate for a sweet addition.

—SANDY KLOCINSKI SUMMERVILLE, SC

PREP: 35 MIN. • **BAKE:** 10 MIN./BATCH + COOLING
MAKES: ABOUT 5 DOZEN

- 1 cup unsalted butter, softened
- 1 cup sugar
- 1 large egg
- 1 large egg yolk
- 2 teaspoons grated lemon peel
- 1 teaspoon vanilla extract
- 2½ cups all-purpose flour
- 1 teaspoon baking powder
- ¼ teaspoon salt
- 6 ounces semisweet chocolate, chopped
- 1 teaspoon shortening

1. Preheat oven to 350°. In a large bowl, cream butter and sugar until light and fluffy. Beat in egg, egg yolk, lemon peel and vanilla. In another bowl, whisk flour, baking powder and salt; gradually beat into the creamed mixture. Cut a small hole in the tip of a pastry bag or in a corner of a food-safe plastic bag; insert a ¾-inch round tip. Transfer dough to bag. Pipe 2-in. S-shaped logs 2 in. apart onto parchment paper-lined baking sheets.

2. Bake 10-12 minutes or until edges are lightly browned. Cool on pans 2 minutes. Remove to wire racks to cool completely.

3. In top of a double boiler or a metal bowl over hot water, melt chocolate and shortening; stir until smooth. Dip one end of cookies in glaze, allowing excess to drip off. Place on waxed paper; let stand until set.

RASPBERRY SNOWFLAKE SANDWICH COOKIES

When my son was growing up, I made these cookies with him every Christmas Eve. He loved using the straws to punch out the holes in the snowflakes. Now he's grown up, so I make them with my niece. It's a wonderful Christmas tradition!

—RENEE BETTICH NELSON STEVENSVILLE, MI

PREP: 20 MIN. + CHILLING • **BAKE:** 10 MIN./BATCH
MAKES: ABOUT 1½ DOZEN

- ½ cup butter, softened
- ¼ cup shortening
- ¾ cup sugar
- 1 large egg
- 1 tablespoon lemon juice
- 2 cups all-purpose flour
- 1½ teaspoons baking powder
- ½ teaspoon ground cinnamon
- ¼ teaspoon salt
- ¼ teaspoon ground nutmeg
- 2 drinking straws (different sizes)
- ½ cup seedless raspberry jam
  Confectioners' sugar

1. In a large bowl, cream the butter, shortening and sugar until light and fluffy. Beat in egg and lemon juice. In another bowl, whisk flour, baking powder, cinnamon, salt and nutmeg; gradually beat into creamed mixture.

2. Divide dough in half. Shape each into a disk; wrap in plastic wrap. Refrigerate 2 hours until firm enough to roll.

3. Preheat oven to 375°. On a floured surface, roll each portion of dough to ⅛-in. thickness. Cut with floured 2½-in. scalloped round cookie cutter. Using straws, cut several holes in half of the cutouts, twisting the straws to release. Place the cutouts 2 in. apart on baking sheets.

4. Bake 6-8 minutes or until edges are light brown. Cool on pan slightly. Remove from pans to wire racks to cool completely.

5. Spread about 1 teaspoon jam on bottoms of solid cookies; top with cutout cookies. Sprinkle tops of cookies with confectioners' sugar.

ORANGE TWISTS

These soft and sweet twists have a long shelf life. You can make many variations on this recipe, including lemon, cherry and almond. I like to add confectioners' sugar glaze.

—RAINE GOTTESS WELLINGTON, FL

PREP: 25 MIN. + CHILLING • **BAKE:** 10 MIN./BATCH
MAKES: ABOUT 3 DOZEN

- 1 cup butter, softened
- 1½ cups confectioners' sugar
- 1 large egg
- 1 teaspoon vanilla extract
- 2½ cups all-purpose flour
- ½ cup cake flour
- ½ teaspoon salt
- 2 teaspoons grated orange peel
- 4 drops yellow food coloring
- 2 drops red food coloring

1. In a large bowl, cream butter and confectioners' sugar until blended. Beat in egg and vanilla. In another bowl, whisk flours and salt; gradually beat into creamed mixture.

2. Divide dough in half. Mix orange peel and food colorings into one half; leave remaining dough plain. Wrap each in plastic wrap; refrigerate 1 hour or until firm enough to roll.

3. Preheat oven to 350°. Divide each half into eight portions. Roll each portion into a 15-in. rope. Place one plain rope and one orange rope side by side; press together lightly. Cut the rope crosswise into 3-in. pieces. Twist each piece several times; place 2 in. apart on ungreased baking sheets. Repeat with the remaining dough. Bake 7-9 minutes or until bottoms are golden brown. Cool on pans for 2 minutes. Remove to wire racks to cool.

ORANGE
TWISTS

WAFFLE IRON COOKIES

WAFFLE IRON COOKIES

The recipe for these cookies is the easiest to find in my book because it's a beautiful mess—covered with fingerprints, flour smudges and memories of more than 30 Christmases! I made these with my daughters, and now I make them with my granddaughters.

—JUDY TAYLOR ELKTON, MD

PREP: 10 MIN. • **BAKE:** 5 MIN./BATCH + COOLING
MAKES: 32 COOKIES (8 BATCHES)

- ½ cup butter, softened
- 1 cup sugar
- 2 large eggs
- 1 teaspoon vanilla extract
- 1½ cups all-purpose flour
- 1 teaspoon baking powder
- ½ teaspoon salt
  Confectioners' sugar

1. In a large bowl, cream butter and sugar until light and fluffy. Beat in eggs and vanilla. In another bowl, whisk flour, baking powder and salt; gradually beat into creamed mixture (mixture will be thick).
2. Drop the dough in batches by tablespoonfuls 3-4 in. apart onto a greased preheated waffle iron. Bake 2-3 minutes or until dark brown.
3. Remove to wire racks to cool completely. Sprinkle with confectioners' sugar.

DATE-FILLED PINWHEELS

My mom made these family favorites when I was growing up. Sliced thin, these cookies are crispy and chewy; sliced thick, they have a cake-like texture. They make an attractive gift.

—KATHRYN WILKINS NORFOLK, VA

PREP: 20 MIN. + CHILLING • **BAKE:** 10 MIN.
MAKES: ABOUT 2½ DOZEN

- ¾ cup firmly packed chopped dates
- ⅓ cup sugar
- ⅓ cup water
- ⅓ cup chopped pecans
- ⅓ cup shortening
- ⅔ cup packed brown sugar
- 1 large egg
- ¼ teaspoon vanilla extract
- 1⅓ cups all-purpose flour
- ¼ teaspoon salt
- ⅛ teaspoon baking soda

1. In a large saucepan, combine dates, sugar and water. Cook and stir over medium heat 10 minutes until very soft. Add pecans; cool. In a large bowl, cream shortening and brown sugar. Beat in egg and vanilla. In another bowl, whisk flour, salt and baking soda; gradually beat into creamed mixture. Refrigerate, covered, 1 hour or until easy to handle.
2. On a lightly floured surface, roll out dough into an 8-in. square. Spread with date mixture; roll up jelly-roll style. Wrap with plastic wrap. Refrigerate 4 hours or until firm.
3. Preheat oven to 400°. Unwrap and cut dough crosswise into ¼-in. slices. Place 2 in. apart on greased baking sheets. Bake 8-10 minutes or until golden brown. Remove from pans to wire racks to cool.

CRANBERRY PRETZEL COOKIES

These salty and sweet delights are perfect for cookie exchanges. I use cream cheese to make the cookies extra rich.

—MEG BAGLEY LOGAN, UT

PREP: 30 MIN. • **BAKE:** 15 MIN./BATCH
MAKES: ABOUT 3½ DOZEN

- 1 cup butter, softened
- 1 package (8 ounces) cream cheese, softened
- ¾ cup sugar
- ¾ cup packed brown sugar
- 2 teaspoons vanilla extract
- 2¼ cups all-purpose flour
- 1 teaspoon baking soda
- ½ teaspoon salt
- 2 cups coarsely crushed pretzels (about ½-inch pieces)
- 1 cup dried cranberries
- 1 cup white baking chips

1. Preheat oven to 350°. In a large bowl, cream butter, cream cheese and sugars until light and fluffy. Beat in vanilla. In another bowl, whisk flour, baking soda and salt; gradually beat into the creamed mixture. Stir in pretzels, cranberries and baking chips.
2. Drop the dough by rounded tablespoonfuls 2 in. apart onto greased baking sheets. Bake for 11-14 minutes or until edges are golden brown. Cool on pans for 2 minutes. Remove to wire racks to cool.

TOP TIP

Pretty Packaging Ideas

You don't have to spend a fortune or valuable time at the mall in search of perfect Christmas gifts. Often the most priceless treasures are your own homemade cookies, brownies or treats presented in decorative tins or in one of the pretty packages suggested below.

- At Christmastime, craft and variety stores sell papier-mache boxes perfect for gift giving. You can stack star-shaped sugar cookies in a star-shaped papier-mache box that's been lined with wax-coated tissue paper.
- Decorative tins, plates and candy dishes often can be found at bargain prices throughout the year at stores and rummage sales and at after-Christmas sales. Keep them on hand for last-minute gifts.
- Stack cookies in a wide-mouth canning jar, cover the lid with fabric and screw on the band. You may also want to include the recipe for the cookies.
- Instead of discarding potato chip cans, coffee tins or shortening cans, wash them, decorate the outside with wrapping paper or Con-Tact paper and fill with cookies or candies. Attach a bow to the lid and close.
- Wrap cookies in plastic wrap, place a bow on top and tuck inside a pretty coffee mug or teacup.

CHOCOLATE CHIP PEPPERMINT BISCOTTI

My family loves peppermint. When I pair it with chocolate in crunchy biscotti, we know that the Christmas season has arrived. Dunk these in a glass of cold milk, hot chocolate or coffee...and ahh.

—KATHERINE WOLLGAST FLORISSANT, MO

PREP: 10 MIN. • **BAKE:** 45 MIN. + COOLING
MAKES: ABOUT 3½ DOZEN

- ½ cup butter, softened
- 1⅓ cups sugar
- 3 large eggs
- ½ teaspoon peppermint extract
- 4 cups all-purpose flour
- 1 teaspoon baking powder
- ½ teaspoon salt
- ½ cup crushed peppermint candies
- ½ cup miniature semisweet chocolate chips

1. Preheat oven to 350°. In a large bowl, cream butter and sugar until light and fluffy. Beat in the eggs and extract. In another bowl, whisk flour, baking powder and salt; gradually beat into creamed mixture. Stir in crushed candies and chocolate chips.
2. Divide the dough in half. On a parchment paper-lined baking sheet, shape each portion into a 10x3-in. rectangle. Bake for 30-35 minutes or until light brown. Cool on pans on wire racks 15 minutes or until firm.
3. Transfer baked rectangles to a cutting board. Using a serrated knife, cut diagonally into ½-in. slices. Place on baking sheets, cut side down.
4. Bake 15-18 minutes or until crisp and golden brown. Remove from pans to wire racks to cool completely. Store between pieces of waxed paper in an airtight container.

PECAN-FILLED MAPLE COOKIES

These festive cookies melt in your mouth, and look and taste just like a personal-size pecan pie. My clan eats them straight from the cooling rack. The treats rarely make it to the cookie jar!

—TAEREE GLOVER SEDAN, KS

PREP: 20 MIN. + CHILLING • **BAKE:** 15 MIN./BATCH
MAKES: 2½ DOZEN

- 1 cup butter, softened
- ½ cup sugar
- ½ cup maple syrup
- 2 large egg yolks
- 2½ cups all-purpose flour

PECAN FILLING
- ¼ cup butter, cubed
- 3 tablespoons maple syrup
- ⅔ cup confectioners' sugar
- ½ cup chopped pecans
- 2 large egg whites

1. In a large bowl, cream butter and sugar until light and fluffy. Beat in maple syrup and egg yolks. Beat in flour. Wrap dough in plastic wrap; refrigerate 2 hours or until firm. Meanwhile, in a small saucepan, combine butter, maple syrup and confectioners' sugar. Cook over medium heat until mixture reaches a rolling boil, stirring occasionally. Remove from heat; fold in pecans. Cool slightly; refrigerate until cooled completely.
2. Preheat oven to 350°. In a small bowl, whisk egg whites. Shape dough into 1-in. balls. Press a 1-inch wide indentation in the center of each ball, leaving a ¼-in. shell. Dip in the egg whites; place 2 in. apart on greased baking sheets. Bake for 6 minutes. Press 1 rounded teaspoon pecan filling into center of each cookie. Bake 7-9 minutes longer or until golden brown. Cool on pans for 2 minutes. Remove to wire racks to cool.

PHOTO GIFT TAGS

Create a personalized gift tag for everyone on your Christmas list this year. If you want to have even more fun with the Secret Santa theme, use photos in place of names. You'll easily remember to whom each gift belongs without having to handwrite "To" and "From" on the tags. Recipients will appreciate the heartfelt creative touch as much as the delicious cookies!

MATERIALS
- Desired photos
- Decorative card stock
- Narrow satin ribbon
- Two circle or square paper punches of slightly different sizes
- Craft glue

DIRECTIONS
1. Using the smaller paper punch, punch out each desired photo. Using the larger paper punch, punch out a card stock shape for each photo.
2. If making circle tags, glue each photo to the center of a card stock circle. Glue the ends of a short length of ribbon to each tag to resemble the hanging loop of an ornament.
3. If making square tags, glue two short lengths of ribbon in a crisscross shape across the front of each card stock square. Glue each photo to the center of a card stock square. Tie a short length of ribbon into a bow and glue to the top of each tag to resemble the bow on a gift.
4. Let tags dry completely. Attach to cookie packaging.

Holiday Cakes

Cake is the royalty of all desserts. So it only stands to reason that it's the perfect Christmas-dinner finale. **Spark your creativity and satisfy your sweet tooth craving all in one** with this scrumptious assortment of festive cakes.

Love the classic combo of mint and chocolate? You won't be able to turn down our impressive triple decker crowned with chopped Andes candies. **A heavenly slice of a rich, velvety cheesecake is sure to win you raves.** Or maybe a light and airy angel food cake or a moist, cream-filled roll is in order this holiday?

Turn the page to find an array of splendid choices, from simple to lavish, to **make the season memorable**.

Red Velvet Cake Roll with White Chocolate Filling (p. 85)

MINT-FROSTED
CHOCOLATE CAKE

MINT-FROSTED CHOCOLATE CAKE

I often make a peanut butter version of this cake but wanted to switch things up by introducing a new flavor. I tinkered with the recipe and decided mint was my new go-to ingredient. My son came up with the idea for the frosting. The rest is delicious history! The cake is fragile, so freezing the layers makes them easier to handle.

—MELANIE COOKSEY MONROE, GA

PREP: 25 MIN. + CHILLING
BAKE: 30 MIN. + COOLING • **MAKES:** 16 SERVINGS

- 2 large eggs
- 1½ cups water
- 1 cup canola oil
- 1 cup (8 ounces) sour cream
- 2 tablespoons white vinegar
- 1 teaspoon vanilla extract
- 2½ cups sugar
- 2 cups all-purpose flour
- ¾ cup baking cocoa
- 2 teaspoons baking soda
- 1 teaspoon salt

MINT FROSTING
- 1 package (8 ounces) cream cheese, softened
- ½ cup butter, softened
- 5 cups confectioners' sugar
- ¾ teaspoon mint extract
- 2 to 3 drops green food coloring
- 24 mint Andes candies, chopped

CHOCOLATE GLAZE
- 8 ounces semisweet chocolate, coarsely chopped
- ½ cup half-and-half cream
- 2 tablespoons light corn syrup
  Additional mint Andes candies, chopped, optional

1. Preheat oven to 350°. Line bottom of three greased 8-in. round baking pans with parchment paper; grease paper.
2. In a large bowl, beat eggs, water, oil, sour cream, vinegar, and vanilla until well blended. In another bowl, whisk sugar, flour, cocoa, baking soda and salt; gradually beat into egg mixture.
3. Transfer to prepared pans. Bake 30-35 minutes or until a toothpick inserted in center comes out clean. Cool in pans for 10 minutes before removing to wire racks; remove paper. Cool completely.
4. In a large bowl, beat cream cheese and butter until blended. Gradually beat in confectioners' sugar until smooth. Beat in mint extract and food coloring.
5. Place one cake layer on a serving plate; spread with ⅔ cup mint frosting. Sprinkle with half of the mints. Repeat the layers. Top with remaining cake layer. Frost the top and sides of cake with remaining frosting. Refrigerate until set.
6. Place chocolate in a small bowl. In a small saucepan, bring cream just to a boil. Pour over chocolate; let stand 5 minutes. Stir with a whisk until smooth. Stir in corn syrup. Cool slightly, stirring occasionally. Pour over cake and quickly spread to edges. If desired, top with additional mints. Refrigerate until serving.

GINGERBREAD CAKE WITH WHIPPED CREAM FROSTING

Pleasantly spiced gingerbread and nuts are the stars in this stunning dessert. Top the delectable delight with spiced whipped cream frosting.

—SARAH HATTER BRODHEAD, WI

PREP: 45 MIN. • **BAKE:** 20 MIN. + COOLING
MAKES: 16 SERVINGS

- 1 cup 2% milk
- ¾ cup honey
- ¾ cup molasses
- ½ cup canola oil
- 2 large eggs
- 1¾ cups whole wheat flour
- 1 cup all-purpose flour
- 2 teaspoons baking powder
- 1 teaspoon ground cinnamon
- 1 teaspoon baking soda
- 1 teaspoon ground ginger
- ½ teaspoon salt

WHIPPED CREAM
- 1½ cups heavy whipping cream
- ¼ cup confectioners' sugar
- ¾ teaspoon ground cinnamon
- ¾ teaspoon vanilla extract
- ¾ cup chopped pecans, toasted

1. Preheat oven to 350°. Line bottoms of three greased 9-in. round baking pans with parchment paper; grease paper.
2. In a large bowl, beat the first five ingredients until well blended. In another bowl, whisk flours, baking powder, cinnamon, baking soda, ginger and salt; gradually beat into milk mixture.
3. Transfer to prepared pans. Bake 20-25 minutes or until a toothpick inserted in center comes out clean. Cool in pans 10 minutes before removing to wire racks; remove paper. Cool completely.
4. In a large bowl, beat cream until it begins to thicken. Add confectioners' sugar, cinnamon and vanilla; beat until stiff peaks form.
5. Place one cake layer on a serving plate; spread with 1 cup of the whipped cream. Sprinkle with ¼ cup pecans. Repeat layers. Top with remaining cake layer, whipped cream and nuts.

TOP TIP

Stacking Layered Cakes

Stacking a layer cake can be tricky because each layer typically has a little "crown" or dome in the center. To make a uniformly shaped cake, you'll need to remove a thin slice from the top of each layer to level it. With level layers, you'll have a much easier time arranging and frosting your cake.

COCONUT DREAM CAKE

My friends and family love this beautiful cake. I keep it refrigerated before serving to keep it moist and sweet.
—DENISE CARROLL MANCHESTER, TN

PREP: 1 HOUR • **BAKE:** 25 MIN. + COOLING
MAKES: 12 SERVINGS

- ⅔ cup butter, softened
- 1¾ cups sugar
- 2 large eggs
- 1½ teaspoons vanilla extract
- 2½ cups all-purpose flour
- 2½ teaspoons baking powder
- ½ teaspoon salt
- 1¼ cups 2% milk

FILLING
- 3 cups flaked coconut
- 1 cup confectioners' sugar
- 1 cup (8 ounces) sour cream

FROSTING
- 1½ cups sugar
- ⅓ cup water
- 2 large egg whites
- ¼ teaspoon cream of tartar
- 1 teaspoon vanilla extract
  Additional flaked coconut, optional

1. Preheat oven to 350°. Line the bottoms of two greased 9-in. round baking pans with parchment or waxed paper; grease paper.
2. In a large bowl, cream butter and sugar until light and fluffy. Add eggs, one at a time, beating well after each addition. Beat in vanilla. In another bowl, mix flour, baking powder and salt; add to the creamed mixture alternately with milk, beating well after each addition.
3. Transfer to prepared pans. Bake 22-27 minutes or until a toothpick inserted in center comes out clean. Cool in pans 10 minutes before removing to wire racks; remove paper. Cool completely.
4. In a small bowl, mix the filling ingredients until blended. Using a long serrated knife, cut each cake layer horizontally in half. Place one cake layer on a serving plate. Top with a third of filling. Repeat twice. Top with the remaining cake layer. Refrigerate while preparing frosting.
5. For the frosting, in a large heavy saucepan, combine sugar, water, egg whites and cream of tartar. Beat on low speed 1 minute. Place the pan over low heat; continue beating on low until a thermometer reads 160°, 8-10 minutes. Transfer to large bowl. Add vanilla; beat on high until stiff glossy peaks form, about 7 minutes.
6. Spread over top and sides of cake. If desired, sprinkle with additional coconut. Refrigerate, covered, until serving.

AMARETTO RICOTTA CHEESECAKE

PREP: 35 MIN. + STANDING
BAKE: 1 HOUR + CHILLING • **MAKES:** 16 SERVINGS

- 2¾ cups (24 ounces) whole-milk ricotta cheese
- ⅓ cup cornstarch
- ¼ cup amaretto
- 2 packages (8 ounces each) cream cheese, softened
- 1½ cups sugar
- 1 cup (8 ounces) sour cream
- 5 large eggs, lightly beaten

TOPPING
- 1 cup (8 ounces) sour cream
- 2 tablespoons sugar
- 2 tablespoons amaretto

GARNISH
- 1 tablespoon light corn syrup
- 1 cup fresh cranberries
- ⅓ cup sugar
- ½ cup sliced almonds, toasted

1. Line a strainer or colander with four layers of cheesecloth or one coffee filter; place over a bowl. Place ricotta in prepared strainer; cover ricotta with sides of cheesecloth. Refrigerate at least 8 hours or overnight. Remove ricotta from cheesecloth; discard liquid in bowl.
2. Preheat oven to 350°. In a small bowl, mix cornstarch and amaretto. In a large bowl, beat cream cheese, sugar, sour cream and drained ricotta until smooth. Beat in the amaretto mixture. Add the eggs; beat on low speed just until blended.
3. Pour the batter into a greased 10-in. springform pan. Place on a baking sheet. Bake 1 to 1¼ hours or until center is almost set. Let stand 5 minutes on a wire rack.
4. In a small bowl, mix topping ingredients; spread over top of cheesecake. Bake 5 minutes longer.
5. Cool on a wire rack 10 minutes. Loosen sides from pan with knife. Cool 1 hour longer. Refrigerate overnight, covering when completely cooled. Remove rim from pan.
6. For garnish, place corn syrup in a small microwave-safe bowl. Microwave, uncovered, 10 seconds or until warm. Add cranberries; toss to coat. Place sugar in a small bowl; add cranberries and toss to coat. Place on waxed paper and let stand until set, about 1 hour.
7. Top cheesecake with almonds and sugared cranberries.

NOTE *To toast nuts, bake in a shallow pan in a 350° oven for 5-10 minutes or cook in a skillet over low heat until lightly browned, stirring occasionally.*

TOP TIP

Making Cheesecakes in Advance

Cool and creamy cheesecakes are a rich, filling dessert that feed a crowd. Often no other dessert is needed. Best of all, cheesecakes can be made in advance, meaning there's one less thing to do on the day you're entertaining. Cheesecakes can be covered and refrigerated for up to 3 days. For even more convenience, bake a cheesecake weeks in advance and freeze it. Place a whole cheesecake or individual slices on a baking sheet; freeze until firm. Wrap in plastic wrap and place in a heavy-duty resealable plastic bag. Freeze for up to 2 months. Defrost whole cheesecakes in the refrigerator overnight. Individual pieces can be defrosted in the refrigerator or at room temperature for 30 minutes before serving.

AMARETTO
RICOTTA
CHEESECAKE

"There's good reason why this cherished recipe was handed down to me by a relative—it's a keeper! The amaretto and ricotta make for a truly unique dessert."

—ISABEL NEUMAN, SURPRISE, AZ

CRANBERRY-FILLED
ORANGE POUND CAKE

CRANBERRY-FILLED ORANGE POUND CAKE

I made this for a holiday dinner with my family. Everyone loved the cran-orange flavor and the sweet glaze drizzled on top. For a fun variation, add ⅔ cup flaked sweetened coconut when including the orange juice to the batter, and sprinkle the finished cake with toasted coconut.

—PATRICIA HARMON BADEN, PA

PREP: 25 MIN. • **BAKE:** 50 MIN. + COOLING
MAKES: 12 SERVINGS

- 1 **cup butter, softened**
- 1 **package (8 ounces) reduced-fat cream cheese**
- 2 **cups sugar**
- 6 **large eggs**
- 3 **tablespoons orange juice, divided**
- 4 **teaspoons grated orange peel**
- 3 **cups all-purpose flour**
- 1 **teaspoon baking powder**
- ½ **teaspoon baking soda**
- ½ **teaspoon salt**
- 1 **can (14 ounces) whole-berry cranberry sauce**
- ½ **cup dried cherries**

GLAZE

- 1 **cup confectioners' sugar**
- ¼ **teaspoon grated orange peel**
- 4 **to 5 teaspoons orange juice**

1. Preheat oven to 350°. Grease and flour a 10-in. fluted tube pan.
2. In a large bowl, cream the butter, cream cheese and sugar until light and fluffy. Add the eggs, one at a time, beating well after each addition. Beat in 2 tablespoons orange juice and peel. In another bowl, whisk flour, baking powder, baking soda and the salt; gradually add to creamed mixture, beating just until combined.
3. In a small bowl, mix cranberry sauce, cherries and remaining orange juice. Spoon two-thirds of the batter into prepared tube pan. Spread with the cranberry mixture. Top with the remaining batter.
4. Bake for 50-60 minutes or until a toothpick inserted in the center of the cake comes out clean. Loosen sides from pan with a knife. Cool in the pan 10 minutes before removing to a wire rack to cool completely.
5. In a small bowl, mix confectioners' sugar, orange peel and enough orange juice to achieve desired consistency. Pour glaze over top of cake, allowing some to flow over sides.

RED VELVET CAKE ROLL WITH WHITE CHOCOLATE FILLING

Get ready for oohs and aahs when you set this on the table. A creamy white chocolate filling rolls up beautifully inside a layer of fluffy red velvet cake. To make it extra festive, dust stripes of confectioners' sugar for a candy cane look.

—TONYA FORSYTH WAURIKA, OK

PREP: 25 MIN. + CHILLING
BAKE: 15 MIN. + COOLING • **MAKES:** 16 SERVINGS

- 4 **large eggs**
- ¾ **cup sugar**
- 2 **tablespoons buttermilk**
- 1 **tablespoon canola oil**
- 1 **tablespoon red food coloring**
- 1 **teaspoon white vinegar**
- 1 **teaspoon vanilla extract**
- 1 **cup all-purpose flour**
- ¼ **cup baking cocoa**
- 1 **teaspoon baking powder**
- ½ **teaspoon salt**

FILLING

- 1 **package (8 ounces) cream cheese, softened**
- ¼ **cup butter, softened**
- 1 **teaspoon vanilla extract**
- 1 **cup confectioners' sugar**
- 5 **ounces white baking chocolate, melted**
  Additional confectioners' sugar, optional

1. Preheat oven to 350°. Line a greased 15x10x1-in. baking pan with parchment paper; grease paper.
2. In a large bowl, beat eggs on high speed 3 minutes. Gradually add sugar, beating until thick and lemon-colored. Beat in buttermilk, oil, food coloring, vinegar and vanilla. In another bowl, whisk flour, cocoa, baking powder and salt; gradually beat into the egg mixture. Beat on high speed for 2 minutes. Transfer to pan, spreading evenly.
3. Bake 12-15 minutes or until top springs back when lightly touched. Cool 5 minutes. Invert onto a tea towel dusted with confectioners' sugar. Gently peel off paper. Roll up cake in the towel jelly-roll style, starting with a short side. Cool cake completely on a wire rack.
4. In a large bowl, beat cream cheese, butter and vanilla until blended. Gradually beat in confectioners' sugar and baking chocolate until smooth. Unroll cake; spread filling on cake to within ½ in. of edges. Roll up again, without towel; trim ends. Place on a platter, seam side down. Refrigerate, covered, at least 2 hours. If desired, place 1-in. strips of waxed paper across cake roll; dust lightly with additional confectioners' sugar. Carefully remove and discard strips.

TOP TIP

Avoid Cracked Cake Rolls

To avoid a cracked cake roll, be sure the cake batter is spread evenly in the pan. This will promote even baking and help your cake remain moist. A moist cake has less chance of cracking. Be sure to not overbake. Doing so can cause the cake to crack when you roll it up. Most cake rolls bake in 10-15 minutes. Check your cake at 8-9 minutes and watch it closely until it tests done. It should be lightly browned, and the top should spring back when lightly touched.

LAYERED CITRUS CAKE

I slightly simplified my mother-in-law's orange cake recipe to come up with this tall, beautiful version. Orange juice and lemon curd give it a delightful tang. It's delicious with a scoop of vanilla ice cream.

—**BARBARA LENTO** HOUSTON, PA

PREP: 35 MIN. + CHILLING
BAKE: 25 MIN. + COOLING • **MAKES:** 12 SERVINGS

- **4 large eggs, separated**
- **1½ cups all-purpose flour**
- **2 teaspoons baking powder**
- **1½ cups sugar, divided**
- **¾ cup orange juice**
- **FILLINGS**
- **2 cups heavy whipping cream**
- **2 tablespoons sugar**
- **1 teaspoon orange extract**
- **2 jars (10 ounces each) lemon curd**
- **¼ cup chopped candied orange peel**

1. Place the egg whites in a small bowl; let stand at room temperature 30 minutes.
2. Meanwhile, preheat oven to 350°. Line bottoms of two greased 8-in. round baking pans with parchment paper; grease paper. Sift flour and baking powder together twice.
3. In another large bowl, beat the egg yolks until slightly thickened. Gradually add 1¼ cups sugar, beating on high speed until thick and lemon-colored. Beat in orange juice. Fold in flour mixture.
4. With clean beaters, beat egg whites on medium until soft peaks form. Gradually add the remaining sugar, 1 tablespoon at a time, beating on high after each addition until sugar is dissolved. Continue beating until soft glossy peaks form. Fold a fourth of the egg whites into batter, then fold in remaining whites.
5. Gently transfer batter to prepared pans. Bake for 25-30 minutes or until the tops spring back when lightly touched. Cool in pans 10 minutes before removing to wire racks; remove paper. Cool completely.
6. In a large bowl, beat cream until it begins to thicken. Add sugar and extract; beat until soft peaks form. Using a long serrated knife, cut each cake horizontally in half.
7. Place one cake layer on a serving plate; spread with one jar lemon curd. Top with another cake layer; spread with 1 cup whipped cream. Top with another cake layer; spread with the remaining lemon curd. Top with the remaining cake layer. Frost top and sides of cake with remaining whipped cream. Sprinkle with candied orange. Refrigerate at least 1 hour before serving.

TOFFEE ANGEL FOOD CAKE

Sometimes I crave the sweet flavor and light, moist texture of angel food cake. Chopped toffee bits and whipped cream make it even more indulgent. For best results, refrigerate the cake for at least one hour before serving.

—**COLLETTE GAUGLER** FOGELSVILLE, PA

PREP: 45 MIN. • **BAKE:** 50 MIN. + COOLING
MAKES: 16 SERVINGS

- **11 large egg whites**
- **1 cup confectioners' sugar**
- **1 cup cake flour**
- **1 teaspoon cream of tartar**
- **1 teaspoon vanilla extract**
- **Pinch salt**
- **1¼ cups superfine sugar**
- **WHIPPED CREAM**
- **2 cups heavy whipping cream**
- **½ cup hot caramel ice cream topping, room temperature**
- **1 teaspoon vanilla extract**
- **4 Heath candy bars (1½ ounces each), chopped**
- **Chocolate curls, optional**

1. Place the egg whites in a large bowl; let stand at room temperature 30 minutes.
2. Meanwhile, preheat oven to 325°. Sift confectioners' sugar and cake flour together twice.
3. Add cream of tartar, vanilla and salt to egg whites; beat on medium speed until soft peaks form. Gradually add superfine sugar, 1 tablespoon at a time, beating on high after each addition until sugar is dissolved. Continue beating until soft glossy peaks form. Gradually fold in flour mixture, about ½ cup at a time.
4. Gently transfer to ungreased 10-in. tube pan. Cut through the batter with a knife to remove air pockets. Bake on lowest oven rack 50-60 minutes or until top crust is golden brown and cracks feel dry. Immediately invert pan; cool completely in pan, about 1½ hours.
5. Run a knife around sides and center tube of pan. Remove cake to a serving plate. Using a long serrated knife, cut cake horizontally into three layers. In a large bowl, beat cream until it begins to thicken. Gradually add caramel topping and vanilla; beat until soft peaks form.
6. Place one cake layer on a serving plate; spread with 1 cup cream mixture. Sprinkle with a third of the chopped candies. Repeat layers. Top with remaining cake layer. Frost top and sides of cake with remaining whipped cream mixture; sprinkle with remaining candy. If desired, sprinkle chocolate curls over top and around bottom of cake.

TOP TIP

Secrets for Successful Angel Food Cakes

Angel food cakes, also called foam cakes, are done when the top springs back when touched and the cracks at the top of the cake look and feel dry. Cool cakes completely in the pan before removing. If your tube pan has legs, invert the pan onto its legs until the cake is completely cool. If your tube pan does not have legs, place the pan over a funnel or the neck of the narrow bottle until cake is completely cool. Cut foam cakes with a serrated knife or electric knife with a sawing motion.

TOFFEE ANGEL
FOOD CAKE

Giving Thanks

There's so much to be thankful for on Thanksgiving: Time to catch up with loved ones, a break from the daily grind of work and a feast so magnificent we look forward to it all year long. Here you'll find all the classics for a top-notch meal, including fresh new favorites and autumn-inspired desserts. If the day still feels a little frenzied, take back that relaxed vibe by using the slow cooker and making the most of leftovers.

All-American Thanksgiving

It's Turkey Day in the USA! We anticipate this meal like no other, and we have the fixings that will make hosting the big meal a snap. Grab that baster—it's time to get cookin'!

First, let's talk turkey. Turn to page 99 to find **the juiciest, crispiest, most golden bird ever** along with handy kitchen secrets for prepping the star attraction. Then get ready to **stuff the table with a bounty of side dishes**—spuds, dressing, greens and more traditional trimmings. As for dessert? Make sweet memories with these after-dinner gems.

Let our classic Thanksgiving Day favorites, along with tempting new creations and a foolproof timeline for getting it all done, inspire you to **make this year's holiday one for the record books.**

Mashed Potatoes with Cheddar (p. 96) **Fresh Herb-Brined Turkey** (p. 99)
Grandma's Cranberry Stuff (p. 96)

CITRUS &
AVOCADO SALAD

CITRUS &
AVOCADO SALAD

The fresh flavors in this salad remind me of my childhood in Southern California. My great-uncle had an orchard, so our family meals were filled with avocados, citrus fruits and nuts of all varieties.

—CATHERINE CASSIDY MILWAUKEE, WI

START TO FINISH: 25 MIN.
MAKES: 12 SERVINGS (1 CUP EACH)

- **10 cups torn Bibb or Boston lettuce**
- **1½ cups orange sections (about 2 medium oranges)**
- **1 cup ruby red grapefruit sections (about 1 medium grapefruit)**
- **2 medium ripe avocados, peeled and cubed**
- **3 tablespoons ruby red grapefruit juice**
- **3 tablespoons extra virgin olive oil**
- **2 teaspoons honey**
- **½ teaspoon salt**
- **¾ cup crumbled queso fresco or feta cheese**
- **¼ cup pistachios, chopped**

Place lettuce, oranges, grapefruit and avocados in a large bowl. In a small bowl, whisk grapefruit juice, oil, honey and salt until blended. Drizzle over salad and toss gently to coat. Sprinkle with cheese and pistachios. Serve immediately.

TOP TIP

Seeding and Chopping Avocados

The easiest avocados to seed and slice are those that are ripe yet firm. (Very ripe, soft avocados are best used for mashing.) Cut the avocado in half lengthwise. Twist the halves in opposite directions to separate. Carefully tap the seed with the blade of a sharp knife. Rotate the knife to loosen the seed and lift it out. To remove the peel, scoop the flesh from each half with a large metal spoon, staying close to the peel. Chop; dip chopped pieces in lemon juice to prevent them from turning brown.

APPLE CIDER SMASH

APPLE CIDER SMASH

A smash is a fruity chilled cocktail. This one is a refreshing adult beverage to serve with your Thanksgiving meal. It's a great way to use cider and any extra apples this fall.

—MOFFAT FRAZIER NEW YORK, NY

START TO FINISH: 20 MIN. • **MAKES:** 16 SERVINGS

- **2 cups finely chopped Gala or other red apples (about 2 small)**
- **2 cups finely chopped Granny Smith apples (about 2 small)**
- **2½ cups bourbon**
- **⅔ cup apple brandy**
- **4 teaspoons lemon juice**
  Ice cubes
- **5⅓ cups chilled sparkling apple cider**

1. In a bowl, toss apples to combine. In a small pitcher, mix bourbon, brandy and lemon juice.

2. To serve, fill each of 16 rocks glasses halfway with ice. To each, add ¼ cup apple mixture and 3 tablespoons of the bourbon mixture; top each drink with ⅓ cup cider.

CURRIED
VEGETABLE DIP

The combination of curry powder and honey gives this dip a sweet and spicy flavor. It's a nice change of pace from traditional onion and ranch dips. Serve with fresh veggies or your favorite potato chips for dipping.

—LOIS KODADA NORTHFIELD, MN

PREP: 15 MIN. + CHILLING • **MAKES:** 1⅔ CUPS

- **1½ cups mayonnaise**
- **2 tablespoons finely chopped onion**
- **2 tablespoons lemon juice**
- **2 tablespoons honey**
- **2 tablespoons ketchup**
- **1 teaspoon curry powder**
- **2 to 4 drops hot pepper sauce**
  Assorted fresh vegetables

Combine the first seven ingredients in a small bowl. Cover the bowl and refrigerate for at least 1 hour. Serve with vegetables.

GLAZED MEATBALLS

Allspice adds an unexpectedly pleasant twist to typical barbecue meatballs. These are likely to be your next Thanksgiving's go-to appetizer.

—NANCY HORSBURGH EVERETT, ON

PREP: 30 MIN. • **COOK:** 15 MIN.
MAKES: ABOUT 3½ DOZEN

- 2 large eggs, lightly beaten
- ⅔ cup milk
- 1 tablespoon prepared horseradish
- 1¼ cups soft bread crumbs
- 1½ pounds ground beef
- 1 cup water
- ½ cup chili sauce
- ½ cup ketchup
- ¼ cup maple syrup
- ¼ cup reduced-sodium soy sauce
- 1½ teaspoons ground allspice
- ½ teaspoon ground mustard

1. In a large bowl, combine the eggs, milk, horseradish and bread crumbs. Crumble beef over mixture and mix well. Shape into 1½-in. balls.
2. Place meatballs on a greased rack in a shallow baking pan. Bake at 375° for 15-20 minutes or until cooked through; drain.
3. In a large saucepan, combine the remaining ingredients. Bring to a boil; add the meatballs. Reduce heat; cover and simmer for 15 minutes or until heated through, stirring occasionally.
SAUCY MEATBALLS *Omit the glaze ingredients. In a saucepan, combine 1¾ cups ketchup, 1 jar (12 ounces) grape jelly and 1 cup chopped onion. Cook and stir over medium heat for 3-5 minutes or until jelly is melted. Transfer meatballs to a greased 13x9-in. baking dish, then pour sauce over the meatballs. Bake, uncovered, 20 minutes longer or until sauce is bubbly.*
CRANBERRY MEATBALLS *Omit the glaze ingredients. In a saucepan, combine 1 can (16 ounces) whole-berry cranberry sauce, 1 bottle (12 ounces) chili sauce, 1 tablespoon each brown sugar, prepared mustard and lemon juice, and 2 minced garlic cloves. Bring mixture to a boil. Reduce the heat and simmer for 10 minutes, stirring occasionally. Pour over meatballs; serve warm.*

SAUSAGE DRESSING

If you're not stuffing the bird this year, rely on the convenience of your slow cooker to make a moist and flavorful dressing. The results are fantastic. Even my family members who don't usually eat stuffing enjoy every bite.

—MARY KENDALL APPLETON, WI

PREP: 20 MIN. • **COOK:** 4 HOURS
MAKES: 12 SERVINGS

- 1 pound bulk pork sausage
- 1 large onion, chopped
- 2 celery ribs, chopped
- 1 package (14 ounces) seasoned stuffing croutons
- 1 can (14½ ounces) chicken broth
- 1 large tart apple, chopped
- 1 cup chopped walnuts or pecans
- ½ cup egg substitute
- ¼ cup butter, melted
- 1½ teaspoons rubbed sage
- ½ teaspoon pepper

1. In a large skillet, cook the sausage, onion and celery over medium heat until the meat is no longer pink; drain. Transfer to a greased 5-qt. slow cooker. Stir in the remaining ingredients.
2. Cover and cook on low for 4-5 hours or until a thermometer reads 160°.

GRANDMA'S CRANBERRY STUFF

What tastes better than turkey and cranberry on Thanksgiving? The classic pairing is even better with my grandma's classic recipe for cranberry stuffing. See photo on page 91.

—CATHERINE CASSIDY MILWAUKEE, WI

PREP: 10 MIN. • **MAKES:** 3 CUPS

- 1 medium navel orange
- 1 package (12 ounces) fresh or frozen cranberries, thawed
- 1 cup sugar
- 1 cup chopped walnuts, toasted

Cut unpeeled orange into wedges, removing any seeds, and place in a food processor. Add cranberries and sugar; pulse until chopped. Add walnuts; pulse just until combined.
NOTE *To toast nuts, bake in a shallow pan in a 350° oven for 5-10 minutes or cook in a skillet over low heat until lightly browned, stirring occasionally.*

MASHED POTATOES WITH CHEDDAR

Everybody loves fluffy homemade mashed potatoes, and they're even better with sharp cheddar cheese. My mother added whipping cream instead of half-and-half. Try her secret to make them extra rich and creamy.

—DARLENE BRENDEN SALEM, OR

PREP: 15 MIN. • **COOK:** 30 MIN.
MAKES: 8 SERVINGS

- 3 pounds potatoes, peeled and cubed (about 6 cups)
- 1 to 1¼ cups half-and-half cream
- 3 tablespoons butter
- 1 teaspoon salt
- 3 cups (12 ounces) shredded extra-sharp cheddar cheese

1. Place potatoes in a 6-qt. stockpot; add water to cover. Bring to a boil. Reduce heat and cook, uncovered, for 15-20 minutes or until tender. Meanwhile, in a small saucepan, heat cream, butter and salt until butter is melted, stirring occasionally.
2. Drain potatoes; return to pot. Mash potatoes, gradually adding the cream mixture. Stir in cheese.

TOP TIP

Slow Cooker Mashed Potatoes

My mom came up with a great idea to beat the clock when hosting a large crowd for dinner. She mashes her potatoes in the afternoon and keeps them warm in a slow cooker. She simply covers the cooker and sets it on low, keeping the potatoes moist. I've tried this technique, and it sure beats mashing the potatoes immediately before serving the meal.

—KIM M. BADGER, IA

MASHED POTATOES
WITH CHEDDAR

"To brine or not to brine? If you want a tender, juicy bird with lots of flavor, the choice is easy. We flavor our brine with parsley, rosemary and a touch of thyme."

—FELICIA SAATHOFF, VASHON, WA

FRESH
HERB-BRINED
TURKEY

Turkey Prep Work

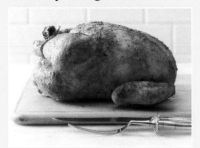

BUY IT When choosing a frozen turkey, size matters. A typical 14-lb. bird serves 16 people. Add an extra pound or so if you're looking forward to leftovers.

THAW IT Every 4 lbs. of frozen turkey needs 24 hours of thawing time. For a 14-lb. bird, plan on pulling your turkey from the freezer five days before the big feast, then move it to the fridge.

RUB IT The day before Thanksgiving, don't forget to pull the giblets from the turkey (check both the neck area and the back area to find them). Save the neck—it's the key to making some seriously good gravy. Then rub a salt or herb mixture over the outside of the turkey or soak it in a brine, cover it and send it back to the fridge.

PREP IT It's the big day! Preheat the oven, give the turkey one last rub and load the broiler pan with veggies and stock ingredients. Don't wing it! Follow the directions on your recipe for a picture-perfect bird.

FRESH HERB-BRINED TURKEY

PREP: 40 MIN. + BRINING
BAKE: 2½ HOURS + STANDING
MAKES: 16 SERVINGS

- 4 **quarts water**
- 2 **cups sugar**
- 1½ **cups salt**
- 10 **fresh parsley sprigs**
- 10 **fresh thyme sprigs**
- 5 **fresh rosemary sprigs**
- 7 **bay leaves**
- 4 **teaspoons crushed red pepper flakes**
- 4 **teaspoons whole peppercorns**
- 4½ **quarts cold water**
- 2 **turkey-size oven roasting bags**
- 1 **turkey (14 to 16 pounds)**

TURKEY
- 2 **tablespoons olive oil**
- ½ **teaspoon pepper**
- ½ **teaspoon salt, optional**

1. In a large stockpot, combine the first nine ingredients; bring to a boil. Cook and stir until sugar and salt are dissolved. Remove from heat. Add cold water to cool the brine to room temperature.

2. Place one oven roasting bag inside the other. Place turkey inside both bags; pour in cooled brine. Seal bags, pressing out as much air as possible; turn to coat turkey. Place in a shallow roasting pan. Refrigerate 18-24 hours, turning occasionally.

3. Preheat oven to 350°. Remove turkey from brine; rinse and pat dry. Discard brine. Place turkey on a rack in a shallow roasting pan, breast side up. Tuck wings under turkey and tie the drumsticks together. Rub oil over the outside of the turkey; sprinkle with pepper and, if desired, salt.

4. Roast, uncovered, for 2½-3 hours or until a thermometer inserted in the thickest part of the thigh reads 170°-175°. (Cover loosely with foil if turkey browns too quickly.)

5. Remove turkey from the oven; tent with foil and let stand for 20 minutes before carving.

NOTE *If using a prebasted turkey, omit salt sprinkled on outside of turkey.*

GIBLET TURKEY GRAVY

Gravy with giblets is a tradition in our house. Try this hearty version accented with sage and a dash of wine, and it will become a tradition in your house, too.

—JEFF LOCKE ARMA, KS

START TO FINISH: 25 MIN.
MAKES: 16 SERVINGS (ABOUT ¼ CUP EACH)

- ¼ **cup cornstarch**
- 4 **cups chicken stock, divided**
- 1 **tablespoon butter**
- 1 **tablespoon olive oil**
  Giblets from 1 turkey, finely chopped
- ½ **cup dry white wine or additional chicken stock**
- 2 **tablespoons minced fresh sage or 2 teaspoons dried sage leaves**
- ¼ **teaspoon salt**
- ¼ **teaspoon pepper**

1. In a small bowl, mix cornstarch and ½ cup stock until smooth. In a large saucepan, heat the butter and oil over medium-high heat. Add giblets; cook and stir 5-8 minutes or until browned.

2. Add wine and sage to pan; cook for 3-5 minutes, stirring to loosen the browned bits from pan. Add remaining stock; bring to a boil. Stir in cornstarch mixture; return to a boil. Reduce heat; simmer 3-5 minutes or until thickened to the desired consistency, stirring occasionally. Stir in salt and pepper.

PUMPKIN CHEESECAKE DESSERT

With its gingersnap crust and maple syrup drizzle, this rich and creamy spiced pumpkin dessert never fails to get accolades. It cuts nicely, too.

—CATHY HALL LYNDHURST, VA

PREP: 25 MIN. • **BAKE:** 40 MIN. + CHILLING
MAKES: 24 SERVINGS

- 32 **gingersnap cookies, crushed (about 1½ cups)**
- ¼ **cup butter, melted**
- 5 **packages (8 ounces each) cream cheese, softened**
- 1 **cup sugar**
- 1 **can (15 ounces) solid-pack pumpkin**
- 1 **teaspoon ground cinnamon**
- 1 **teaspoon vanilla extract**
- 5 **large eggs, lightly beaten**
  Dash ground nutmeg
  Maple syrup

1. Combine gingersnap crumbs and butter in a small bowl. Press onto the bottom of a greased 13x9-in. baking dish; set aside.

2. In a large bowl, beat cream cheese and sugar until smooth. Beat in the pumpkin, cinnamon and vanilla. Add the eggs; beat on low speed just until combined. Pour over crust; sprinkle with nutmeg.

3. Bake at 350° for 40-45 minutes or until the center is almost set. Cool on a wire rack for 10 minutes. Carefully run a knife around edge of baking dish to loosen; cool 1 hour longer and then refrigerate overnight.

4. Cut into squares; serve with syrup. Refrigerate leftovers.

CARROT CAKE WITH PECAN FROSTING

This impressive carrot cake is one of my husband's favorites. The recipe is homey and old-fashioned, making it perfect for special holidays like Thanksgiving.

—ADRIAN BADON DENHAM SPRINGS, LA

PREP: 35 MIN. • **BAKE:** 40 MIN. + COOLING
MAKES: 16 SERVINGS

- 1 **cup shortening**
- 2 **cups sugar**
- 4 **large eggs**
- 1 **can (8 ounces) unsweetened crushed pineapple, undrained**
- 2½ **cups all-purpose flour**
- 2 **teaspoons ground cinnamon**
- 1 **teaspoon baking powder**
- 1 **teaspoon baking soda**
- ¾ **teaspoon salt**
- 3 **cups shredded carrots (about 6 medium carrots)**

FROSTING
- 1 **package (8 ounces) reduced-fat cream cheese**
- ½ **cup butter, softened**
- 1 **teaspoon vanilla extract**
- 3¾ **cups confectioners' sugar**
- 1 **cup chopped pecans**

1. Preheat oven to 325°. Line bottoms of two greased 9-in. round baking pans with parchment paper; grease paper.

2. In a large bowl, cream shortening and sugar until fluffy. Add the eggs, one at a time, beating well after each addition. Beat in pineapple. In another bowl, whisk the flour, cinnamon, baking powder, baking soda and salt; gradually add to creamed mixture. Stir in carrots.

3. Transfer batter to prepared pans. Bake for 40-45 minutes or until a toothpick inserted in center comes out clean. Cool in pans 10 minutes before removing to wire racks; remove paper. Cool completely.

4. In a large bowl, beat cream cheese, butter and vanilla until blended. Gradually beat in confectioners' sugar until smooth. Stir in pecans.

5. Spread frosting between layers and over top and sides of cake. Refrigerate until serving.

Dress Up Your Table

Add a little warmth and cheer to your Thanksgiving Day table with these charming ideas.

- If you have white dishes, add a pop of color to the table with festive napkins or linens. Or consider a bright centerpiece such as flowers in a vase or potted plants.

- Place tea light candles on tables, countertops and mantels. Nothing creates a warm and inviting atmosphere quite like candles.

- Fill clear bowls with apples or pears to add a seasonal touch and a wonderful fragrance.

- Another "scent-sational" idea is to simmer some apple cider on the stove. The aroma appeals to all, adds a little coziness to the home, and makes a delicious sipper.

- Framed word art makes a gorgeous accent for walls, mantels and buffet tables. Home decor and department stores sell a variety of designs and styles. Or take a look at **etsy. com** for artists who sell their own digital designs or hand-lettered calligraphy.

CARROT CAKE WITH
PECAN FROSTING

Slow Cooker Side Dishes

The turkey may take center stage on Thanksgiving, but **it's the accompaniments that make the meal.** From the famous mashed potatoes to the essential green bean casserole, there's something for everyone in this special lineup of side dishes.

The best part? Each of these wonders is made in a slow cooker. **The magic of this appliance is that it will do most of the work** for you on your busiest cooking day of the year. Not to mention it will leave you with valuable stovetop space and plenty of room in the oven for that bird to bake to perfection.

Bring new life to the ultimate holiday feast with a little slow-cooked action on the side. **These tempting creations promise to satisfy!**

Slow-Cooked Golden Mashed Potatoes (p. 109) **Savory Sausage Dressing** (p. 110)

**EASY GREEN BEANS
WITH MUSHROOMS**

EASY GREEN BEANS WITH MUSHROOMS

My family looks forward to this dish every holiday. I add sliced almonds for crunch and garlic for a little kick.
—**CHERYL WITTMAN** BERGEN, NY

PREP: 10 MIN. • **COOK:** 5 HOURS
MAKES: 10 SERVINGS

- **2 pounds fresh green beans, trimmed**
- **1 pound sliced fresh mushrooms**
- **1 large onion, finely chopped**
- **2 tablespoons butter, melted**
- **2 tablespoons olive oil**
- **3 garlic cloves, minced**
- **¼ teaspoon pepper**
- **1 package (2¼ ounces) sliced almonds, toasted**

In a 6-qt. slow cooker, combine the first seven ingredients. Cook, covered, on low 5-6 hours or until the beans are tender. Remove with a slotted spoon. Sprinkle with almonds.

HONEY-BUTTER PEAS AND CARROTS

The classic combination of peas and carrots is made even better with a handful of flavor enhancers. Slow cooking allows the ingredients to meld for maximum richness and taste.
—**THERESA KREYCHE** TUSTIN, CA

PREP: 15 MIN. • **COOK:** 5¼ HOURS
MAKES: 12 SERVINGS (½ CUP EACH)

- **1 pound carrots, sliced**
- **1 large onion, chopped**
- **¼ cup water**
- **¼ cup butter, cubed**
- **¼ cup honey**
- **4 garlic cloves, minced**
- **1 teaspoon salt**
- **1 teaspoon dried marjoram**
- **⅛ teaspoon white pepper**
- **1 package (16 ounces) frozen peas**

In a 3-qt. slow cooker, combine the first nine ingredients. Cook, covered, on low for 5 hours. Stir in peas. Cook, covered, on high 15-25 minutes longer or until vegetables are tender.

SLOW COOKER CRAN-APPLE CHUTNEY

SLOW COOKER CRAN-APPLE CHUTNEY

My clan isn't crazy for cranberries, but they can't get enough of this delicious chutney. I recommend it for Thanksgiving as it tastes amazing paired with turkey, but it's also good on its own.
—**RAQUEL HAGGARD** EDMOND, OK

PREP: 10 MIN. • **COOK:** 3 HOURS + CHILLING
MAKES: 3 CUPS

- **1 package (12 ounces) fresh or frozen cranberries, thawed**
- **1 medium Gala apple, peeled and finely chopped**
- **⅔ cup sugar or sugar substitute equivalent to ⅔ cup sugar**
- **⅓ cup honey**
- **2 tablespoons brown sugar**
- **2 tablespoons frozen orange juice concentrate, thawed**
- **1 teaspoon ground cinnamon**
- **1 teaspoon cider vinegar**
  Dash ground ginger

1. In a 1½-qt. slow cooker, combine all the ingredients. Cook, covered, on low 3-4 hours or until cranberries pop and mixture is slightly thickened.
2. Transfer chutney to a small bowl; cool slightly. Refrigerate until cold.

TOP TIP

Leftover Chutney

If you have leftover chutney, try one of these delicious ways to use it up.

- Warm chutney in the microwave and serve over pound cake, angel food cake or ice cream.
- Spread chutney on a flour tortilla. Layer with sliced cooked turkey and lettuce. Roll up to make a wrap.
- Stir a few tablespoons of chutney into hot, cooked oatmeal for a comforting breakfast.

DREAMY POLENTA

I grew up eating polenta, so it's a must at my holiday gatherings. It usually requires constant stirring, but using a handy slow cooker allows me to turn my attention to the lineup of other foods on the spread.
—**ANN VOCCOLA** MILFORD, CT

PREP: 10 MIN. • **COOK:** 5 HOURS
MAKES: 12 SERVINGS (¾ CUP EACH)

- 1 tablespoon butter
- 5 cups whole milk
- 4 cups half-and-half cream
- 12 tablespoons butter, divided
- 2 cups yellow cornmeal
- ¾ teaspoon salt
- ½ teaspoon minced fresh rosemary
- ¼ teaspoon pepper
- 2 cups shredded Asiago cheese

1. Generously grease a 5-qt. slow cooker with 1 tablespoon butter. Add the milk, cream, 6 tablespoons butter, cornmeal, salt, rosemary and pepper; stir to combine.
2. Cook, covered, on low 5-6 hours or until the polenta is thickened, whisking every hour. Just before serving, whisk again; stir in cheese and remaining butter.

MAPLE-WALNUT SWEET POTATOES

Thanksgiving isn't complete without the sweet potatoes. But these aren't your grandma's marshmallow-fluffed spuds. Dried cherries, maple syrup, apple cider and walnuts for crunch make this dish one to remember.
—**SARAH HERSE** BROOKLYN, NY

PREP: 15 MIN. • **COOK:** 5 HOURS
MAKES: 12 SERVINGS (¾ CUP EACH)

- 4 pounds sweet potatoes (about 8 medium)
- ¾ cup coarsely chopped walnuts, divided
- ½ cup packed light brown sugar
- ½ cup dried cherries, coarsely chopped
- ½ cup maple syrup
- ¼ cup apple cider or juice
- ¼ teaspoon salt

1. Peel and cut the sweet potatoes lengthwise in half; cut crosswise into ½-in. slices. Place in a 5-qt. slow cooker. Add ½ cup walnuts, brown sugar, cherries, syrup, cider and salt; toss to combine.
2. Cook, covered, on low for 5-6 hours or until potatoes are tender. Sprinkle with remaining walnuts.

SLOW COOKER CREAMED CORN

I'm a teacher, and this is one of my go-to recipes for faculty potlucks. It's great for Thanksgiving, too, when you're looking for an easy, comforting dish that has just a little bit of bite.
—**SHELBY WINTERS** BONNER SPRNGS, KS

PREP: 15 MIN. • **COOK:** 3 HOURS
MAKES: 8 SERVINGS

- ½ cup butter, cubed
- 1 medium onion, finely chopped
- ¼ cup finely chopped sweet red pepper
- 6 cups frozen corn (about 30 ounces), thawed
- 1 package (8 ounces) cream cheese, cubed
- 1 can (4 ounces) chopped green chilies
- 1 teaspoon salt
- ½ teaspoon garlic powder
- ¼ teaspoon pepper

In a large skillet, heat butter over medium-high heat. Add onion and red pepper; cook and stir 3-4 minutes or until tender. Transfer to a greased 3-qt. slow cooker. Stir in remaining ingredients. Cook, covered, on low for 3-4 hours or until heated through. Stir just before serving.

**SLOW COOKER
CREAMED CORN**

SLOW COOKER
SPICED FRUIT

SLOW COOKER SPICED FRUIT

My aunt who lived in Hawaii gave me this cherished recipe. She would prepare a traditional tropical meal for us whenever we visited, and this fruity side was always included. I love to think of her when I make it, whether it's for the holidays or for an everyday meal.

—**JOAN HALLFORD** NORTH RICHLAND HILLS, TX

PREP: 10 MIN. • **COOK:** 3 HOURS
MAKES: 8 SERVINGS

- 1 can (20 ounces) pineapple chunks, drained
- 1 can (15¼ ounces) sliced peaches, drained
- 1 can (15¼ ounces) sliced pears, drained
- 1 can (15 ounces) apricot halves, drained
- 1 can (11 ounces) mandarin oranges, drained
- 1 jar (10 ounces) maraschino cherries, drained
- 8 whole cloves
- 2 cinnamon sticks (3 inches)
- ½ cup packed brown sugar
- ½ teaspoon curry powder
- 1 cup white wine or white grape juice
- ½ cup slivered almonds, toasted

1. In a 3- or 4-qt. slow cooker, combine the first six ingredients. Place cloves and cinnamon sticks on a double thickness of cheesecloth. Gather the corners of the cloth to enclose the seasonings; tie securely with string. Place bag in the slow cooker. In a small bowl, mix brown sugar, curry powder and wine; pour over fruit.
2. Cook, covered, on low for 3-4 hours or until heated through. Discard spice bag; sprinkle with almonds. Remove with a slotted spoon.
NOTE *To toast nuts, bake in a shallow pan in a 350° oven for 5-10 minutes or cook in a skillet over low heat until lightly browned, stirring occasionally.*

SLOW-COOKED GOLDEN MASHED POTATOES

SLOW-COOKED GOLDEN MASHED POTATOES

Making a grand meal on Thanksgiving can be a little daunting, even for the most experienced cook. The convenience of a slow cooker for classic potatoes makes prep one step easier and allows you to spend more time with the family.

—**SAMANTHA SIX** FREDERICKSBURG, IN

PREP: 20 MIN. • **COOK:** 4 HOURS
MAKES: 14 SERVINGS (¾ CUP EACH)

- 5 pounds Yukon Gold potatoes (about 10 medium), chopped
- 1 cup butter, cubed
- 1 cup water
- 3 teaspoons salt
- ¾ teaspoon pepper
- ½ cup mayonnaise
- ¼ cup grated Parmesan cheese
- 1 to 1½ cups 2% milk

1. In a 6-qt. slow cooker, combine the first five ingredients. Cook, covered, on high for 4-5 hours or until potatoes are tender (do not drain liquid).
2. Mash potatoes, gradually adding mayonnaise, cheese and enough milk to achieve desired consistency.

MUSHROOM & RICE PILAF

Simple rice pilaf is a lifesaver when you are hosting Thanksgiving. Just place the ingredients in the slow cooker and forget about it until it's time to serve.

—**KATHLEEN HEDGER** FAIRVIEW HEIGHTS, IL

PREP: 15 MIN. • **COOK:** 3 HOURS
MAKES: 10 SERVINGS

- ½ cup butter, cubed
- 2 cups uncooked long grain rice
- ½ pound sliced fresh mushrooms
- 8 green onions, chopped
- 2 teaspoons dried oregano
- 2 cans (10½ ounces each) condensed beef broth, undiluted
- 1½ cups water

In a large saucepan, heat butter over medium heat. Add rice; cook and stir 5-6 minutes or until lightly browned. Transfer to a 3-qt. slow cooker. Add the mushrooms, green onions and oregano. Stir in the broth and water. Cook, covered, on low for 3-4 hours or until the rice is tender and liquid is absorbed.

WILD RICE WITH DRIED BLUEBERRIES

I love the combination of rice and fruit, so this is a go-to Thanksgiving side dish at my house. I toss in mushrooms and toasted almonds to enhance the flavor. You can also include dried cherries or cranberries if you like.

—**JANIE COLLE** HUTCHINSON, KS

PREP: 15 MIN. • **COOK:** 3 HOURS
MAKES: 16 SERVINGS (¾ CUP EACH)

- 2 **tablespoons butter**
- 8 **ounces sliced fresh mushrooms**
- 3 **cups uncooked wild rice**
- 8 **green onions, sliced**
- 1 **teaspoon salt**
- ½ **teaspoon pepper**
- 4 **cans (14½ ounces each) vegetable broth**
- 1 **cup chopped pecans, toasted**
- 1 **cup dried blueberries**

In a large skillet, heat the butter over medium heat. Add mushrooms; cook and stir 4-5 minutes or until tender. In a 5-qt. slow cooker, combine rice, mushrooms, onions, salt and pepper. Pour broth over rice mixture. Cook, covered, on low for 3-4 hours or until the rice is tender. Stir in pecans and blueberries. Cook, covered, 15 minutes longer or until heated through.

NOTE *To toast nuts, bake in a shallow pan in a 350° oven for 5-10 minutes or cook in a skillet over low heat until lightly browned, stirring occasionally.*

SAVORY SAUSAGE DRESSING

I used to make the same old dressing every year for Thanksgiving. About 10 years ago, I decided to jazz up my recipe by adding pork sausage. Now everyone requests it for all our holiday meals.

—**URSULA HERNANDEZ** WALTHAM, MN

PREP: 30 MIN. • **COOK:** 2 HOURS
MAKES: 16 SERVINGS (¾ CUP EACH)

- 1 **pound sage pork sausage**
- ½ **cup butter, cubed**
- ½ **pound fresh mushrooms, finely chopped**
- 6 **celery ribs, finely chopped**
- 2 **small onions, finely chopped**
- 2 **garlic cloves, minced**
- 1 **loaf (13 ounces) French bread, cut into ½-inch cubes (about 17 cups)**
- 4 **cups cubed multigrain bread (½ inch cubes)**
- 1 **tablespoon rubbed sage**
- 1 **cup chicken stock**
- ½ **cup white wine or chicken stock**
- 1 **cup dried cranberries**
- ½ **cup sunflower kernels, optional**

1. In a large skillet, cook sausage over medium heat 4-6 minutes or until no longer pink, breaking into crumbles; drain. In a stockpot, melt butter over medium heat. Add mushrooms, celery and onions; cook and stir 3-4 minutes or until tender. Add the garlic; cook 1 minute longer. Remove from heat.
2. Stir in sausage. Add bread cubes and sage; toss to combine. Add chicken stock and wine. Stir in the cranberries and, if desired, the sunflower kernels. Transfer to a greased 6-qt. slow cooker. Cook, covered, on low for 2-3 hours or until heated through, stirring once.

TOP TIP

Thanksgiving Timesaver

To save time on Thanksgiving morning, begin some of the preparation for the dressing (or stuffing if you're using a recipe that will be baked inside the bird) the night before. Wash, chop and saute vegetables. Cut bread into cubes or measure out store-bought stuffing croutons. Combine seasonings. Store wet ingredients separate from dry ones, and refrigerate perishable items.

Leveraging Leftovers

The joy of the Thanksgiving meal extends to the days following and **the anticipation of twice-as-nice leftovers**. This year, skip ho-hum turkey sandwiches and re-heated mashed potatoes. Be adventurous and turn your surplus fare into one of these unique creations that give new life to turkey, stuffing, cranberries and more.

Make use of every inch of that bird with croquettes, a melty panini or zesty rellenos. **Folks will clamor for second slices** of a pizza that features all the beloved Turkey Day fixings. And don't forget to end the meal with a splurge-worthy dessert.

You'll quickly see there's **no need to make a post-Thanksgiving grocery run** when you serve these second-time-around specialties!

Thanksgiving Lover's Pizza (p. 119)

**TURKEY & CORN BREAD
STUFFING RELLENOS**

TURKEY & CORN BREAD STUFFING RELLENOS

Give your Thanksgiving leftovers a south of the border vibe with these rellenos. They're easy to make any time of year with roasted deli turkey and a box of corn stuffing. Adjust the heat by adding more or fewer peppers or adobo sauce.

—CHRISTINE FRIESENHAHN BOERNE, TX

PREP: 30 MIN. + STANDING • **COOK:** 5 MIN.
MAKES: 6 SERVINGS

- 6 large poblano peppers (about 1½ pounds)
- 1½ cups chopped cooked turkey
- 1½ cups cooked cornbread stuffing
- 2 packages (8½ ounces each) corn muffin mix
- 1 carton (8 ounces) egg substitute Oil for deep-fat frying
- 1 can (14 ounces) whole-berry cranberry sauce
- 1 chipotle pepper in adobo sauce plus 1 tablespoon adobo sauce

1. Place peppers on a broiler pan. Broil 4 in. from heat until skins blister, about 5 minutes. With tongs, rotate peppers a quarter turn. Broil and rotate until all sides are blistered and blackened. Immediately place peppers in a large bowl; let stand, covered, 10 minutes.
2. Peel off and discard charred skin. Cut and discard tops from peppers; remove the seeds. In a small bowl, combine turkey and stuffing. Fill peppers with turkey mixture. Place corn muffin mix and egg substitute in separate shallow bowls. Roll the stuffed peppers in corn muffin mix, then in egg substitute, then again in corn muffin mix.
3. In an electric skillet, heat ½ in. of oil to 375°. Fry stuffed peppers, a few at a time, 2-4 minutes on each side or until browned. Drain on paper towels.
4. Place the cranberry sauce, pepper and adobo sauce in a blender; cover and process until blended, about 10 seconds. Serve with peppers.

LEFTOVER TURKEY CROQUETTES

I grew up with a family that looked forward to leftovers, especially on the day after Thanksgiving. But we didn't just reheat turkey and spuds in the microwave—we took our culinary creativity to a new level with recipes likes these croquettes. Serve three per plate along with a crisp green salad for an unforgettable meal.

—MEREDITH COE CHARLOTTESVILLE, VA

PREP: 20 MIN. • **COOK:** 20 MIN.
MAKES: 6 SERVINGS

- 2 cups mashed potatoes (with added milk and butter)
- ½ cup grated Parmesan cheese
- ½ cup shredded Swiss cheese
- 1 shallot, finely chopped
- 2 teaspoons minced fresh rosemary or ½ teaspoon dried rosemary, crushed
- 1 teaspoon minced fresh sage or ¼ teaspoon dried sage leaves
- ½ teaspoon salt
- ¼ teaspoon pepper
- 3 cups finely chopped cooked turkey
- 1 large egg
- 2 tablespoons water
- 1¼ cups panko (Japanese) bread crumbs
- ¼ cup butter, divided Sour cream, optional

1. In a large bowl, combine mashed potatoes, cheeses, shallot, rosemary, sage, salt and pepper; stir in turkey. Shape into twelve 1-in.-thick patties.
2. In a shallow bowl, whisk egg and water. Place bread crumbs in another shallow bowl. Dip the croquettes in egg mixture, then in bread crumbs, patting to help coating adhere.
3. In a large skillet, heat 2 tablespoons butter over medium heat. Add half of croquettes; cook 4-5 minutes on each side or until browned. Remove and keep warm. Repeat. If desired, serve with sour cream.

TURKEY, BACON & FETA PANINIS

No more boring turkey sandwiches! These flavorful paninis are the perfect way to use up leftover cranberry sauce and turkey. Use ready-made bacon and pre-washed spinach for a quick and delicious meal. These are also great assembled on leftover corn bread.

—LISA SPEER PALM BEACH, FL

START TO FINISH: 25 MIN.
MAKES: 4 SERVINGS

- 12 thick-sliced applewood smoked bacon
- ¼ cup mayonnaise
- ¼ cup jellied cranberry sauce
- 8 slices sourdough bread
- 12 ounces thinly sliced cooked turkey
- 1 cup (4 ounces) crumbled feta cheese
- 2 cups fresh baby spinach

1. Preheat panini maker or indoor electric grill. In a large skillet, cook bacon over medium heat until crisp. Remove to paper towels to drain. Discard drippings. In a small bowl, mix mayonnaise and cranberry sauce. Spread bread slices with mayonnaise mixture. Layer turkey, bacon, feta cheese and spinach on four bread slices; top with remaining bread.
2. Cook sandwiches 4-6 minutes or until bread is browned and cheese is melted.

CRAN-APPLE BAKED OATMEAL

Put leftover cranberries, apples and walnuts to good use in this comforting baked oatmeal. I also serve it at my church's breakfast potlucks. Feel free to use blueberries in place of the cranberries if you like.
—**SHARON GERST** NORTH LIBERTY, IA

PREP: 15 MIN. • **BAKE:** 30 MIN.
MAKES: 8 SERVINGS

- 4 cups old-fashioned oats
- 2 teaspoons baking powder
- 1 teaspoon salt
- 1 teaspoon ground cinnamon
- 3 large eggs
- 2 cups 2% milk
- ⅔ cup sugar
- ⅔ cup canola oil
- 1 medium apple, chopped
- 1 cup fresh cranberries, chopped
- 1 cup chopped walnuts, toasted
- ½ cup packed brown sugar

1. Preheat oven to 350°. In a large bowl, mix oats, baking powder, salt and cinnamon. In another bowl, whisk eggs, milk, sugar and oil until blended; stir into oat mixture. Stir in apple, cranberries and walnuts.
2. Transfer to a greased 13x9-in. baking dish. Sprinkle with the brown sugar. Bake, uncovered, 30-35 minutes or until set and edges are lightly browned.

APPLE-PIE ICE CREAM PIE

If you serve more than one type of pie at Thanksgiving, you're likely to have leftovers. Turn what's left into a gourmet dessert for the day after. This recipe also works with leftover pumpkin or blueberry pie. Omit the caramel if you use blueberry.
—**AYSHA SCHURMAN** AMMON, ID

PREP: 20 MIN. • **BAKE:** 10 MIN. + FREEZING
MAKES: 8 SERVINGS

- 1½ cups graham cracker crumbs
- ¼ cup sugar
- ⅓ cup butter, melted
- 1 cup hot caramel ice cream topping
- 2 cups coarsely chopped apple pie (about half of an 8-inch pie)
- 4 cups vanilla ice cream, softened if necessary

1. Preheat oven to 375°. In a small bowl, mix cracker crumbs and sugar; stir in butter. Press onto bottom and up sides of a greased 9-in. pie plate. Bake 8-10 minutes or until lightly browned. Cool on a wire rack.
2. Drizzle ⅓ cup caramel topping over crust. Layer with 1 cup pie pieces and 2 cups ice cream. Repeat layers. Drizzle with remaining caramel topping. Freeze, covered, until firm, about 3 hours.

BREAD PUDDING WITH PRALINE SAUCE

Here's a sweet way to make use of the day-old dinner rolls that didn't get gobbled up at Thanksgiving. The combination of the soft pudding with the sweet, velvety smooth sauce is a match made in heaven.
—**ANITA GEOGHAGAN** WOODSTOCK, GA

PREP: 15 MIN. + SOAKING • **BAKE:** 45 MIN.
MAKES: 12 SERVINGS

- 5 large eggs
- 4 cups half-and-half cream
- 1 cup sugar
- 1 teaspoon vanilla extract
- 10 cups cubed day-old dinner rolls
PRALINE SAUCE
- ½ cup unsalted butter, cubed
- 1 cup packed brown sugar
- 1 cup heavy whipping cream
- ¼ teaspoon vanilla extract
   Sweetened whipped cream and toasted chopped walnuts, optional

1. Preheat oven to 350°. In a large bowl, whisk eggs, cream, sugar and vanilla until blended. Gently fold in cubed rolls; let stand about 15 minutes or until bread is softened.
2. Transfer to greased 13x9-in. baking dish. Bake for 45-50 minutes or until puffed, golden and knife inserted near center comes out clean. Meanwhile, in a small saucepan, melt the butter over medium-high heat. Stir in the brown sugar. Bring to a boil. Boil 2 minutes. Stir in cream; return to a boil. Remove from heat. Stir in vanilla. Serve with warm pudding. If desired, top with whipped cream and walnuts.

TOP TIP

Safely Storing Thanksgiving Leftovers

Follow these guidelines to ensure that the leftovers you keep will be safe to eat.

- When in doubt, throw it out. This is a good rule of thumb, whether you're questioning the safety of food you're about to store or of food you're taking out of the refrigerator or freezer to eat.
- Stock up on plastic storage bags and containers so you're prepared to store leftovers soon after the meal.
- Immediately after cooking, remove stuffing from the turkey, chicken, duck or goose. Within 2 hours, carve all meat off the bones. Place the meat and stuffing in separate containers and refrigerate. For faster cooling, don't stack the containers.

- Leftover turkey, stuffing and pumpkin pie can be refrigerated for 3 to 4 days.
- Meat combined with gravy and gravy by itself should be used within 1 to 2 days.
- Cranberry sauce and relish can be refrigerated for 5 to 7 days.
- Cooked vegetables should be eaten within 3 to 5 days.
- Freeze any leftovers you won't eat within 3 days. Frozen cooked meat and gravy should be used within 2 to 3 months.
- When reheating leftovers, bring gravy to a full rolling boil and all others foods to a temperature of 165°.

BREAD PUDDING WITH PRALINE SAUCE

**CINNAMON-SUGAR
SWEET POTATO
PASTRIES**

CINNAMON-SUGAR SWEET POTATO PASTRIES

We always have leftover mashed sweet potatoes after our Thanksgiving Day meal. I take what's left to make an indulgent filling for empanadas.
—**SARAH VASQUES** MILFORD, NH

PREP: 25 MIN. • **BAKE:** 10 MIN.
MAKES: 32 APPETIZERS

- ½ **cup mashed sweet potato**
- 2 **ounces cream cheese, softened**
- 1 **tablespoon brown sugar**
- ½ **teaspoon grated orange peel**
- 2 **tubes (8 ounces each) refrigerated crescent rolls**
- ½ **cup sugar**
- 2 **teaspoons ground cinnamon**
- ¼ **cup butter, melted**

1. Preheat oven to 375°. In a small bowl, combine sweet potato, cream cheese, brown sugar and orange peel. Unroll crescent dough and separate into four rectangles; press perforations to seal. Cut each rectangle into four triangles. Repeat with remaining dough. Place 1 teaspoon potato filling in center of each triangle. Fold dough over filling and pinch seams to seal.
2. Place 2 in. apart on parchment paper-lined baking sheets. Bake for 10-12 minutes or until golden brown. Cool slightly. In a bowl, mix sugar and cinnamon. Brush pastries with butter; coat with cinnamon-sugar mixture.

TOP TIP

Taco-Inspired Pizza

If you think that a Thanksgiving-inspired pizza is fun, you'll love this Southwestern twist that uses leftover taco ingredients. Top a ready-made frozen pizza crust with a mixture of sour cream and refried beans. Then sprinkle on leftover taco-seasoned ground beef. Add shredded cheddar or Monterey Jack cheese, chopped green peppers, onions and tomatoes. Baked for 15 minutes or until heated through.

THANKSGIVING LOVER'S PIZZA

THANKSGIVING LOVER'S PIZZA

Forget the standard next-day turkey sandwich and try this delicious take on pizza instead. Get creative with different variations of all the leftover favorites: use whole berry or jelly cranberry sauce; add dollops of mashed potatoes on top; drizzle with turkey gravy; sprinkle with stuffing or dressing; or try unique pizza crust varieties.
—**CARLA PARKER** ANDERSON, SC

PREP: 25 MIN. • **BAKE:** 10 MIN.
MAKES: 6 SERVINGS

- 1 **tablespoon olive oil**
- 1 **large sweet onion, thinly sliced**
- 2 **cups shredded cooked turkey**
- 1½ **teaspoons dried thyme**
- 1½ **teaspoons rubbed sage**
- ½ **teaspoon salt**
- ¼ **teaspoon pepper**
- 1 **prebaked 12-inch pizza crust**
- ½ **cup whole-berry cranberry sauce**
- 1 **medium sweet potato, baked, peeled and thinly sliced**
- 1 **cup (4 ounces) shredded part-skim mozzarella cheese**
- 1 **cup (4 ounces) Gruyere cheese**
- ½ **cup dried cranberries**
- ½ **teaspoon dried rosemary, crushed**

1. Preheat oven to 425°. In a large skillet, heat oil over medium-high heat. Add onion; cook and stir for 6-8 minutes or until tender. Stir in turkey, thyme, sage, salt and pepper.
2. Place crust on an ungreased 12-in. pizza pan. Top with cranberry sauce, turkey mixture, sweet potato, cheeses cranberries; sprinkle with rosemary. Bake 10-15 minutes or until cheese is melted.

NOTE *To prepare potato, scrub potato and pierce several times with a fork. Microwave, uncovered, on high on microwave-safe plate 8-10 minutes or until tender, turning once.*

SPICED SWEET POTATO BREAD

I love experimenting with leftovers. There are a lot of tasty twists on sweet potatoes, but my favorite way to repurpose them is in this delicious quick bread. The loaves freeze well and make a great gift.
—**KATIE FERRIER** HOUSTON, TX

PREP: 15 MIN. • **BAKE:** 50 MIN. + COOLING
MAKES: 2 LOAVES (16 SLICES EACH)

- 2 **cups all-purpose flour**
- 1⅓ **cups whole wheat flour**
- 2 **teaspoons baking powder**
- 1 **teaspoon ground cinnamon**
- ½ **teaspoon salt**
- ½ **teaspoon baking soda**
- 4 **large eggs**
- 2 **cups sugar**
- 2 **cups mashed sweet potatoes**
- ⅔ **cup orange juice**
- ½ **cup unsweetened applesauce**
- ⅓ **cup canola oil**
- 1 **finely chopped chipotle pepper in adobo sauce plus 1½ teaspoons adobo sauce**
- 1 **cup coarsely chopped pecans**

1. Preheat the oven to 350°. In a large bowl, whisk the first six ingredients. In another bowl, whisk eggs, sugar, sweet potatoes, orange juice, applesauce, oil, chipotle pepper and adobo sauce until blended. Add to flour mixture; stir just until moistened. Fold in pecans.
2. Transfer to two greased 9x5-in. loaf pans. Bake 50-60 minutes or until a toothpick inserted in center comes out clean. Cool in pans 10 minutes before removing to wire racks to cool.

STUFFIN' MUFFINS

If you love stuffing, you won't be able to get enough of these fun muffin cups that not only make use of leftover stuffing but also green beans, turkey, mashed potatoes, cheddar and gravy. It's a taste of Thanksgiving in every bite!
—**PAULINE PORTERFIELD** ROXBORO, NC

PREP: 10 MIN. • **BAKE:** 30 MIN. + STANDING.
MAKES: 4 SERVINGS

- 2 **cups cooked stuffing**
- 1 **cup cooked cut green beans**
- 1 **cup chopped cooked turkey**
- 1 **cup mashed potatoes**
- ¼ **cup shredded cheddar cheese**
- 1 **cup turkey gravy**

1. Preheat oven to 425°. Press stuffing onto bottom of eight greased muffin cups. Layer with beans and turkey. In a small bowl, combine the mashed potatoes and cheese; spoon over turkey.
2. Bake 15 minutes. Reduce oven setting to 350°. Bake 15-20 minutes longer or until potatoes begin to brown. Let stand 10 minutes. Run a knife around sides of muffin cups to remove muffins. Serve with gravy.

CRANBERRY SMOOTHIE

When you think of Thanksgiving leftovers, a smoothie probably isn't the first thing that comes to mind. I promise after you try my nutrient-packed beverage, it will be your new next-day favorite!
—**DEBRA TORRES** LYNCHBURG, VA

START TO FINISH: 5 MIN. • **MAKES:** 6 SERVINGS

- 2 **cups cranberry-apple juice**
- 2 **cups whole-berry cranberry sauce, divided**
- 1 **cup plain Greek yogurt**
- 2 **cups ice cubes**

Place juice, 1 cup cranberry sauce, yogurt and ice cubes in a blender; cover and process until blended. Add remaining cranberries; cover and pulse until combined. Serve immediately.

STUFFIN'
MUFFINS

Autumnal Desserts

The first cool breeze of fall can be a shock to our senses, especially when it's the precursor of what's to come. But once our eyes descend on the first sugar maple awash with color, **we become giddy with excitement for all the autumnal pleasures in store.** Among them is the trademark flavors of the season. And what better way to enjoy them than in a luscious dessert?

Here you'll find **a delicious array of after-dinner delights** bursting with your favorite fall flavors: pumpkin-style tiramisu, sinfully gooey creme brulee, from-scratch fruit pies and other sweet indulgences.

So when the air turns crisp and leaves start dancing across your path, **embrace all the cozy comforts of fall** with these fine desserts.

Pear Gruyere Pie (p. 130)

S'MORES
CREME BRULEE

SWEET POTATO & MARSHMALLOW SWIRL CHEESECAKE

I make a sweet potato souffle that I've always thought tastes like a dessert. I finally decided to use that idea for an actual dessert, and the result was a smooth, rich cheesecake.

—JESSICA SILVA EAST BERLIN, CT

PREP: 35 MIN. • **BAKE:** 1¼ HOURS + CHILLING
MAKES: 16 SERVINGS

- 2 pounds sweet potatoes, halved

CRUST
- 1 cup crushed gingersnap cookies (about 20 cookies)
- 1 cup finely chopped macadamia nuts
- ¼ cup butter, melted

FILLING
- 3 packages (8 ounces each) cream cheese, softened
- ¾ cup sugar
- ¼ cup packed brown sugar
- ⅓ cup sour cream
- ¼ cup heavy whipping cream
- 2 tablespoons butter, softened
- 2 teaspoons vanilla extract
- 1 teaspoon pumpkin pie spice
- 3 large eggs, lightly beaten

MARSHMALLOW SWIRL
- 1 jar (7 ounces) marshmallow creme
- 4 ounces cream cheese, softened
- 1 large egg, lightly beaten
- 4 teaspoons all-purpose flour
- 1 teaspoon vanilla extract

1. Preheat oven to 350°. Place sweet potatoes on a greased baking sheet, cut side down. Bake 25-30 minutes or until tender. Cool slightly. Remove peel; place the potatoes in a food processor. Cover and process until potatoes are smooth. (There should be about 2 cups.)

2. Place a greased 9-in. springform pan on a double thickness of heavy-duty foil (about 18 in. square). Wrap foil securely around pan. Place on a baking sheet.

3. In a small bowl, mix cookie crumbs, macadamia nuts and butter. Press onto the bottom of prepared pan. Bake 15 minutes. Cool on a wire rack. Reduce oven setting to 325°.

4. In a large bowl, beat cream cheese and sugars until smooth. Beat in sour cream, whipping cream, butter, vanilla, pie spice and sweet potato puree. Add eggs; beat on low speed just until blended.

5. In a small bowl, beat marshmallow creme, cream cheese, egg, flour and vanilla until smooth. Pour half of the sweet potato mixture over crust. Pour half of the marshmallow mixture over sweet potato mixture; swirl gently with a knife. Repeat.

6. Place springform pan in a large baking pan; add 1-in. of hot water to larger pan. Bake 1¼ hours or until center is just set and top appears dull. Remove springform pan from water bath. Cool cheesecake on a wire rack 10 minutes. Loosen sides of pan with a knife; remove foil. Cool 1 hour longer. Refrigerate overnight, covering when completely cooled.

S'MORES CREME BRULEE

A big bite into a scrumptious s'more brings back sweet campfire memories. This fancy take on the classic treat is perfect for a fall meal and will be adored by young and old alike.

—ROSE DENNING OVERLAND PARK, KS

PREP: 30 MIN. • **BAKE:** 25 MIN. + CHILLING
MAKES: 6 SERVINGS

- 1 cup 2% milk
- 3 large eggs
- ⅔ cup sugar
- ⅓ cup baking cocoa
- 2 tablespoons coffee liqueur or strong brewed coffee
- ⅔ cup graham cracker crumbs
- 2 tablespoons butter, melted
- ⅓ cup coarse or granulated sugar
- 2 cups miniature marshmallows
- 1 milk chocolate candy bar (1.55 ounces), broken into 12 pieces

1. Preheat the oven to 325°. In a small saucepan, heat milk until bubbles form around sides of pan; remove from heat. In a large bowl, whisk eggs, sugar, cocoa and liqueur until blended but not foamy. Slowly whisk in hot milk.

2. Place six 4-oz. broiler-safe ramekins in a baking pan large enough to hold them without touching. Pour egg mixture into ramekins. Place pan on oven rack; add very hot water to pan to within ½ in. of top of ramekins. Bake for 20-25 minutes or until a knife inserted near the center comes out clean; centers will still be soft. Remove ramekins from water bath immediately to a wire rack; cool 10 minutes. Refrigerate until cold.

3. In a small bowl, mix cracker crumbs and the butter. To caramelize topping with a kitchen torch, sprinkle custards evenly with sugar. Hold flame about 2 in. above custard surface. Rotate it slowly until sugar is caramelized. Sprinkle the custards with crumb mixture; top with marshmallows. Using torch, heat marshmallows until browned. Top with chocolate pieces. Serve immediately or refrigerate up to 1 hour.

4. To caramelize topping in a broiler, place ramekins on a baking sheet; let stand at room temperature 15 minutes. Preheat broiler. Sprinkle custards evenly with the sugar. Broil 3-4 in. from heat 3-5 minutes or until sugar is caramelized. Sprinkle custards with crumb mixture; top with the marshmallows. Broil 30-45 seconds or until marshmallows are browned. Top with the chocolate pieces. Serve the creme brulee immediately or refrigerate up to 1 hour.

TOP TIP

Water Bath Basics

A water bath is a cooking technique in which you place a small baking dish or ramekin containing food, such as a custard or souffle, inside a larger baking pan. Using a kettle or large measuring cups, carefully pour hot or boiling water into the larger baking pan. Fill according to the recipe directions, generally to a depth of 1 in. or halfway up the sides of the larger pan. Place the pan on a rack in the oven. The food is then baked in the water bath to promote even cooking. To easily remove ramekins from a water bath after cooking, wrap rubber bands around the ends of your tongs to get a firm grip.

HONEY-ROASTED FIGS IN PUFF PASTRY

I created this recipe for a national honey contest and won third place! I was thrilled, and you will be, too, when you try these tasty but elegant desserts.

—**KELLY WILLIAMS** FORKED RIVER, NJ

PREP: 45 MIN. + CHILLING • **BAKE:** 25 MIN.
MAKES: 8 SERVINGS

- 4 ounces cream cheese, softened
- 2 teaspoons dark brown sugar
- ½ teaspoon vanilla extract
- 1 vanilla bean
- ¼ cup spun or regular honey
- ½ teaspoon balsamic vinegar
- 8 fresh figs
- 1 package (17.3 ounces) frozen puff pastry, thawed

EGG WASH

- 1 large egg
- 1 tablespoon water
- ¼ cup pistachios, chopped

1. In a small bowl, mix cream cheese, brown sugar and vanilla. Divide into eight small mounds. Refrigerate 30 minutes or until firm.

2. Meanwhile, preheat oven to 400°. Split vanilla bean lengthwise. Using the tip of a sharp knife, scrape seeds from the center; place in a small microwave-safe bowl. Add the honey and the balsamic vinegar. Microwave, uncovered, at 80% power for 20 seconds, stir to mix.

3. Slice each fig lengthwise into six slices; place on a parchment paper-lined 15x10x1-in. baking pan. Drizzle with 2 tablespoons honey sauce. Roast 8-10 minutes or until softened. Cool on pan on a wire rack.

4. Unfold one sheet of puff pastry. On a lightly floured surface, roll out pastry just enough to smooth surface. Cut into four equal pieces; trim off corners to round. Cut in about half way from each rounded corner in toward the center. Place a cream cheese mound in the center of each. Top with six slices cooled roasted figs; drizzle tops with ¼ teaspoons honey sauce.

5. In a small bowl, whisk egg with water; brush pastry with egg wash. Fold up 1 "petal" of dough wrapping around filling. Wrap the second petal around first one from the opposite side lightly pressing ends to stick. Continue

with other two petals. Tuck last two points under "rose" and cup in hand gently to round the base.

6. Place on parchment paper-lined baking sheet. Repeat. Use the excess corner trimmings to make leaves and place slightly under and next to roses. Brush outside of pastries with egg wash. Bake 25-30 minutes or until golden brown. Remove to a cooling rack. Place roses on a serving plate; drizzle with re-warmed remaining honey sauce. Top with pistachios; serve warm.

ORANGE-KISSED APPLE STRUDEL

My mom used to make the best apple turnovers using store-bought phyllo dough. I created a quick and delicious variation on her recipe by making one apple strudel in a log. It's a time-saver, but just as delicious. You can easily double the recipe for a larger crowd.

—**ELENA IORGA** HELENA, MT

PREP: 20 MIN. • **BAKE:** 15 MIN. + COOLING
MAKES: 6 SERVINGS

- 2 medium Granny Smith apples, peeled and grated
- ¼ cup sugar
- 2 tablespoons butter
- 1 tablespoon grated orange peel
- 2 teaspoons lemon juice
- ¼ teaspoon ground cinnamon
- 1 teaspoon vanilla extract
- 6 tablespoons finely ground almonds, toasted
- ¼ teaspoon ground cinnamon
- ⅛ teaspoon ground nutmeg
- 6 sheets phyllo dough (14x9-inch size)
- ¼ cup butter, melted Confectioners' sugar Vanilla ice cream, optional

1. In a large saucepan, combine apples, sugar, butter, orange peel, lemon juice and cinnamon. Cook, uncovered, over medium heat 5-7 minutes or until thickened and liquid is evaporated, stirring occasionally. Remove from heat; stir in vanilla. Cool.

2. Preheat oven to 375°. In a bowl, mix almonds, cinnamon and nutmeg. Place one sheet of phyllo dough on a work surface; brush with some butter.

Sprinkle with about 1 tablespoon almond mixture. Layer with five additional phyllo sheets, brushing each sheet with butter and sprinkling with almond mixture. (Keep the remaining phyllo covered with plastic wrap and a damp towel to prevent it from drying out.) Spoon apple filling down a long side to within ½ in. of edges. Roll up jelly-roll style, starting with long side. Transfer to a baking sheet, seam side down. Brush top with remaining melted butter. Bake for 15-17 minutes or until golden brown.

3. Cool completely on a wire rack. Using a serrated knife, cut into slices; dust with confectioners' sugar. If desired, serve with ice cream.

TOFFEE CARAMEL SQUARES

Layers of caramel and chocolate cover a cookie crust, creating these rich treats. I made several pans for our son's wedding and received many requests for the recipe. The scrumptious bars are also perfect for cookie exchanges.

—**KAREN BOURNE** MAGRATH, AB

PREP: 20 MIN. • **BAKE:** 20 MIN.
MAKES: 3 DOZEN

- 1¼ cups all-purpose flour
- ¼ cup sugar
- ½ cup plus 2 tablespoons cold butter

FILLING

- ½ cup butter, cubed
- ½ cup packed brown sugar
- ½ cup sweetened condensed milk
- 2 tablespoons light corn syrup

GLAZE

- 2 cups (12 ounces) semisweet chocolate chips
- 1 tablespoon shortening

1. Preheat the oven to 350°. In a large bowl, combine flour and sugar. Cut in the butter until crumbly. Press into greased 9-in. square baking pan. Bake 18-20 minutes or until golden brown.

2. In a small saucepan, combine the filling ingredients. Bring to a boil over medium heat; boil, stir 5 minutes. Pour over warm crust.

3. In a microwave, melt chocolate chips and shortening; stir until smooth. Spread over filling. Cool on a wire rack. Cut into squares.

**HONEY-ROASTED
FIGS IN PUFF PASTRY**

PUMPKIN CREAM
TIRAMISU

PUMPKIN CREAM TIRAMISU

Pumpkin isn't only for pies. Now you can take the classic fall vegetable and enjoy it in a tiramisu-style dessert. I promise that after one bite you'll add this recipe to your keeper files.

—**PAM PETERS** FERNIE, BC

PREP: 1 HOUR + CHILLING • **BAKE:** 10 MIN./BATCH + COOLING
MAKES: 12 SERVINGS

- ½ cup butter, softened
- 1 cup sugar
- 1 large egg
- ¼ cup honey
- ½ cup solid-pack pumpkin
- 1 teaspoon dark rum
- 2⅓ cups all-purpose flour
- 2 teaspoons ground cinnamon
- 1½ teaspoons baking soda
- 1½ teaspoons ground ginger
- 1 teaspoon ground cloves
- ½ teaspoon salt

TIRAMISU

- 2¼ cups solid-pack pumpkin
- 1½ teaspoons ground cinnamon
- ¾ teaspoon ground ginger
- ¼ teaspoon ground cloves
- 2 cups heavy whipping cream
- ¾ cup sugar
- 1 package (8 ounces) cream cheese, softened
- ¼ cup dark rum
- ½ teaspoon ground cinnamon or nutmeg

1. Preheat oven to 350°. In a large bowl, cream butter and sugar until light and fluffy. Gradually beat in egg and honey. Add pumpkin and rum; mix well. In another bowl, whisk flour, cinnamon, baking soda, ginger, cloves and the salt; gradually beat into creamed mixture.

2. Cut a ¾-in. hole in the tip of a pastry bag or in a corner of a food-safe plastic bag. Working in batches, pipe dough to form 2½-in. logs, 2 in. apart, onto parchment paper-lined baking sheets. Bake 12-14 minutes or until cookies are golden and set. Cool on a wire rack.

3. In a large bowl, mix pumpkin and spices. In a small bowl, beat cream until it begins to thicken. Add the sugar; beat until soft peaks form. Fold a third of whipped cream mixture into pumpkin mixture.

In a small bowl, beat cream cheese until smooth. Beat in remaining whipped cream until combined. Arrange a third of the cookies in a single layer in a 13x9-in. baking dish; brush with rum. Top with a third of pumpkin filling. Spread with a third of the cream cheese mixture. Repeat layers twice. Refrigerate, covered, 8 hours or overnight. Sprinkle with cinnamon.

BUTTERNUT SQUASH APPLE CRISP

I had this recipe in my box for years before I finally tried it—and now we love it! It has become my son-in-law's favorite.

—**BARBARA ELLIS** BRIDGEWATER, MA

PREP: 25 MIN. • **BAKE:** 45 MIN.
MAKES: 8 SERVINGS

- 1 small butternut squash (about 1 pound)
- 3 medium tart apples, peeled and sliced
- ¼ cup corn syrup
- 2 tablespoons lemon juice
- ¾ cup packed brown sugar
- 1 tablespoon cornstarch
- 1 teaspoon ground cinnamon
- ½ teaspoon salt

OAT TOPPING

- ½ cup all-purpose flour
- ½ cup quick-cooking oats
- ¼ cup packed brown sugar
- 6 tablespoons cold butter
  Vanilla ice cream

1. Preheat oven to 375°. Peel and cut squash lengthwise in half; discard seeds. Cut squash into thin slices. In a large bowl, combine squash, apples, corn syrup and lemon juice; toss to coat. Mix brown sugar, cornstarch, cinnamon and salt; stir into squash mixture.

2. Transfer mixture to a greased 13x9-in. baking dish. Bake, covered, 20 minutes.

3. In a small bowl, mix flour, oats and brown sugar; cut in butter until crumbly. Sprinkle over the squash mixture. Bake 25 minutes longer or until squash and apples are tender and topping is lightly browned. Serve warm with ice cream.

CINNAMON CRUNCH ICE CREAM

Is your ice cream feeling a little vanilla? Take the flavor up a notch with my cinnamon- and spice-enhanced recipe. It's great for special occasions or a treat to make with the kids on a fall afternoon. Use your favorite nuts or a mixture for some variety.

—**CATHERINE JOHNSTON** STAFFORD, NY

PREP: 1 HOUR + CHILLING • **PROCESS:** 25 MIN. + FREEZING
MAKES: 1½ QUARTS

- 8 large egg yolks
- 1 cup sugar
- 2 cups heavy whipping cream
- 1 cup 2% milk
- 2 teaspoons vanilla extract

WALNUTS

- 1 tablespoon large egg white
- 2 cups walnut or pecan halves
- ⅓ cup sugar
- ¾ teaspoon ground cinnamon
- ¼ teaspoon ground nutmeg
- ¼ teaspoon ground allspice

1. In a large heavy saucepan, whisk egg yolks and sugar until blended; stir in cream and milk. Cook over medium-low heat until mixture is just thick enough to coat a metal spoon and a thermometer reads at least 175°, stirring constantly. Do not allow to boil. Remove from heat immediately.

2. Quickly transfer to a large bowl; stir in vanilla. Place bowl in a pan of ice water. Stir gently and occasionally for 2 minutes. Press plastic wrap onto surface of custard. Refrigerate several hours or overnight.

3. Preheat oven to 325°. In a large bowl, whisk egg white. Add the walnuts; toss to coat. In a small bowl, mix sugar and spices. Sprinkle over the walnuts; toss to coat. Spread into a 15x10x1-in. baking pan. Bake for 30-35 minutes or until crisp, stirring every 10 minutes. Cool completely.

4. Fill cylinder of ice cream maker no more than two-thirds full; freeze according to the manufacturer's directions.

5. Transfer ice cream to freezer containers, allowing head space for expansion. Fold in nut mixture. Freeze 4-6 hours or until firm.

PRALINE CHOCOLATE DESSERT

A cookie crumb crust, luscious layers of praline and cream cheese, and a chocolate glaze make this dessert a showstopper. It's worth the extra time and effort to make, and it freezes well, too.

—**KORRIE BASTIAN** CLEARFIELD, UT

PREP: 25 MIN. + CHILLING • **BAKE:** 10 MIN. + COOLING
MAKES: 16 SERVINGS

- 2 cups cream-filled chocolate sandwich cookie crumbs
- ½ cup butter, melted
- 1 cup chopped pecans

PRALINE

- 1½ cups butter, cubed
- 1 cup packed brown sugar
- 1 teaspoon vanilla extract

FILLING

- 2 packages (8 ounces each) cream cheese, softened
- ½ cup confectioners' sugar
- ⅓ cup packed brown sugar

GANACHE

- 1 cup (6 ounces) semisweet chocolate chips
- ½ cup heavy whipping cream
  Pecan halves

1. Preheat oven to 350°. In a small bowl, combine the cookie crumbs and butter. Press onto bottom of a greased 9-in. springform pan. Place the pan on a baking sheet. Bake 10 minutes. Cool on a wire rack. Sprinkle with pecans.
2. In a large saucepan over medium heat, bring butter and brown sugar to a boil, stirring constantly. Reduce the heat; simmer, uncovered, 10 minutes. Remove from heat; stir in vanilla. Pour over pecans. Refrigerate 1-2 hours or until set.
3. In a large bowl, beat the filling ingredients until smooth. Spread over praline layer. Refrigerate for 1-2 hours or until set.
4. For ganache, place chocolate chips in a small bowl. In a small saucepan, bring cream just to a boil. Pour over chocolate; whisk until smooth. Spread over filling. Refrigerate 1-2 hours or until set.
5. Loosen sides of pan with a knife. Remove rim from pan. Sprinkle with pecans. Refrigerate leftovers.

FINISHING TOUCHES FOR PIE CRUSTS

To top off double-crust pies before baking, use a pastry brush to lightly and evenly apply one of the following washes to the top crust, avoiding the edges.

- For a shine and light browning, brush with an egg white that was lightly beaten with 1 teaspoon of water.
- For a glossy, golden appearance, brush with an egg yolk that was beaten with 1 teaspoon of water.
- For a slight shine, brush with half-and-half cream or heavy whipping cream.

- For a crisp brown crust, brush with water.
- For a little sparkle, sprinkle with the sugar or decorator sugar after brushing with one of the washes.
- To give a little more shine to a baked double-crust pie, warm 1 tablespoon of light corn syrup. Gently brush over the baked warm crust.

PEAR GRUYERE PIE

I love cheese and fruit, so this pie was a natural pairing for me. Sweet and spicy wine-poached pears and a flaky, buttery cheese crust make for a winning dessert you'll want to create again and again. If you're serving this for Thanksgiving, bake leaf-shaped pie pastry on top for a festive look (see directions on opposite page).

—**ALEXANDRA PENFOLD** BROOKLYN, NY

PREP: 30 MIN. + CHILLING
BAKE: 40 MIN. + COOLING • **MAKES:** 8 SERVINGS

- 2½ cups all-purpose flour
- 3 ounces Gruyere cheese, finely grated
- 1 tablespoon sugar
- 1 teaspoon salt
- 1 cup cold unsalted butter, cubed
- 6 to 8 tablespoons ice water

FILLING

- 1½ cups water
- ¾ cup port wine
- ¼ cup sugar
- 1 cinnamon stick (3 inches)
- 2 teaspoons vanilla extract
- ½ teaspoon ground ginger
- ¼ teaspoon ground nutmeg
- ¼ teaspoon ground cloves
- 6 medium pears (about 3 pounds) peeled and thinly sliced
- 2 teaspoons cornstarch
- 1 tablespoon water
- 1 large egg, lightly beaten
  Vanilla ice cream, optional

1. Place flour, cheese, sugar and salt in a food processor; pulse until blended. Add butter; pulse until butter is the size of peas. While pulsing, add just enough of the ice water to form moist crumbs. Divide dough in half. Shape each into a disk; wrap in plastic wrap. Refrigerate 1 hour or overnight.
2. In a large saucepan, combine water, wine, sugar, cinnamon stick, vanilla and spices; bring to a boil. Add pears to poaching liquid. Cook, uncovered, 10-15 minutes or until tender.
3. Using a slotted spoon, remove pears and cool slightly. Refrigerate until cooled; discard cinnamon stick. Meanwhile, return poaching liquid to a boil. Cook 12-15 minutes or until liquid is reduced to ¾ cup. In a small bowl, mix cornstarch and water until smooth; stir into the reduced liquid. Return to a boil, stirring constantly; cook and stir 1-2 minutes or until thickened. Pour the mixture into a 1-cup measuring cup. Cool slightly; refrigerate until chilled.
4. Preheat oven to 400°. On a well floured surface, roll one half of dough to a ⅛-in.-thick circle; transfer to a 9-in. pie plate. Trim pastry to ½ in. beyond edge of plate; flute edges. Add pear filling; pour syrup over pears. Roll remaining dough to a ⅛-in.-thick circle. Cut decorative cutouts from remaining pastry and arrange over pie filling; re-roll pastry scraps as needed. Brush pastry with the egg. Place pie on a baking sheet.
5. Bake 30-40 minutes or until crust is golden brown and filling is bubbly. Cover edges with foil during the last 15 minutes to prevent over-browning if necessary. Cool on a wire rack. If desired, serve with ice cream.

PEAR
GRUYERE PIE

Easy Pie Pastry Cutouts

A golden homemade crust made up of thin, crisp layers is the hallmark of a perfect pie. Give your pie crush a fancy finishing touch with a decorative upper crust. With some simple but snappy finger work, you can turn out pie that's as yummy to look at as it is to eat.

ROLL out dough to a ⅛-in.-thick circle; cut out shapes using a leaf-shaped cookie cutter. Reroll scrap dough; cut out more shapes as desired.

LAYER dough shapes over pie filling (brush with water to make them stick together).

Easter
Gatherings

At long last...spring has sprung! Once again Mother Nature beckons us outdoors to soak up her warm, supple breezes and golden light. From Easter dinners and brunches to long, sunny evenings entertaining friends on the patio, there's a host of springtime celebrations to enjoy. As each breathtaking day folds into the next, savor all the food the season has to offer.

Make-Ahead Easter Dinner

Easter celebrates rebirth and the promise of a new start.
This is the time of year when the air is fresh, the days are longer
and the first graceful flowers are raising their heads to the sky.

But with church services, egg hunts and other activities, it can be
a day filled with flurry. This year, make dinner an afternoon affair
with **a bounty of make-ahead dishes.**

A succulent maple-glazed ham will win you raves, while a citrus-
infused asparagus salad and a colorful fruit medley highlight **the
season's best flavors.** Round out the meal with slow-cooked spuds,
warm yeast rolls and a heavenly cream torte that will have the
kids—and the grown-ups!—passing on the chocolate bunnies.

Maple-Glazed Ham (p. 138) **Citrus-Tarragon Asparagus Salad** (p. 138)
Overnight Yeast Rolls (p. 142) **Refreshing Raspberry Iced Tea** (p. 141)

Easter Dinner Agenda

Hop to it this Easter with a make-ahead menu that lets you hightail it out of the kitchen. Please everyone at the table with a succulent maple-glazed ham, homemade rolls, the season's best veggies and other sunny selections. **Hallelujah!**

A FEW WEEKS BEFORE

- Prepare two grocery lists— one of nonperishables to buy now and one for perishable items to buy a few days before Easter.

TWO DAYS BEFORE

- Buy remaining grocery items.

- Make the Raspberry Crumb Bars; cool. Store in an airtight container.

THE DAY BEFORE

- Set the table. See page 37 for a guide.

- Mix together the Raspberry Iced Tea; refrigerate.

- Prepare the Roasted Garlic & Onion Dip; cover and refrigerate until serving.

- Prepare Cool and Creamy Fruit Salad; cover and store in the refrigerator for up to 24 hours.

- Make the Chocolate & Coconut Cream Torte; cover and refrigerate until serving.

THE NIGHT BEFORE

- Prepare dough for Overnight Yeast Rolls; cover and refrigerate overnight.

- Prepare Marinated Shrimp; cover and refrigerate until serving.

EASTER MORNING

- Prepare the ingredients for Slow-Cooked Potatoes with Spring Onions and place in the slow cooker. Cook for 6-8 hours.

- Prepare the Citrus-Tarragon Asparagus Salad and refrigerate up to 4 hours before serving.

- For Maple-Glazed Ham, place ham in the oven and bake at 300 degrees.

- Bake the Overnight Yeast Rolls; cover.

- Slice the strawberries and remove rind from Brie for Brie-Berry Bruschetta.

RIGHT BEFORE DINNER

- Mix together the glaze for the ham; pour over ham and bake an additional 15-30 minutes before serving.

- Boil the carrots for the Peach-Glazed Carrots and mix together the glaze; toss the carrots with glaze right before serving.

- Toast French bread and top with Brie and strawberries.

- Warm rolls in the oven.

ROASTED GARLIC & ONION DIP

I'm known for the variety of appetizers I serve at holiday gatherings. I continually try to include new recipes, but this one is always on the table. It takes a little more time to make than most onion dips, but I promise the savory results are worth it!
—**KIM CONOVER** EGG HARBOR, NJ

PREP: 10 MIN. • **COOK:** 45 MIN.
MAKES: 1½ CUPS

- 2 **large sweet onions, cut into four wedges**
- 2 **tablespoons honey**
- 2 **tablespoons olive oil, divided**
- 1 **tablespoon balsamic vinegar**
- 2 **teaspoons Dijon mustard**
- ¼ **teaspoon coarsely ground pepper**
- 2 **whole garlic bulbs**
- 1 **package (8 ounces) cream cheese, softened and cubed**
- ½ **teaspoon salt**
  Assorted fresh vegetables or crackers

1. Preheat oven to 375°. Place onions in a greased 15x10x1-in. baking pan. In a small bowl, mix honey, 1 tablespoon oil, vinegar, mustard and pepper. Drizzle over onions; toss to coat. Roast 40-45 minutes or until golden brown, stirring occasionally.

2. Remove papery outer skin from garlic bulbs, but do not peel or separate the cloves. Cut off top of garlic bulbs, exposing individual cloves. Drizzle cut cloves with remaining oil. Wrap in foil. Bake 30-45 minutes or until cloves are soft. Unwrap and cool 10 minutes. Squeeze garlic from skins.

3. Transfer onions and pan drippings to a food processor; add garlic. Pulse until finely chopped. Add the cream cheese and salt; pulse until blended. Transfer to a small bowl. Refrigerate until serving. Serve with vegetables.

PEACH-GLAZED CARROTS

PEACH-GLAZED CARROTS

My kids have no problem eating all their vegetables when this dish is on the table. These peach-sweetened carrots are a great companion to our Easter ham.
—**CHRISTINE MOHN** NEW PROVIDENCE, PA

START TO FINISH: 30 MIN. • **MAKES:** 10 SERVINGS

- 3½ **pounds medium carrots, sliced diagonally**
- ½ **cup butter, cubed**
- ½ **cup peach preserves**
- ¼ **cup orange juice**
- ½ **teaspoon salt**
- ⅛ **teaspoon ground nutmeg**
  Coarsely ground pepper, optional

1. Place carrots in a 6-qt. stockpot; add water to cover. Bring to a boil. Cook, covered, 5-8 minutes or until tender. Drain.

2. Meanwhile, in a small saucepan, combine butter, preserves, orange juice, salt and nutmeg. Cook and stir over medium-low heat 3-5 minutes or until blended. Pour over carrots; toss to coat. If desired, sprinkle with ground pepper.

**CITRUS-TARRAGON
ASPARAGUS SALAD**

MAPLE-GLAZED HAM

I cook this ham for Christmas and for Easter, but my husband thinks that twice a year is not enough. If it were up to him, we'd eat this every day! When I have larger hams, I double the glaze. If any glaze is left, we use it on pancakes the next day.

—JEANIE BEASLEY TUPELO, MS

PREP: 10 MIN. • **COOK:** 1¾ HOURS
MAKES: 15 SERVINGS

- 1 **spiral-sliced fully cooked bone-in ham (7 to 9 pounds)**
- **GLAZE**
- ½ **cup packed brown sugar**
- ½ **cup maple syrup**
- 2 **tablespoons prepared mustard**
- ½ **teaspoon ground cinnamon**
- ¼ **teaspoon ground nutmeg**

1. Preheat oven to 300°. Place ham on a rack in a shallow roasting pan. Cover ham and bake for 1½-2 hours or until a thermometer reads 130°.
2. Meanwhile, in a large saucepan, combine glaze ingredients. Bring to a boil; cook and stir 2-3 minutes or until slightly thickened.
3. Remove ham from oven. Pour the glaze over ham. Bake ham, uncovered, for another 15-30 minutes or until a thermometer reads 140°.

TOP TIP

Freeze Pan Juices

After baking a ham, I refrigerate the pan juices. The next day, I skim off the fat and heat the juice just enough to pour it into ice cube trays I save for this purpose. I store the trays in my freezer. Then I pull a cube or two out as needed to season dishes like green beans or boiled potatoes.

—DOROTHY P. WARSAW, IN

CITRUS-TARRAGON ASPARAGUS SALAD

I created this colorful salad when I was invited to a friend's Easter egg hunt and potluck picnic. The guests were begging to get my recipe. Let the flavors infuse overnight for the best taste.

—CHERYL A. MAGNUSON APPLE VALLEY, CA

PREP: 40 MIN. + CHILLING • **BROIL:** 15 MIN.
MAKES: 12 SERVINGS

- 3 **medium sweet red peppers**
- 3 **pounds fresh asparagus, trimmed**
- ½ **cup minced shallots**
- **DRESSING**
- ⅓ **cup white balsamic vinegar**
- 2 **tablespoons grated orange peel**
- 2 **tablespoons minced fresh tarragon**
- 1 **tablespoon honey**
- 1 **teaspoon sea salt**
- ¼ **teaspoon pepper**
- ⅔ **cup walnut or olive oil**

1. Preheat broiler. Place peppers on a foil-lined baking sheet. Broil 4 in. from heat until skins blister, about 5 minutes. With tongs, rotate peppers a quarter turn. Broil and rotate until all sides are blistered and blackened. Immediately place peppers in a large bowl; let stand, covered, 20 minutes.
2. Meanwhile, in a 6-qt. stockpot, bring 8 cups of water to a boil. Add asparagus in batches; cook, uncovered, 1-2 minutes or just until crisp-tender. Remove asparagus and immediately drop into ice water. Drain and pat dry; cut into halves.
3. Peel off and discard charred skin on peppers. Remove stems and seeds. Cut peppers into ¼-in.-wide strips. In a large bowl, combine asparagus, red peppers and shallots. For dressing, in a small bowl, whisk vinegar, orange peel, tarragon, honey, salt and pepper. Gradually whisk in oil until blended. Drizzle over asparagus mixture; toss to coat. Refrigerate up to 4 hours before serving, stirring occasionally.

MAPLE-GLAZED HAM

**SLOW-COOKED
POTATOES WITH
SPRING ONIONS**

SLOW-COOKED POTATOES WITH SPRING ONIONS

I love the simplicity of this recipe as well as the ease of preparation with my slow cooker. And everyone always likes roasted potatoes, even my pickiest child! If desired, top with shredded or crumbled cheese.

—THERESA GOMEZ STUART, FL

PREP: 5 MIN. • **COOK:** 6 HOURS
MAKES: 12 SERVINGS

- 4 pounds small red potatoes
- 8 green onions, chopped (about 1 cup)
- 1 cup chopped sweet onion
- ¼ cup olive oil
- ½ teaspoon salt
- ½ teaspoon pepper

In a 5- or 6-qt. slow cooker, combine all ingredients. Cook, covered, on low 6-8 hours or until potatoes are tender.

BRIE-BERRY BRUSCHETTA

I love fresh strawberries and look forward to when they are in season. Because these berries appear in so many desserts that are sweet, I wanted to come up with a way to use them in something savory. This bruschetta was the tasty result.

—MARY LEVERETTE COLUMBIA, SC

START TO FINISH: 15 MIN. • **MAKES:** 1 DOZEN

- 12 slices French bread baguette (¼ inch thick)
- 1 tablespoon olive oil
- 1 round (8 ounces) Brie cheese, rind removed
- 1 cup sliced fresh strawberries
- 1 tablespoon balsamic vinegar
- 1½ teaspoons minced fresh thyme or ½ teaspoon dried thyme

1. Place bread on an ungreased baking sheet; brush with oil. Broil 3-4 in. from the heat for 1-2 minutes or until bread is golden brown.
2. Spread Brie over toast; top with strawberries. Drizzle with vinegar and sprinkle with thyme.

RASPBERRY CRUMB BARS

I take advantage of fruit that's in season when I make desserts. These bars are so delectable. It's hard to eat just one!

—ROSIE NEWCOMER BOWDOIN, ME

PREP: 30 MIN. • **BAKE:** 20 MIN. + COOLING
MAKES: 2 DOZEN

- 3 cups all-purpose flour
- 1½ cups sugar
- ½ teaspoon baking soda
- 1 cup cold butter, cubed
- 1 large egg, beaten

FILLING
- 1¼ cups sugar
- 3 tablespoons cornstarch
- ¼ cup water
- 2 cups fresh or frozen raspberries, thawed
- ½ teaspoon vanilla extract

GLAZE
- 1¼ cups confectioners' sugar
- 2 tablespoons water
- 1 tablespoon butter, melted

1. Preheat oven 350°. In a large bowl, mix the flour, sugar and baking soda; cut in butter until crumbly. Stir in the egg. Reserve 2 cups of the crumb mixture for topping. Press remaining mixture onto bottom of an ungreased 15x10x1-in. baking pan. Bake crust for 9-11 minutes or until lightly browned. Cool on a wire rack.
2. In a large saucepan, mix sugar and cornstarch; stir in water until smooth. Add raspberries. Bring to a boil; cook and stir mixture over medium heat until thickened, about 2 minutes. Remove from heat; stir in vanilla.
3. Spread raspberry mixture over crust; top with the reserved topping. Bake 20-25 minutes or until topping is golden brown. Cool slightly.
4. In a small bowl, mix the glaze ingredients until smooth; drizzle over warm bars. Cool completely in pan on a wire rack. Cut into bars.

REFRESHING RASPBERRY ICED TEA

This recipe makes two gallons, so it's a great choice for a springtime party when you have a medium-size crowd. It freezes well, so feel free to make it ahead of time.

—ARLANA HENDRICKS MANCHESTER, TN

PREP/TOTAL: 20 MIN.
MAKES: 16 SERVINGS (1 CUP EACH)

- 6 cups water
- 1¾ cups sugar
- 8 individual tea bags
- ¾ cup frozen apple-raspberry juice concentrate
- 8 cups cold water
  Ice cubes
  Fresh raspberries, optional

In a large saucepan, bring 6 cups water and sugar to a boil; remove from the heat. Add tea bags; steep, covered, for 3-5 minutes according to taste. Discard tea bags. Add the juice concentrate; stir in cold water. Serve over ice with raspberries if desired.

OVERNIGHT YEAST ROLLS

It's easy to make light and flavorful rolls with this no-fuss recipe. The dough can also be used for cinnamon rolls, herb bread or coffee cake. (Or try one of the tasty toppings listed below right.)

—TRISHA KRUSE EAGLE, ID

PREP: 20 MIN. + CHILLING • **BAKE:** 15 MIN.
MAKES: 2 DOZEN

- 1 tablespoon sugar
- 1 tablespoon active dry yeast
- 1½ teaspoons salt
- 5½ to 6 cups all-purpose flour
- 1 cup buttermilk
- ½ cup water
- ½ cup butter, cubed
- 3 large eggs
- 2 tablespoons butter, melted

1. In a bowl, mix sugar, yeast, salt and 3 cups flour. In a small saucepan, heat buttermilk, water and ½ cup butter to 120°-130°. Add to dry ingredients; beat on medium speed 2 minutes. Add eggs; beat on high 2 minutes. Stir in enough remaining flour to form a soft dough (dough will be sticky).
2. Do not knead. Place dough in a large greased bowl. Cover with plastic wrap; refrigerate overnight.
3. Punch down dough. Turn onto a lightly floured surface; divide and shape into 24 balls. Place 2 in. apart on greased baking sheets. Cover with kitchen towels; let rise in a warm place until almost doubled, about 1½ hours.
4. Preheat oven to 400°. Bake for 15-20 minutes or until golden brown. Brush with melted butter. Remove from pans to wire racks; serve warm.

MARINATED SHRIMP

I'm always on the lookout for new and unique appetizers. I like that I can make this colorful party starter ahead of time.
—PAT WAYMIRE YELLOW SPRINGS, OH

PREP: 10 MIN. • **COOK:** 5 MIN. + CHILLING
MAKES: 6 SERVINGS

- 1 pound uncooked shrimp (31-40 per pound), peeled and deveined
- ¾ cup white vinegar
- ½ cup lemon juice
- ½ cup olive oil
- ¼ cup honey
   Hot pepper sauce, salt and pepper to taste
- 2 medium onions, thinly sliced and separated into rings
- 1 jar (5¾ ounces) pimiento-stuffed olives, undrained

1. Place shrimp in a steamer basket. Place in a saucepan over 1 in. of water; bring to boil. Cover; steam 3-5 minutes or until shrimp are pink. Cool.
2. In a large bowl, whisk the vinegar, lemon juice, oil, honey, pepper sauce, salt and pepper until blended. Stir in onions, olives with juice and shrimp. Cover and refrigerate for 4 hours or overnight. Serve with a slotted spoon.

COOL AND CREAMY FRUIT SALAD

PREP/TOTAL: 30 MIN. • **MAKES:** 12 SERVINGS

- 1 package (8 ounces) reduced-fat cream cheese
- 2 teaspoons grated lemon peel
- 1 tablespoon lemon juice
- ½ cup heavy whipping cream
- ¼ cup confectioners' sugar
- 2 cups fresh or frozen sliced peeled peaches, thawed
- 2 cups fresh blueberries
- 2 cups sliced fresh strawberries
- 2 cups green grapes, halved
- 2 tablespoons chopped pecans

1. In a large bowl, beat cream cheese, lemon peel and juice until blended. In a small bowl, beat cream until it begins to thicken. Add confectioners' sugar; beat until stiff peaks form. Fold into cream cheese mixture.
2. Layer fruit in a 2-qt. glass bowl; spread cream cheese mixture over top. Refrigerate, covered, until serving or up to 24 hours. Just before serving, sprinkle with pecans.

TOP TIP

Toppings for Yeast Rolls

Add some flair to homemade yeast rolls with one of these quick and easy toppers. If you can't decide which one to use, just make them all!

PARM-GARLIC 2 Tbsp. grated Parmesan cheese and ½ tsp. dried minced garlic.

ALMOND-HERB 2 Tbsp. chopped sliced almonds and ½ tsp. each kosher salt, dried basil and dried oregano.

EVERYTHING 1 tsp. each poppy seeds, kosher salt, dried minced garlic, sesame seeds and dried minced onion.

"My mom found this recipe in a magazine 25 years ago, and we've been enjoying it ever since. I refrigerate it overnight before serving."

—SUSAN SCHILLER, TOMAHAWK, WI

COOL AND CREAMY
FRUIT SALAD

CHOCOLATE & COCONUT CREAM TORTE

What could be a better way to end an Easter feast than with a spring-inspired torte? My grandmother passed this recipe down to me years ago, and now I make it for my own grandchildren. When preparing, make sure the chocolate layer is properly chilled before adding the next layer, or the coconut will sink into it.

—JASON PURKEY OCEAN CITY, MD

PREP: 25 MIN. + CHILLING
COOK: 10 MIN. + CHILLING
MAKES: 12 SERVINGS

- 1 **package (12 ounces) vanilla wafers, crushed**
- ½ **cup butter, melted**
- 8 **ounces dark baking chocolate, chopped**
- 1 **cup heavy whipping cream**

FILLING

- 1 **can (13½ ounces) coconut milk**
- 3 **cups flaked coconut**
- 1 **cup sugar**
- 2 **tablespoons cornstarch**
- 4 **tablespoons cold water, divided**
- 1 **large egg**
- 1 **large egg yolk**
- 2 **teaspoons unflavored gelatin**
- 1¼ **cups heavy whipping cream**
- ½ **cup flaked coconut, toasted**

1. In a large bowl, mix the wafer crumbs and butter. Press onto bottom and 2 in. up sides of a greased 9-in. springform pan.

2. Place chocolate in a small bowl. In a small saucepan, bring 1 cup cream just to a boil. Pour over chocolate; let stand 5 minutes. Stir with a whisk until smooth. Pour over prepared crust. Refrigerate 1 hour.

3. In a large saucepan, combine the coconut milk, coconut and sugar; bring just to a boil. Strain through a fine-mesh strainer into a bowl, reserving strained coconut; return coconut milk mixture to saucepan. In a small bowl, mix cornstarch and 2 tablespoons water until smooth; stir into coconut milk mixture. Return to a boil, stirring constantly; cook and stir 1-2 minutes or until thickened. Remove from heat.

4. In a small bowl, whisk egg and egg yolk. Whisk a small amount of hot mixture into egg mixture; return all to pan, whisking constantly. Bring to a gentle boil; cook and stir 2 minutes. Remove from heat.

5. In a microwave-safe bowl, sprinkle gelatin over remaining cold water; let stand 1 minute. Microwave on high for 30-40 seconds. Stir and let stand for 1 minute or until gelatin is completely dissolved. Whisk gelatin mixture into coconut milk mixture. Refrigerate, covered, for 1 hour, whisking every 15 minutes.

6. In a large bowl, beat cream until stiff peaks form; fold into coconut milk mixture. Spoon reserved strained coconut into prepared crust. Spread filling over coconut. Refrigerate for 6 hours or overnight before serving.

7. Remove rim from pan. Top with toasted coconut.

NOTE *To toast coconut, bake in shallow pan in a 350° oven for 5-10 minutes or cook in a skillet over low heat until golden brown, stirring occasionally.*

TOP TIP

Soften Shredded Coconut

To soften shredded coconut that's turned hard, soak it in milk for 30 minutes. Drain it and pat it dry on paper towels before using. The leftover coconut-flavored milk can be used within 5 days in baked goods or blended with fresh fruit for a tasty beverage.

Easter Egg Favorites

Easter morning will be off to an eggs-cellent start when you're greeted with any one of these rise-and-shine brunch specialties. **Here you'll find farm-fresh ideas by the dozen**, and each recipe calls for the exceptional egg as one of its main ingredients.

Hatch a plan to make the holiday extra special with scrambled eggs tucked in puff pastry. **For heartier fare, try a frittata, egg bake or quiche.** Fancy something sweet? Custard, meringue torte and angel food cake all make a fitting finale.

Whether you're feeding just a few, hosting a crowd or simply need a dish to pass, you can't go wrong with these scrumptious delights. **Get ready for endless ways to enjoy eggs!**

"Easter brunch will be an event to remember with this elegant egg pastry as the main dish. Everyone will love the bold flavors and light texture."

—JAMIE BROWN-MILLER, NAPA, CA

SHIITAKE SCRAMBLED EGGS IN PUFF PASTRY

SHIITAKE SCRAMBLED EGGS IN PUFF PASTRY

START TO FINISH: 30 MIN.
MAKES: 4 SERVINGS

- 1 sheet frozen puff pastry, thawed
- 2 tablespoons butter, divided
- 1½ cups sliced fresh shiitake mushrooms
- 1 cup fresh baby spinach
- 6 large eggs, lightly beaten
- ½ cup crumbled goat cheese
- 1 tablespoon Sriracha Asian hot chili sauce
- 4 thin slices prosciutto
- 1 tablespoon minced fresh tarragon

1. Preheat oven to 425°. Place four 6-ounce ramekins or custard cups upside-down on a large baking sheet. Grease outsides of ramekins well. Cut puff pastry into quarters; shape each quarter around a ramekin. Bake for 14-16 minutes or until golden brown.
2. Meanwhile, in a large skillet, melt 1 tablespoon butter over medium-high heat. Add mushrooms; cook and stir 2-3 minutes or until lightly browned. Stir in spinach until wilted; remove from pan.
3. In same pan, heat remaining butter over medium heat. Pour in eggs; cook and stir until eggs are thickened and no liquid egg remains. Gently stir in goat cheese, Sriracha and mushroom mixture.
4. Carefully remove pastries from the ramekins and place right-side up on individual serving plates. Line bottoms and sides of pastries with prosciutto. Fill with egg mixture; sprinkle with tarragon.

CRAB DEVILED EGGS

My family loves crab salad and deviled eggs, so I combined the two. The crab meat adds a lot of flavor. What a hit!
—**KEVON SHULER** CHELSEA, MI

START TO FINISH: 30 MIN.
MAKES: 2 DOZEN

- 12 hard-cooked large eggs
- 1 can (6 ounces) crabmeat, drained, flaked and cartilage removed
- ½ cup mayonnaise
- 1 green onion, finely chopped
- 1 tablespoon finely chopped celery
- 1 tablespoon finely chopped green pepper
- 2 teaspoons Dijon mustard
- 1 teaspoon minced fresh parsley
- ½ teaspoon salt
- ⅛ teaspoon pepper
- 3 dashes hot pepper sauce
- 3 dashes Worcestershire sauce
  Additional minced fresh parsley

1. Cut eggs in half lengthwise. Remove yolks; set whites aside. In a bowl, mash the yolks. Add the crab, mayonnaise, onion, celery, green pepper, mustard, parsley, salt, pepper, hot pepper sauce and Worcestershire sauce; mix well.
2. Pipe or spoon into egg whites. Sprinkle with additional parsley. Refrigerate until serving.

LEMON-THYME ANGEL FOOD CAKE

Thyme adds a new twist to the classic angel food cake. The flavors pair well together. We enjoy it alongside strawberry ice cream.
—**JANIE COLLE** HUTCHINSON, KS

PREP: 40 MIN. • **BAKE:** 30 MIN. + COOLING
MAKES: 12 SERVINGS

- 1¼ large egg whites (about 10 eggs)
- 1 cup cake flour
- ½ cup confectioners' sugar
- 3 tablespoons lemon juice
- 1 teaspoon cream of tartar
- ½ teaspoon salt
- 1 cup granulated sugar
- 2 tablespoons minced fresh thyme
- 2 tablespoons finely grated lemon peel

1. Place egg whites in a bowl; let stand at room temperature for 30 minutes.
2. Meanwhile, preheat oven to 350°. Sift flour and confectioners' sugar together twice.
3. Add lemon juice, cream of tartar and salt to egg whites; beat on medium speed until soft peaks form. Gradually add granulated sugar, 1 tablespoon at a time, beating on high after each addition until sugar is dissolved. Continue beating until soft glossy peaks form. Beat in thyme and lemon peel. Gradually fold in flour mixture, about ½ cup at a time.
4. Gently transfer to an ungreased 10-in. tube pan. Cut through the batter with a knife to remove air pockets. Bake on lowest oven rack 30-35 minutes or until top crust is golden brown and cracks feel dry. Immediately invert the pan; cool completely in pan, about 1½ hours.
5. Run a knife around sides and center tube of pan. Remove cake to a serving plate.

HAM & TWO-CHEESE STRATA

The youth group at my church makes a scrumptious brunch every year on Easter morning. This strata is always part of the spread. Feel free to change the amount of cheese. In our family, the cheesier the better!
—**DEVIN WISMAN** PLYMOUTH, WI

PREP: 15 MIN. + CHILLING • **BAKE:** 50 MIN.
MAKES: 12 SERVINGS

- 12 cups cubed French bread (about 11 ounces)
- 2 cups cubed fully cooked ham
- 1 cup (4 ounces) shredded sharp cheddar cheese
- 1 cup (4 ounces) shredded Swiss cheese
- 6 large eggs
- 3 cups 2% milk
- ½ teaspoon onion salt
- ½ teaspoon ground mustard
- ⅛ teaspoon garlic powder
- 2 cups crushed cornflakes
- ¼ cup butter, melted

1. In greased 13x9-in. baking dish, layer half of each of the following: bread, ham, cheddar cheese and Swiss cheese. Repeat layers.
2. In a large bowl, whisk eggs, milk and seasonings. Pour over layers. Refrigerate, covered, several hours or overnight.
3. Preheat the oven to 375°. Remove strata from refrigerator while oven heats. Bake, covered, 40-45 minutes or until a knife inserted near the center comes out clean. In a small bowl, combine the cornflakes and melted butter; sprinkle over strata. Bake, uncovered, 10-15 minutes longer or until golden brown.

ROASTED VEGETABLE FRITTATA

The great thing about frittatas is that you can make them with whatever you have available in the garden and in the pantry. This version uses spring produce to its advantage. Roasting intensifies the natural sweetness of the asparagus and onion, and the earthiness of the potatoes. See photo on page 147.

—TRISHA KRUSE EAGLE, ID

PREP: 25 MIN. • **BAKE:** 15 MIN.
MAKES: 6 SERVINGS

- 1 pound fresh asparagus, trimmed and cut into 2-inch pieces.
- 2 small red potatoes, halved and thinly sliced
- 1½ cups sliced sweet onion (½ inch thick)
- 2 tablespoons olive oil, divided
- 1 teaspoon salt, divided
- ½ teaspoon pepper, divided
- 4 large eggs
- ½ cup 2% milk
- 1 cup finely chopped fully cooked ham
- 3 garlic cloves, minced
- ½ cup shredded part-skim mozzarella cheese
- ¼ cup grated Parmesan cheese
- 2 tablespoons minced fresh basil

1. Preheat oven to 450°. In a large bowl, combine asparagus, potatoes and the onion. Mix 1 tablespoon oil, ½ teaspoon salt and ¼ teaspoon pepper; drizzle over vegetables. Toss to coat. Transfer to an ungreased baking sheet. Roast 15-20 minutes or until vegetables are golden and tender, stirring halfway.

2. Meanwhile, whisk eggs, milk and remaining salt and pepper until blended.

3. Reduce oven setting to 350°. In a large ovenproof skillet, heat the remaining oil over medium-high heat. Add the ham; cook and stir 2-3 minutes or until lightly browned. Reduce heat to medium. Add roasted vegetables and garlic; cook 1 minute longer. Pour in egg mixture; sprinkle with cheeses and basil.

4. Bake, uncovered, 15-18 minutes or until eggs are completely set. Let stand 5 minutes. Cut into wedges.

CRESCENT EGG BAKE WITH HOLLANDAISE SAUCE

What's better than eggs mixed with bacon and cheese over a fluffy crust and topped with hollandaise sauce? You also can use egg whites instead of yolks if you like.

—GIDGET GORGONE MABLETON, GA

PREP: 20 MIN. • **BAKE:** 15 MIN.
MAKES: 8 SERVINGS

- 3 large egg yolks
- 1 tablespoon water
- 1 tablespoon lemon juice
- ½ cup butter, melted
- ¼ teaspoon salt

CASSEROLE

- 1 tube (8 ounces) refrigerated crescent rolls
- 4 large eggs
- 2 tablespoons 2% milk
- ¼ teaspoon onion powder
- ¼ teaspoon pepper
- 8 thick-sliced bacon strips, cooked and crumbled
- 1 cup (4 ounces) shredded cheddar cheese
- 4 green onions, sliced

1. Preheat oven to 350°. In top of a double boiler or a metal bowl over simmering water, whisk egg yolks, water and lemon juice until blended; cook until mixture is just thick enough to coat a metal spoon and temperature reaches 160°, whisking constantly. Remove from heat. Very slowly drizzle in warm melted butter, whisking constantly. Whisk in salt. Transfer to a small bowl if necessary. Place bowl in a larger bowl of warm water. Keep warm, stirring occasionally, until ready to serve, up to 30 minutes.

2. Unroll crescent dough into one long rectangle; press perforations to seal. Press onto the bottom of a greased 13x9-in. baking dish. Bake 5 minutes. Meanwhile, in a small bowl, whisk eggs, milk, onion powder and pepper; stir in bacon and cheese. Spoon over crescent dough. Bake 10-15 minutes longer or until golden brown. Serve casserole with sauce; sprinkle with green onions.

BURNT CUSTARD

I got the recipe for this smooth-as-silk custard from a restaurant years ago. With its broiled topping, it looks pretty in individual cups.

—HEIDI MAIN ANCHORAGE, AK

PREP: 25 MIN. • **BAKE:** 45 MIN. + CHILLING
MAKES: 6 SERVINGS

- 4 large egg yolks
- ½ cup plus 6 teaspoons sugar, divided
- 2 cups heavy whipping cream
- 3 teaspoons vanilla extract
  Fresh raspberries, optional

1. In a small bowl, whisk egg yolks and ½ cup sugar. In a small saucepan, heat cream over medium heat until bubbles form around sides of the pan. Remove from the heat; stir a small amount of hot cream into the egg yolk mixture. Return all of the mixture to the pan, stirring constantly. Stir in vanilla.

2. Transfer to six 6-oz. broiler-safe ramekins or custard cups. Place cups in a baking pan; add 1 in. of boiling water to pan. Bake, uncovered, at 300° for 30-35 minutes or until centers are just set (mixture will jiggle). Remove ramekins from water bath; cool for 10 minutes. Cover and refrigerate for at least 4 hours.

3. Before serving, let stand at room temperature for 15 minutes. Sprinkle with remaining sugar. Broil 8 in. from the heat for 2-4 minutes or until sugar is caramelized. If desired, garnish with fresh raspberries.

TOP TIP

Keys to Perfect Custard

The two keys to perfect custard are timing and proper oven temperature. Underbaking results in a runny custard that won't set, while overbaking can cause a weeping or watery custard. To check for the proper doneness, insert a clean knife near the center of the custard a few minutes before the recommended baking time has elapsed. If the knife comes out clean, the custard is done. (The center may still jiggle, but it will firm up while cooling.)

BURNT
CUSTARD

**STRAWBERRY-CHOCOLATE
MERINGUE TORTE**

STRAWBERRY-CHOCOLATE MERINGUE TORTE

I make this rich torte whenever I'm asked to bring dessert to any occasion. Use reduced-calorie whipped topping to create a lighter version.

—CHRISTINE MCCULLOUGH AUBURN, MA

PREP: 45 MIN. • **BAKE:** 70 MIN. + COOLING
MAKES: 6 SERVINGS

- 4 **large egg whites**
- 3 **cups sliced fresh strawberries**
- 1 **teaspoon plus 1 cup sugar, divided**
- 1½ **cups heavy whipping cream**
- ⅓ **cup confectioners' sugar**
- ¾ **teaspoon vanilla extract**
- ¼ **teaspoon cream of tartar**
- ¼ **teaspoon salt**
- ½ **cup semisweet chocolate chips**

1. Place the egg whites in a large bowl; let stand at room temperature 30 minutes. Meanwhile in a small bowl, combine strawberries and 1 teaspoon sugar. In another bowl, beat cream until it begins to thicken. Add confectioners' sugar and vanilla; beat until soft peaks form. Refrigerate the strawberries and whipped cream, covered, until assembly.

2. Preheat oven to 250°. Line a baking sheet with parchment paper. Trace two 8-in. circles 1 in. apart on paper; set aside. Add cream of tartar and salt to egg whites; beat on medium speed until foamy. Gradually add remaining sugar, 1 tablespoon at a time, beating on high after each addition until sugar is dissolved. Continue beating until stiff glossy peaks form. Spread evenly over circles.

3. Bake 70-80 minutes or until set and dry. Turn off oven (do not open oven door); leave meringues in oven for 1½ hours. Remove from oven; cool completely.

4. In a microwave, melt chocolate chips; stir until smooth. Spread evenly over tops of meringues. Carefully remove one meringue to a serving plate. Remove whipped cream from refrigerator; beat until stiff peaks form. Spread half of the whipped cream over the meringue; top with half of the strawberries. Repeat layers. Serve immediately.

CINNAMON-RAISIN BREAD PUDDING WITH HONEY CREAM

My boyfriend loves bread pudding, but it's hard to find a restaurant that serves it. So I put together this tasty delight, and now we can enjoy it whenever we like. It makes an excellent addition to an Easter spread.

—DIANE WRIGHT STACY, MN

PREP: 20 MIN. + STANDING • **BAKE:** 45 MIN.
MAKES: 8 SERVINGS

- 4 **large eggs**
- 3 **cups 2% milk**
- ½ **cup sugar**
- ½ **teaspoon ground cinnamon**
- ⅛ **teaspoon salt**
- ½ **cup raisins**
- 6 **cups cubed French bread (about 5 ounces)**

HONEY CREAM
- 2 **teaspoons cornstarch**
- ¾ **cup heavy whipping cream, divided**
- ¼ **cup butter, cubed**
- ¼ **cup honey**
- ½ **teaspoon vanilla extract**
  Sweetened whipped cream

1. Preheat oven to 350°. In a large bowl, whisk the first five ingredients. Stir in raisins. Gently stir in bread; let stand about 15 minutes or until bread is softened.

2. Transfer the mixture to a greased 11x7-in. baking dish. Bake mixture for 45-50 minutes or until puffed, golden and a knife inserted near the center comes out clean.

3. Meanwhile, in a small bowl, mix cornstarch and 2 tablespoons cream until smooth. In a small heavy saucepan combine butter, honey and remaining cream. Stir in cornstarch mixture. Bring to a boil. Reduce the heat; simmer, uncovered, 1-2 minutes or until thickened. Remove from heat; stir in vanilla. Serve with bread pudding; top with whipped cream.

BRUNCH HASH & EGG BAKE

When my kids were growing up, I was cooking for a family of eight. I couldn't conveniently fry eggs for that many people, so I devised this recipe that quickly became a favorite in our house. Mild and salty feta cheese is my favorite for the dish, but shredded cheddar or Parmesan works, too.

—LILY JULOW LAWRENCEVILLE, GA

PREP: 45 MIN. • **BAKE:** 15 MIN.
MAKES: 8 SERVINGS

- 2 **pounds Yukon Gold potatoes, peeled and cut into ¾-inch pieces**
- 1 **pound bulk Italian sausage**
- 1 **large onion, finely chopped**
- ¼ **cup olive oil**
- ¼ **teaspoon salt**
- ¼ **teaspoon pepper**
- 8 **large eggs**
- 1 **cup (4 ounces) crumbled feta cheese**
- 3 **tablespoons minced fresh parsley**

1. Preheat oven to 375°. Place potatoes in a large saucepan; add water to cover. Bring to a boil. Reduce the heat; cook, uncovered, 5-7 minutes or until almost tender. Drain.

2. Meanwhile, in a 12-in. ovenproof skillet, cook sausage and onion over medium heat 8-10 minutes or until sausage is no longer pink, breaking up sausage into crumbles. Remove with a slotted spoon. Discard drippings, wiping skillet clean.

3. In same skillet, heat oil over medium-high heat. Add drained potatoes; sprinkle with salt and pepper. Cook 10-15 minutes or until golden brown, turning potatoes occasionally. Stir in sausage mixture. Remove from heat.

4. With the back of a spoon, make eight wells in potato mixture. Break one egg into each well. Sprinkle with cheese.

5. Bake 12-15 minutes or until egg whites are set and yolks begin to thicken but are not hard. Sprinkle with parsley.

LEEK AND BABY PORTOBELLO QUICHES

If you are looking for something to serve at a relaxing weekend brunch, look no further. My family always asks for this dish. The leeks and mushrooms make a terrific flavor combo.

—AMY MUELLER COOPERSVILLE, MI

PREP: 15 MIN. • **BAKE:** 40 MIN. + STANDING
MAKES: 2 QUICHES (6 SERVINGS EACH)

Pastry for two single-crust pies (9 inches)
2 cups sliced baby portobello mushrooms
2 tablespoons olive oil
1 small leek (white portion only), sliced
3 garlic cloves, minced
⅓ cup cream sherry
⅓ cup Miracle Whip
10 large eggs
2 cups half-and-half cream
1 tablespoon Italian seasoning
1 teaspoon salt
½ teaspoon pepper
⅓ cup grated Parmesan cheese

1. Preheat oven to 350° On a lightly floured surface, roll each pastry dough into a ⅛-in.-thick circle; transfer to a 9-in. pie plate. Trim pastry to ½ in. beyond rim of plate; flute edge. Divide mushrooms between pastry shells. In a large skillet, heat oil over medium heat. Add leek and garlic; cook and stir 4-6 minutes or until leeks are tender. Add sherry. Remove from heat. Stir in Miracle Whip. Divide leek mixture between pastry shells.
2. In a large bowl, whisk eggs, cream, Italian seasoning, salt and pepper; pour into shells. Bake on a lower oven rack 40-50 minutes or until a knife inserted near the center comes out clean. Sprinkle with the cheese. Let stand 10 minutes before cutting.
NOTE *Pastry for a single-crust pie (9 inches): Combine 1¼ cups all-purpose flour and ¼ tsp. salt; cut in ½ cup cold butter until crumbly. Gradually add 3-5 Tbsp. ice water, tossing with a fork until dough holds together when pressed. Wrap in plastic wrap and refrigerate 1 hour.*

PUFF PANCAKE WITH ROASTED BLACKBERRY SAUCE

What a treat on Easter morning! This puff pancake with its fruity sauce makes a great brunch entree. The blackberry sauce is tasty and versatile. Try it with ice cream, crepes, French toast or waffles.

—GERALDINE SAUCIER ALBUQUERQUE, NM

PREP: 15 MIN. + STANDING • **BAKE:** 30 MIN.
MAKES: 4 SERVINGS

2 cups fresh blackberries
2 tablespoons sugar
1 tablespoon balsamic vinegar
1 teaspoon cornstarch
2 tablespoons butter, melted
PANCAKE BATTER
2 tablespoons butter
2 large eggs
½ cup 2% milk
½ cup all-purpose flour
2 tablespoons sugar
¼ teaspoon grated lemon peel
¼ teaspoon ground cinnamon
Dash ground nutmeg
⅛ teaspoon salt

1. Preheat the oven to 425°. In an 8-in.-square baking dish, combine berries, sugar, vinegar and cornstarch; let stand 20 minutes. Pour melted butter over berry mixture. Bake for 15-20 minutes or until berries soften and juices are slightly thickened. Remove from oven; set aside.
2. Place butter in a 9-in. pie plate. Place in oven 3-4 minutes or until butter is melted; carefully swirl to coat bottom and sides of dish.
3. Meanwhile, in a large bowl, whisk eggs until frothy; add milk. Whisk in flour, sugar, lemon peel, spices and salt. Pour into prepared dish. Bake for 12-15 minutes or until puffed and sides are golden brown.
4. Remove from oven; serve immediately with sauce.

BLOWING OUT EGGS

Before you dress up your eggs using the technique on the following page, empty out the liquid contents with this simple method.

MATERIALS

Large eggs and carton
Large bowl
Straw cut to 4 inches
Thumbtack
Wood skewer
Kitchen or tea towel

DIRECTIONS

1. With the egg in a carton, press thumbtack firmly into the top and bottom of egg to puncture shell.
2. At the bottom of the egg, insert the sharp end of a skewer and rotate it to break up the yolk. Wrap the egg in a towel and shake it several times to further break up the contents.
3. Place a straw over the hole at the top of the egg and blow out contents into a bowl. If yolk does not flow easily out of the egg, repeat steps 2 and 3 as needed until egg is empty. Discard the egg contents or reserve for another use.
4. Wash egg in warm soapy water; dry. Blow through egg one final time to ensure that the inside of the shell is completely clear.
NOTE *If you don't have time to decoupage, layer strips of washi tape—instead of washi paper— onto your eggs.*

WASHI PAPER EGGS

Skip those messy dyes! This year, decorate eggs with colorful washi paper to create a cheerful Easter centerpiece.

MATERIALS

- **Blown large eggs**
- **Washi or origami paper in various colors**
- **Measuring tape**
- **Ruler**
- **Cutting mat**
- **Decoupage glue**
- **Craft knife**
- **Paintbrush**

DIRECTIONS

1. Start with an empty egg shell. See opposite page for directions.

2. Cut washi paper ⅛ in. bigger than circumference and height of the egg.

3. Fold paper in half lengthwise, then again crosswise.

4. Cut ¼ in. strips along the long side of the paper, stopping ¼ in. before the center fold.

5. Trim the ends of each ¼-in. strip to a point. Unfold paper and place wrong side up on a piece of parchment paper.

6. Use a brush to spread on a thin layer of glue.

7. Lay egg against a short side and wrap paper around the egg. Press each strip toward the tip of the egg, one piece at a time. Each strip should slightly overlap the previous one. Work your way slowly around egg, smoothing out the paper strips with your fingers. Brush glue over the top of each strip of paper as you go. Repeat on bottom half of the egg.

8. Apply a layer of glue over the entire egg and set on parchment paper to dry.

NOTE *Washi, or origami paper, can be found at most craft stores and online.*

WASHI
PAPER EGGS

Springtime Salads

Glorious springtime! The arrival, or at least the anticipation, of warmer weather sets taste buds craving **big, fresh, sunny salads.**

Featuring greens, veggies, slaw, pasta, spuds and more, these recipes offer **ingenious ways to sass up old favorites.** They're versatile, too—some can be enjoyed on their own, while others make the perfect complement to a main dish. And **many can be made in advance and are easily carried to a picnic or potluck.**

Bursting with intriguing flavors and cool, crisp textures, **these mouthwatering medleys make the best of spring's bounty.** Flip the page to see just how easy it is to mix together the right ingredients for fresh and tasty toss-ups!

Four-Berry Spinach Salad (p. 161)

PEAS & PEPPER PASTA SALAD

I made this recipe to go with ham and other goodies for our Easter buffet. Any leftover pasta salad is great stuffed into halved and cored plum tomatoes. For a little tang and color, add a tablespoon or two of drained capers.

—ANN SHEEHY LAWRENCE, MA

PREP: 20 MIN. • **COOK:** 10 MIN. + STANDING
MAKES: 10 SERVINGS

- 1 package (16 ounces) acini di pepe pasta
- 1½ cups coarsely chopped Cubanelle peppers or miniature sweet peppers (in assorted colors)
- 1 cup loosely packed fresh Italian parsley leaves
- 4 radishes, trimmed and quartered
- ½ medium red onion, coarsely chopped
- 2 green onions, cut into 1-inch pieces
- 1¾ cups frozen petite peas (about 8 ounces), thawed
- ½ cup creamy Caesar salad dressing
- ¾ teaspoon salt
- ½ teaspoon freshly ground pepper Thinly sliced radishes, optional

1. Cook pasta according to package directions. Drain; rinse with cold water and drain well. Place peppers, parsley, radishes, red onion and green onions in a food processor; pulse until finely chopped, scraping sides of food processor bowl as necessary.
2. In a large bowl, combine pasta, chopped vegetables and peas. Add dressing, salt and pepper; toss to coat. Let stand 15 minutes to allow flavors to blend. If desired, top with sliced radishes.

JAPANESE STEAK SALAD

With its sweet soy marinade and fresh veggies, this salad has a lot to love.

—DIANE HALFERTY CORPUS CHRISTI, TX

PREP: 25 MIN. + MARINATING • **COOK:** 20 MIN.
MAKES: 4 SERVINGS

- 3 tablespoons sherry or reduced-sodium chicken broth
- 3 tablespoons rice vinegar
- 3 tablespoons reduced-sodium soy sauce
- 2 tablespoons hoisin sauce
- ½ teaspoon minced fresh gingerroot
- 1 boneless beef sirloin steak (1 inch thick and 1¼ pounds)
- 2 green onions, chopped
- 1 tablespoon sugar
- 1 tablespoon sesame oil
- ⅓ cup fresh snow peas
- 3 cups sliced Chinese or napa cabbage
- 3 cups torn romaine
- ⅓ cup uncooked instant rice
- ½ cup julienned carrot
- ½ cup thinly sliced cucumber
- ½ cup sliced radishes

1. In a small bowl, combine first five ingredients. Pour ⅓ cup into a large resealable plastic bag; add beef. Seal bag and turn to coat; refrigerate for at least 2 hours. For dressing, add onions, sugar and sesame oil to the remaining marinade. Cover and refrigerate until serving.
2. Preheat broiler. In a saucepan, bring 1 in. of water to a boil. Add peas. Reduce heat; cover and simmer for 2-3 minutes or until crisp-tender. Drain; immediately place the peas in ice water. Drain and pat dry. Combine cabbage, romaine and peas; place on a platter.
3. Drain and discard marinade. Place beef on broiler pan. Broil beef 4-6 in. from the heat 8-10 minutes on each side or until meat reaches desired doneness (for medium-rare, a meat thermometer should read 145°; medium, 160°; well-done, 170°). Let stand 5 minutes before slicing.
4. Meanwhile, cook rice according to package directions. Arrange the carrot, cucumber and radishes on cabbage mixture. Top with rice and beef; drizzle with dressing.

ARTICHOKE & LEMON PASTA

While sailing in the Mediterranean, I tasted a lemony pasta and quickly fell in love with it. I developed my own version of it that our guests now love. Try it with shrimp and kalamata olives, too.

—PETER HALFERTY CORPUS CHRISTI, TX

PREP: 20 MIN. • **COOK:** 20 MIN.
MAKES: 6 SERVINGS

- 2½ teaspoons salt, divided
- ½ pound fresh asparagus, trimmed and cut into 1½-inch pieces
- 4 cups uncooked bow tie pasta (about 12 ounces)
- 3 tablespoons olive oil, divided
- 1 can (14 ounces) water-packed quartered artichoke hearts, well drained
- 2 garlic cloves, minced
- 1 cup crumbled goat cheese
- 2 tablespoons minced fresh parsley
- 1 tablespoon grated lemon peel
- 2 to 3 tablespoons lemon juice
- ⅓ cup grated Parmesan cheese

1. Fill a 6-qt. stockpot three-fourths full with water; add 2 teaspoons salt and bring to a boil. Add asparagus; cook, uncovered, 1-2 minutes or just until crisp-tender. Remove asparagus and immediately drop into ice water. Drain and pat dry.
2. In same pot of water, cook pasta according to package directions for al dente. Drain, reserving 1 cup pasta water. Return pasta to pot.
3. Meanwhile, in a large skillet, heat 1 tablespoon oil over medium-high heat. Add artichoke hearts; cook and stir for 3-4 minutes or until lightly browned. Add garlic; cook 1 minute longer. Add to pasta.
4. Add asparagus, goat cheese, parsley, lemon peel, lemon juice and the remaining salt and oil; toss to combine, adding enough reserved pasta water to coat. Heat through. Serve with Parmesan cheese.

ARTICHOKE &
LEMON PASTA

CILANTRO BLUE
CHEESE SLAW

CILANTRO BLUE CHEESE SLAW

Folks will love the fresh, tangy twist that cilantro and blue cheese give to traditional coleslaw. It makes a great picnic dish, or use it to top your favorite fish taco recipe.

—**CHRISTI DALTON** HARTSVILLE, TN

START TO FINISH: 25 MIN.
MAKES: 8 SERVINGS

- 8 cups shredded cabbage
- 1 small red onion, halved and thinly sliced
- ⅓ cup minced fresh cilantro
- 1 jalapeno pepper, seeded and minced
- ¼ cup crumbled blue cheese
- ¼ cup fat-free mayonnaise
- ¼ cup reduced-fat sour cream
- 2 tablespoons rice vinegar
- 2 tablespoons lime juice
- 1 garlic clove, minced
- 1 teaspoon sugar
- 1 teaspoon grated lime peel
- ¾ teaspoon salt
- ½ teaspoon coarsely ground pepper

In a large bowl, combine cabbage, onion, cilantro and jalapeno. In a small bowl, combine the remaining ingredients; pour dressing over salad and toss to coat.
NOTE *Wear disposable gloves when cutting hot peppers; the oils can burn skin. Avoid touching your face.*

TOP TIP

Shredding Cabbage

To shred cabbage by hand, cut cabbage into wedges. Place cut side down on a cutting board. With a large sharp knife, cut into thin slices.

RASPBERRY-CHILI TUNA ON GREENS

Turn grilled tuna into something sensational with a zippy marinade featuring raspberry preserves and Thai chili sauce. Serve the tuna on romaine lettuce and garnish with fresh veggies to create a truly special meal for guests.

—**KATHY HAWKINS** INGLESIDE, IL

PREP: 15 MIN. + MARINATING • **GRILL:** 10 MIN.
MAKES: 4 SERVINGS

- 6 tablespoons seedless raspberry preserves
- ¼ cup balsamic vinegar
- 2 teaspoons minced fresh basil or ½ teaspoon dried basil
- 2 teaspoons Thai chili sauce
- ½ teaspoon salt
- ¼ teaspoon pepper
- 4 tuna steaks (6 ounces each)
- 1 package (10 ounces) torn romaine
- ½ cup shredded carrot
- ½ cup thinly sliced cucumber

1. In a small bowl, combine the first six ingredients. Pour ¼ cup marinade into a large resealable plastic bag. Add tuna; seal bag and turn to coat. Refrigerate 30 minutes, turning occasionally. Cover and refrigerate remaining marinade for dressing.
2. Drain tuna, discarding marinade in bag. Moisten a paper towel with cooking oil; using long-handled tongs, rub on grill rack to coat lightly. Grill tuna, covered, over high heat or broil 3-4 in. from heat 3-4 minutes on each side for medium-rare or until slightly pink in the center.
3. In a large bowl, combine romaine, carrot and cucumber; drizzle with remaining marinade and toss to coat. Divide among four plates. Top with grilled tuna.

APRICOT-CHILI TUNA ON GREENS
Substitute apricot preserves for the raspberry and white balsamic vinegar for the balsamic vinegar.

FOUR-BERRY SPINACH SALAD

Enjoy some of nature's candy in this colorful, berry-filled salad. Its slightly tart dressing contrasts deliciously with sweet in-season fruit.

—**BETTY LISE ANDERSON** GAHANNA, OH

START TO FINISH: 15 MIN. • **MAKES:** 4 SERVINGS

- 1 tablespoon canola oil
- 1 tablespoon orange juice
- 1 tablespoon red wine vinegar
- 1 tablespoon balsamic vinegar
- 1 tablespoon water
- 2 teaspoons lemon juice
- ½ teaspoon sugar
- ½ teaspoon poppy seeds
- ⅛ teaspoon ground allspice
  Dash ground cinnamon
- 4 cups fresh baby spinach
- ½ cup each fresh raspberries, blueberries, blackberries and sliced strawberries
- 2 teaspoons chopped walnuts, toasted

In a small bowl, whisk the first 10 ingredients until blended. In a small bowl, combine spinach and berries. Drizzle with dressing and sprinkle with walnuts; toss to coat.

STRAWBERRY CHICKEN SALAD

I received this zesty salad idea from a friend who served it at a shower I attended years ago. If you take it to a potluck, make copies of the recipe—everyone will ask you for it!

—EDIE DESPAIN LOGAN, UT

PREP: 20 MIN. + CHILLING • **MAKES:** 4 SERVINGS

- ⅓ cup reduced-fat mayonnaise
- 2 tablespoons chutney
- ¾ teaspoon grated lime peel
- 2 teaspoons lime juice
- ¾ teaspoon curry powder
- ½ teaspoon salt
- 2 cups cubed cooked chicken breast
- 2 celery ribs, thinly sliced
- ¼ cup chopped red onion
- 2 cups sliced fresh strawberries
- 4 Bibb or Boston lettuce leaves

1. In a large bowl, mix the first six ingredients. Stir in the chicken, celery and onion. Refrigerate, covered, at least 1 hour.

2. To serve, stir strawberries into chicken mixture. Serve over lettuce.

TANGY POTATO SALAD

Springtime makes my family think of potato salad. This tangy side is also yummy in the winter when it's served hot with cubed ham.

—PEGGY GWILLIM STRASBOURG, SK

PREP: 40 MIN. + CHILLING
MAKES: 13 SERVINGS (¾ CUP EACH)

- 4 pounds red potatoes, cubed
- 3 tablespoons plus ⅔ cup white wine vinegar, divided
- 8 hard-cooked large eggs, sliced
- 6 radishes, thinly sliced
- ½ cup minced chives
- 1 cup buttermilk
- ½ cup mayonnaise
- 2 tablespoons prepared mustard
- 1 tablespoon dried minced onion
- 1 tablespoon dill weed
- ¼ teaspoon salt
- ¼ teaspoon pepper

1. Place potatoes in Dutch oven; cover with water. Bring to a boil. Reduce the heat; cover and cook for 10-15 minutes or until tender. Drain. Immediately sprinkle potatoes with 3 tablespoons vinegar; cool.

2. Place potatoes in a large bowl. Add the eggs, radishes and the chives. In a small bowl, combine the buttermilk, mayonnaise, mustard, onion, dill, salt, pepper and remaining vinegar. Pour over potato mixture and gently stir to coat. Refrigerate until chilled.

TOP TIP

Keep Potato Salad Chilled

Since food often sits on a buffet line for quite a while, I like to make sure my favorite potato salad stays chilled. I serve it in a stainless steel bowl that is set in another stainless steel bowl with ice cubes in it. I stir the salad occasionally to ensure that the entire salad stays cold.

— SANDRA V. TEMECULA, CA

Easter Breads

Featuring lovely arrays of flavors and textures, Easter breads are a delicious way to round out your holiday menu. Our sweet and savory assortment of breads, muffins, scones, rolls and more will help you **find the right baked beauty to accompany your meal.**

If you're welcoming morning guests, treat them to muffins inspired by carrot cake or a berry-studded quick bread. **Kids will go wild for rolls shaped like bunnies or flowers.** And if you really want to show off your baking prowess, give traditional honey challah a try.

Tender and delicate, drizzled with icing or braided for a fanciful touch, **there's simply nothing like the blissful, old-fashioned comfort** of these fresh-from-the-oven specialties.

Easter Bunny Rolls (p. 168) **Flower Petal Sweet Rolls** (p. 168)

COCONUT CARROT MUFFINS
STRAWBERRIES 'N' CREAM BREAD

COCONUT CARROT MUFFINS

If you like carrot cake, you'll love these muffins. They make an indulgent treat for an Easter brunch. I use canned carrots to save time in the kitchen.

—**BRITTANY CARRINGTON** TEHACHAPI, CA

PREP: 15 MIN. • **BAKE:** 20 MIN. + COOLING
MAKES: 1 DOZEN

- 1 can (15 ounces) sliced carrots, drained
- ½ cup canola oil
- 1¾ cups all-purpose flour
- 1¼ cups sugar, divided
- 1 teaspoon baking soda
- ½ teaspoon salt
- ½ teaspoon ground cinnamon
- ½ teaspoon pumpkin pie spice
- ¾ cup plus ½ cup flaked coconut, divided
- 1 package (8 ounces) cream cheese, softened

1. Preheat oven to 350°. Place carrots and oil in a food processor; cover and process until smooth. In a large bowl, whisk flour, 1 cup sugar, baking soda, salt, cinnamon and pie spice. Add the carrot mixture to flour mixture; stir just until moistened. Fold in ¾ cup coconut.
2. For filling, in another bowl, beat cream cheese and remaining sugar until smooth. Fill greased or paper-lined muffin cups half full with batter. Drop filling by rounded tablespoonful into center of each muffin; cover with remaining batter. Sprinkle with the remaining coconut.
3. Bake 20-25 minutes or until golden brown. Cool 15 minutes before removing from pan to a wire rack. Serve warm.

STRAWBERRIES 'N' CREAM BREAD

Both my husband and I love strawberries, so this quick bread is a must at our house. To make it even better, pair a slice with a creamy scoop of vanilla ice cream or a warm cup of coffee.

—**SUZANNE RANDALL** DEXTER, ME

PREP: 15 MIN. • **BAKE:** 65 MIN. + COOLING
MAKES: 1 LOAF (12 SLICES)

- ½ cup butter, softened
- ¾ cup sugar
- 2 large eggs
- ½ cup sour cream
- 1 teaspoon vanilla extract
- 1¾ cups all-purpose flour
- ½ teaspoon baking powder
- ½ teaspoon baking soda
- ½ teaspoon salt
- ¼ teaspoon ground cinnamon
- ¾ cup chopped fresh strawberries
- ¾ cup chopped walnuts, toasted, divided

1. Preheat oven to 350°. In a large bowl, cream butter and sugar until light and fluffy. Beat in eggs. Add sour cream and vanilla; mix well.
2. In another bowl, whisk flour, baking powder, baking soda, salt and cinnamon; gradually stir into the creamed mixture just until moistened. Fold in strawberries and ½ cup nuts.
3. Pour into a greased 8x4-in. loaf pan. Sprinkle with remaining nuts. Bake 65-70 minutes or until a toothpick inserted in center comes out clean. Cool in pan 10 minutes before removing to a wire rack to cool completely.

WHOLE WHEAT OATMEAL ROLLS

This long-time family favorite is a staple at my house. To change it up, instead of 2 cups of milk, substitute 1 cup milk and 1 cup potato water, reserved from boiled potatoes.

—**TOM BARLOW** HILDALE, UT

PREP: 1¾ HOURS + RISING • **BAKE:** 15 MIN.
MAKES: 2 DOZEN

- 2 cups 2% milk
- ¾ cup water
- 2 tablespoons canola oil
- ⅓ cup quick-cooking oats
- ½ cup all-purpose flour
- 1 tablespoon active dry yeast
- 1 tablespoon sugar
- 2 teaspoons salt
- 5 to 5½ cups whole wheat flour
- 1 large egg, beaten

TOPPING
- 1 large egg
- 1 tablespoon water
- ⅓ cup quick-cooking oats

1. In a large saucepan, combine milk, water and oil; bring just to a boil over medium heat. Place oats in a small bowl; pour boiling liquid over oats. Cool to 110°-115°.
2. In a large bowl, mix all-purpose flour, yeast, sugar, salt and 2 cups whole wheat flour. Add oat mixture; beat on medium speed 2 minutes. Add egg; beat until smooth. Stir in enough remaining flour to form a soft dough (dough will be sticky).
3. Turn dough onto a floured surface; knead until smooth and elastic, about 6-8 minutes. Place in a greased bowl, turning once to grease the top. Cover with plastic wrap and let rise in a warm place until doubled, about 45 minutes.
4. Punch down dough. Turn onto a lightly floured surface; divide and shape into 24 balls. Place 2 in. apart on greased baking sheets. Cover with kitchen towels; let rise in a warm place until doubled, about 30 minutes.
5. Preheat oven to 375°. In a small bowl, whisk egg with water; brush over rolls. Sprinkle with oats. Bake 12-15 minutes or until lightly browned. Remove from pans to wire racks; serve warm.

TOP TIP

Successful Quick Breads

For best results with quick breads, bake in a light aluminum pan rather than a darker nonstick pan. (If you use a glass pan, lower your oven temperature by 25°.) Position the oven rack so the top of the loaf is in the center of the oven. Bake until a toothpick inserted near the center comes out clean. Cool in the pan for 10 minutes, then remove bread to a wire rack to cool completely. Tightly wrap a cooled quick bread and wait a day to enjoy it—you'll find the flavors have mellowed and the sides have softened.

EASTER BUNNY ROLLS

If you're planning an Easter feast, why not hop to it and roll out a bevy of bunnies? They'll multiply quicker than you think, and your hearty eaters will "cotton" to them! See photo on page 165.

—**BONNIE MYERS** CALLAWAY, NE

PREP: 30 MIN. + RISING • **BAKE:** 10 MIN.
MAKES: 2 DOZEN

- 1 package (¼ ounce) active dry yeast
- ¼ cup warm water (110° to 115°)
- ¾ cup warm milk (110° to 115°)
- 2 tablespoons sugar
- 2 tablespoons shortening
- 1 large egg, beaten
- 2 teaspoons celery seed
- 1 teaspoon salt
- 1 teaspoon rubbed sage
- ½ teaspoon ground nutmeg
- 3 to 3½ cups all-purpose flour
  Melted butter

1. In a small bowl, dissolve yeast in warm water. In a large bowl, combine milk, sugar, shortening, egg, celery seed, salt, sage, nutmeg, yeast mixture and 2 cups flour; beat on medium speed until smooth. Stir in enough remaining flour to form a soft dough. Turn dough onto a floured surface; knead until smooth and elastic; about 6-8 minutes. Place in a greased bowl, turning once to grease the top. Cover with plastic wrap and let rise in a warm place until doubled, about 1 hour. Punch dough down; let rest for 10 minutes.
2. Divide dough into 24 pieces. For each bunny, roll one piece of dough into a 20-in. rope. Cut rope into one 10-in. piece, one 5-in. piece, two 2-in. pieces and one 1-in. piece. Coil 10-in. piece for body; place on a greased baking sheet. Coil 5-in. piece for head; place next to body. Form ears from the 2-in. pieces and tail from the 1-in. piece; add to bunny. Pinch and seal pieces together. Repeat, placing bunnies 2 in. apart on the baking sheet. Cover with a kitchen towel; let rise until doubled, about 25 minutes.
3. Preheat the oven to 375°. Bake for 10-12 minutes or until lightly browned. Brush with melted butter. Serve warm.

FLOWER PETAL SWEET ROLLS

I adapted this recipe from the back of a frozen dinner roll package. What's great is that you can prepare these the night before and bake them the next morning. They make a lasting impression on guests when they step into the kitchen and smell the sweet aroma. See photo on page 165.

—**CELINDA SKOGSBERG** BROOKLYN, NY

PREP: 35 MIN. + RISING • **BAKE:** 20 MIN.
MAKES: 11 PETAL ROLLS PLUS CENTER ROLL

- ⅔ cup plain yogurt
- 1 package (¼ ounce) active dry yeast
- ¼ cup warm water (110° to 115°)
- 3 tablespoons canola oil
- 4½ teaspoons sugar
- 2¼ cups all-purpose flour
- ½ teaspoon baking soda
- ¼ teaspoon salt

FILLING

- ¼ cup seedless raspberry jam or flavors of your choice

GLAZE

- ¼ cup confectioners' sugar
- 1½ teaspoons butter, melted
- ¼ teaspoon vanilla extract

1. Let the yogurt stand at room temperature 15 minutes. In a large bowl, dissolve yeast in warm water. Add yogurt, oil and sugar. In another bowl, whisk flour, baking soda and salt. Add to yeast mixture; beat until smooth. Let stand 10 minutes.
2. Turn dough onto a floured surface; punch down. Divide and shape dough into 13 balls. For center of flower, combine two balls and place in the center of a greased pizza pan. Place remaining balls around the center, allowing room for balls to rise. Cover with a kitchen towel; let rise in a warm place until doubled, about 1 hour. Preheat oven to 350°.
3. Depress centers of petals and pistil; fill each with 1 teaspoon jam. Bake 20-25 minutes or until golden brown. Cool on pan 5 minutes. Remove to a wire rack. Meanwhile, in a small bowl, mix glaze ingredients until smooth. Drizzle over warm rolls.

HAM & CHEESE SCONES

PREP: 20 MIN. • **BAKE:** 40 MIN.
MAKES: 1 DOZEN (½ CUP PEACH SAUCE)

SAUCE

- ½ cup peach preserves
- 1 tablespoon horseradish
- 1 teaspoon wasabi powder
- ½ teaspoon ground mustard
- ¼ teaspoon ground ginger

SCONES

- 4 cups all-purpose flour
- 4 teaspoons baking powder
- 2 teaspoons salt
- 2 cups finely chopped fully cooked ham
- 2 cups (8 ounces) shredded cheddar cheese
- 2 cups heavy whipping cream

TOPPING

- 1 large egg
- 1 tablespoon water
- 1 tablespoon poppy seeds

1. For sauce, combine all ingredients. Refrigerate until serving. Preheat oven to 375°.
2. For scones, in a large bowl, whisk flour, baking powder and salt. Add ham and cheese; toss to combine. Stir in whipping cream just until moistened.
3. Turn onto a lightly floured surface; knead gently 10 times. Pat dough into two 7-in. circles. Cut each into six wedges. Place wedges on a greased baking sheet.
4. For topping, whisk egg with water; brush over the scones. Sprinkle with poppy seeds. Bake 40-45 minutes or until golden brown. Serve warm with peach sauce.

DID YOU KNOW?

History of Scones

It's believed this Scottish quick bread originated between 1505 and 1515. Scones are named after the Stone of Destiny (or Scone), the place where Scottish kings were once crowned.

> "I make these scones as a way to use
> up leftover ham. The cheesy, savory
> wonders are a delight as an appetizer
> or an afternoon snack."
>
> —BARBARA LENTO, HOUSTON, PA

FLAKY DANISH BRAIDS

Pinch ends to seal; tuck under. Place rolls on greased baking sheets. Cover with kitchen towels; let rise in a warm place until almost doubled, about 1 hour.

5. Preheat oven to 350°. Bake for 18-20 minutes or until lightly browned. Remove from pans to wire racks to cool slightly. For icing, in a small bowl, mix confectioners' sugar and enough milk to reach desired consistency. Drizzle over warm braids.

BLUEBERRY-CITRUS MINI LOAVES

These moist treats hit the spot. With subtle orange and blueberry flavor, and hearty whole wheat flour, this recipe offers a welcome way to get your family going in the morning!

—**HEIDI LINDSEY** PRAIRIE DU SAC, WI

PREP: 15 MIN. • **BAKE:** 40 MIN. + COOLING
MAKES: 2 LOAVES (6 SLICES EACH)

- 1 cup all-purpose flour
- 1 cup whole wheat pastry flour
- ¾ cup sugar
- ½ teaspoon salt
- ½ teaspoon baking soda
- 1 large egg
- ¾ cup orange juice
- ¼ cup canola oil
- 1 tablespoon grated orange peel
- ½ cup fresh or frozen blueberries
- ¼ cup chopped pecans

1. Preheat oven to 350°. In a large bowl, combine flours, sugar, salt and baking soda. In a small bowl, whisk egg, orange juice, oil and orange peel. Stir into dry ingredients just until moistened. Fold in blueberries and pecans.

2. Transfer to two 5¾x3x2-in. loaf pans coated with cooking spray. Bake 40-45 minutes or until a toothpick inserted near the center comes out clean. Cool in pans 10 minutes before removing to a wire rack to cool.

NOTE *If using frozen blueberries, use without thawing to avoid discoloring the batter.*

FLAKY DANISH BRAIDS

Though this recipe takes a bit of time to make, it's completely worth it. The braids are a special breakfast treat on occasions like Easter or a family birthday. People will take seconds and thirds!

—**DEBBIE EWALD** OAK GROVE, MO

PREP: 45 MIN. + RISING • **BAKE:** 20 MIN. + COOLING
MAKES: 4 BRAIDS (6 SLICES EACH)

- 1 tablespoon active dry yeast
- ¼ cup warm water (110° to 115°)
- 1 cup warm 2% milk (110° to 115°)
- 1 cup butter, softened
- 1 large egg
- 6 tablespoons sugar
- 1 teaspoon salt
- 4½ to 5 cups all-purpose flour

FILLING

- 1 cup butter, melted
- 2 cups packed brown sugar
- 2 cups chopped pecans
- 1 cup all-purpose flour

GLAZE

- 2 cups confectioners' sugar
- 3 to 4 tablespoons 2% milk

1. In a small bowl, dissolve yeast in warm water. In a large bowl, combine milk, butter, egg, sugar, salt, yeast mixture and 2½ cups flour; beat on medium speed 3 minutes. Stir in enough remaining flour to form a soft dough (dough will be sticky).

2. Turn dough onto a floured surface; knead until smooth and elastic, about 6-8 minutes. Place in a greased bowl, turning once to grease the top. Cover with plastic wrap and let rise in a warm place until doubled, about 1 hour.

3. In a large bowl, combine the filling ingredients. Punch down dough. Turn onto a lightly floured surface; divide into four portions. Roll each portion into a 12x8-in. rectangle. Spread each with a quarter of the filling to within ½ in. of the edges. Roll up jelly-roll style, starting with a long side; pinch seam to seal.

4. For each roll, starting 1 in. from one end, make two lengthwise cuts, making three sections. Braid the sections together, cut sides up.

GOOEY LEMON ROLLS

My mother made these hard-to-resist rolls when I was young. I always warm up after having one, and so will your family.
—CORA PATTERSON LEWISTON, ID

PREP: 25 MIN. + RISING • **BAKE:** 20 MIN.
MAKES: 1 DOZEN

- 1 **tablespoon active dry yeast**
- ½ **cup warm water (110° to 115°)**
- ½ **cup warm 2% milk (110° to 115°)**
- ¼ **cup butter, melted**
- 1 **large egg**
- ½ **cup sugar**
- 1 **teaspoon salt**
- 3 **to 3½ cups all-purpose flour**

FILLING
- ½ **cup sugar**
- 2 **teaspoons grated lemon peel**
- ½ **teaspoon ground cinnamon**
- 1 **tablespoon poppy seeds, optional**
- ¼ **cup butter, melted**
- 1 **cup slivered almonds, toasted**

GLAZE
- ½ **cup sugar**
- 1 **can (12 ounces) frozen lemonade concentrate, thawed**
- 1 **tablespoon butter**
- 2 **teaspoons grated lemon peel**

1. In a small bowl, dissolve yeast in warm water. In a large bowl, combine milk, butter, egg, sugar, salt, yeast mixture and 2 cups flour; beat on medium speed until smooth. Stir in enough remaining flour to form a soft dough (dough will be sticky).
2. Turn dough onto a floured surface; knead until smooth and elastic, about 6-8 minutes. Place in a greased bowl, turning once to grease the top. Cover with plastic wrap and let rise in a warm place until doubled, about 1 hour.
3. For filling, in a small bowl, mix sugar, lemon peel, cinnamon and, if desired, poppy seeds. Punch down dough; roll into an 18x12-in. rectangle. Brush with melted butter to within ¼ in. of edges; sprinkle with sugar mixture and almonds. Roll up jelly-roll style, starting with a long side; pinch seam to seal. Cut into 12 slices.
4. Place in a greased 13x9-in. baking pan, cut side down. Cover with a kitchen towel; let rise in a warm place until almost doubled, about 45 minutes.

5. Preheat oven to 400°. Bake rolls 15 minutes. Meanwhile, for glaze, in a small saucepan, combine sugar and lemonade concentrate. Cook and stir over medium-low heat until sugar is dissolved. Stir in the butter and the lemon peel; simmer, uncovered, 10-12 minutes or until slightly thickened. Remove rolls from oven; pour glaze over rolls. Bake 5-10 minutes longer or until golden brown. Cool in pan 5 minutes. Run a knife around sides of pan before inverting onto a serving plate. Serve warm.

DILL BATTER BREAD

Even those who don't consider themselves bakers can make this bread with success. And your guests will be delighted!
—DONNA LINDECAMP MORGANTON, NC

PREP: 15 MIN. + RISING • **BAKE:** 45 MIN. + COOLING
MAKES: 8 SERVINGS

- ¼ **cup sugar**
- 2 **packages (¼ ounce each) active dry yeast**
- 2 **teaspoons dill weed**
- 1½ **teaspoons salt**
- 4½ **cups all-purpose flour**
- 1 **cup water**
- 1 **cup 2% milk**
- ¼ **cup canola oil**
- 1 **large egg**
- 2 **teaspoons butter, melted**
- ½ **teaspoon kosher salt**

1. In a large bowl, mix sugar, yeast, dill weed, salt and 2 cups flour. In a small saucepan, heat water, milk and oil to 120°-130°. Add to dry ingredients; beat on medium speed 2 minutes. Add egg; beat on high 2 minutes. Stir in the remaining flour to form a stiff batter. Cover with plastic wrap and let rise until doubled, about 1 hour.
2. Preheat the oven to 375°. Stir down batter. Transfer to a greased 2½-qt. round baking dish. Bake 45-50 minutes or until deep golden brown and bread sounds hollow when tapped.
3. Cool 5 minutes before removing to a wire rack. Brush with butter; sprinkle with salt. Cool completely.

BRIE & CARAMELIZED ONION FLATBREAD

Saute the onions and garlic for this flatbread a day ahead so it's easy to put together on the day of a party. Prepared pizza dough makes it a snap.
—TRISHA KRUSE EAGLE, ID

PREP: 45 MIN. • **BAKE:** 20 MIN. + STANDING
MAKES: 1 FLATBREAD (12 PIECES)

- 2 **tablespoons butter**
- 3 **large sweet onions, halved and thinly sliced (about 6 cups)**
- 2 **garlic cloves, minced**
- 1 **tablespoon brown sugar**
- 1 **tablespoon balsamic vinegar**
- ½ **teaspoon salt**
- ¼ **teaspoon pepper**
- 1 **loaf (1 pound) frozen pizza dough, thawed**
- 8 **ounces Brie cheese, cut into ½-inch pieces**

1. Grease a 15x10x1-in. baking pan; set aside. In a large skillet, heat butter over medium heat. Add onions; cook and stir 4-6 minutes or until softened. Reduce heat to medium-low; cook 25-30 minutes or until deep golden brown, stirring occasionally. Add garlic; cook and stir 1 minute longer.
2. Preheat oven to 425°. Add brown sugar, vinegar, salt and pepper to onion mixture. Cook and stir 5 minutes longer. Press dough into a 12x10-in. rectangle onto prepared pan. Top with the onion mixture and cheese. Bake 20-25 minutes or until golden brown. Let stand 10 minutes before cutting.

TOP TIP

Proofing Yeast

To make sure active dry yeast (not quick-rise yeast) is alive and active, you may first want to proof it. Dissolve one package of yeast and 1 teaspoon sugar in ¼ cup warm water (110° to 115°). Let stand for 5 to 10 minutes. If the mixture foams up, the yeast mixture can be used because the yeast is active. If it does not foam, the yeast should be discarded.

HONEY CHALLAH

I use these shiny beautiful loaves as the centerpiece of my spread. I love the springtime taste of honey, but feel free to get creative by adding chocolate chips, cinnamon, orange zest or almond. Leftover slices work well with bread pudding or French toast.

—JENNIFER NEWFIELD LOS ANGELES, CA

PREP: 45 MIN. + RISING • **BAKE:** 30 MIN. + COOLING
MAKES: 2 LOAVES (6 SERVINGS EACH)

- 2 **packages (¼ ounce each) active dry yeast**
- ½ **teaspoon sugar**
- 1½ **cups warm water (110° to 115°), divided**
- 5 **large eggs**
- ⅔ **cup plus 1 teaspoon honey, divided**
- ½ **cup canola oil**
- 2 **teaspoons salt**
- 6 **to 7 cups bread flour**
- 1 **cup boiling water**
- 2 **cups golden raisins**
- 1 **tablespoon water**
- 1 **tablespoon sesame seeds**

1. In a small bowl, dissolve yeast and sugar in 1 cup warm water. Separate 2 eggs; refrigerate 2 egg whites. Place remaining egg yolks and eggs in a large bowl. Add ⅔ cup honey, oil, salt, yeast mixture, 3 cups flour and remaining water; beat the mixture on medium speed 3 minutes. Stir in enough remaining flour to form a soft dough (dough will be sticky).

2. Pour boiling water over raisins in a small bowl; let stand 5 minutes. Drain and pat dry. Turn dough onto a floured surface; knead until smooth and elastic, about 6-8 minutes. Knead in the raisins. Place in a greased bowl, turning once to grease the top. Cover with plastic wrap and let rise in a warm place until almost doubled, about 1½ hours.

3. Punch down dough. Turn onto a lightly floured surface. Divide the dough in half. Divide one portion into six pieces. Roll each into a 16-in. rope. Place ropes parallel on a greased baking sheet; pinch ropes together at the top.

4. To braid, take the rope on the left and carry it over the two ropes beside it, then slip it under the middle rope and carry it over the last two ropes. Lay the rope down parallel to the other ropes; it is now on the far right side. Repeat these steps until you reach the end. As the braid moves to the right, you can pick up your loaf and recenter it on your work surface as needed. Pinch ends to seal and tuck under. For a fuller loaf, using your hands, push the ends of the loaf closer together. Repeat process with remaining dough. Cover with clean kitchen towels; let dough rise in a warm place until almost doubled, about 30 minutes.

5. Preheat oven to 350°. In a small bowl, whisk remaining egg whites and honey with water; brush over loaves. Sprinkle with sesame seeds. Bake 30-35 minutes or until golden brown and bread sounds hollow when tapped. Remove loaves from pans to a wire rack to cool.

HOW-TO

Easy Braided Dough

Challah bread, sometimes called egg bread, is made from yeast dough enriched with sugar—and in this recipe honey—for a slightly sweet flavor. Follow these steps to braid. You also can braid using three strands of dough instead of six.

PINCH ropes together at the top before starting braid.

TO BRAID, take the rope on the left and carry it over the two ropes beside it, under the middle rope and over the last two ropes.

CONTINUE the same braiding pattern. As the braid moves to the right, pick up the loaf and recenter it on your work surface as needed.

PINCH ends to seal and tuck under.

HONEY
CHALLAH

Special Celebrations

Amid all the big holidays and grand parties throughout the year, there are smaller moments worth celebrating—special occasions shared with family and friends over good food and good conversation. Honor a returning soldier with a picnic, reveal a baby's gender in style and put the bash in a Halloween monster mash. With seven fun themes for celebrations, playing host to a happy gathering has never been easier!

Valentine's Day Candy

The crystal-cold days of winter may be far from over. But no matter how crisp the air is, **the magic of Valentine's Day** is enough to send Jack Frost packing—at least for one blissful day in February.

Spark a little fun and satisfy your sweet tooth craving all in one with a gleeful Valentine's Day party! Invite friends, family, little ones, your main squeeze and anyone else who melts your heart to join in the fun of sampling **a lovey-dovey lineup of candies and confections.**

From truffles and mints to bonbons and gumdrops, each of these homemade heavenlies will make the most dreamy day of the year even sweeter. **Will you be my Valentine?**

Creamy Pastel Mints (p. 184)

**EASY PEANUT
BUTTER TRUFFLES**

CHERRY DIVINITY

It's not a Valentine's Day party without these light and airy confections on my dessert platter. The recipe is versatile because you can replace the cherry gelatin with any flavor to suit your tastes.
—**CRYSTAL RALPH-HAUGHN**
BARTLESVILLE, OK

PREP: 35 MIN. • **COOK:** 25 MIN. + STANDING
MAKES: 5 DOZEN

- 2 **large egg whites**
- 3 **cups sugar**
- ¾ **cup water**
- ¾ **cup light corn syrup**
- 1 **package (3 ounces) cherry gelatin**
- 1 **cup chopped walnuts**

1. Place egg whites in the bowl of a large stand mixer; let stand at room temperature for 30 minutes. Meanwhile, line three 15x10x1-in. baking pans with waxed paper.
2. In a heavy saucepan, combine the sugar, water and corn syrup; cook and stir until sugar is dissolved and mixture comes to a boil. Cook over medium heat, without stirring, until a candy thermometer reads 250° (hard-ball stage).
3. Just before the temperature is reached, beat egg whites until foamy. Gradually beat in gelatin. Beat until stiff peaks form. With mixer running on high speed, carefully pour hot syrup in a slow, steady stream into the bowl. Beat just until candy loses its gloss and holds its shape, about 5 minutes. Immediately stir in the walnuts.
4. Quickly drop by tablespoonfuls onto prepared pans. Let stand at room temperature overnight or until dry to the touch. Store divinity in an airtight container at room temperature.

EASY PEANUT BUTTER TRUFFLES

I make a batch or two of these homemade truffles on special occasions. My husband grew up around—and now works in—the beekeeping industry, so honey is a staple in our house. It pairs well with peanut butter and makes these treats so soft and sweet.
—**TAMI KUEHL** LOUP CITY, NE

PREP: 20 MIN. • **COOK:** 10 MIN. + CHILLING
MAKES: 64 TRUFFLES

- 1 **teaspoon plus ¼ cup butter, divided**
- ¼ **cup honey**
- 2 **cups creamy peanut butter**
- 1¼ **cups confectioners' sugar**
- 1 **teaspoon vanilla extract**
- 1½ **cups finely chopped honey-roasted peanuts or miniature semisweet chocolate chips**

1. Line an 8-in. square pan with foil; grease foil with 1 teaspoon butter.
2. In a small saucepan, combine honey and remaining butter over medium heat; cook and stir until blended. Stir in peanut butter until smooth. Remove from heat; whisk in confectioners' sugar and vanilla. Spread into prepared pan. Refrigerate, covered, 2 hours or until firm.
3. Place peanuts in a shallow bowl. Using foil, lift candy out of the pan. Remove the foil; cut the candy into 64 squares. Shape squares into balls; roll in peanuts. Store between layers of waxed paper in an airtight container in the refrigerator.
NOTE *Reduced-fat peanut butter is not recommended for this recipe.*

CHERRY
DIVINITY

DARK CHOCOLATE RASPBERRY FUDGE

The combination of dark chocolate and raspberry is a match made in heaven. This fudge makes a heartfelt valentine, or just a treat that's worth sharing with someone you love.
—**BARBARA LENTO** HOUSTON, PA

PREP: 15 MIN. + FREEZING
COOK: 5 MIN. + CHILLING
MAKES: 3 POUNDS (81 PIECES)

- 1 **package (10 to 12 ounces) white baking chips**
- 1 **teaspoon butter, softened**
- 3 **cups dark chocolate chips**
- 1 **can (14 ounces) sweetened condensed milk**
- ¼ **cup raspberry liqueur**
- ⅛ **teaspoon salt**

1. Place baking chips in a single layer on a small baking sheet. Freeze for 30 minutes. Line a 9-in. square pan with foil; grease foil with butter.
2. In a large microwave-safe bowl, combine dark chocolate chips and milk. Microwave, uncovered, on high for 2 minutes; stir. Microwave in additional 30-second intervals, stirring until smooth. Stir in the liqueur and salt. Add the white baking chips; stir just until partially melted. Spread into prepared pan. Refrigerate 1 hour or until firm.
3. Using foil, lift fudge out of pan. Remove foil; cut fudge into 1-in. squares. Store in an airtight container in the refrigerator.
NOTE *This recipe was tested in a 1,100-watt microwave.*

LEMON CREAM BONBONS

These bonbons with a lemony twinge are perfect for any special occasion. But they're in such high demand with my family that I now keep them on hand all year long.
—**ANN BARBER** CREOLA, OH

PREP: 30 MIN. + FREEZING
MAKES: ABOUT 4 DOZEN

- 2 **packages (8 ounces each) cream cheese, softened**
- 2 **tablespoons grated lemon peel**
- 3 **tablespoons lemon juice**
- 1 **teaspoon lemon extract**
- 1 **cup confectioners' sugar**
- 1 **pound dark chocolate candy coating, melted**
- 4 **ounces white candy coating, melted**

1. In a large bowl, beat cream cheese, lemon peel, juice, extract. Gradually beat in confectioners' sugar. Cover and freeze for 2 hours.
2. Using a small ice cream scoop, drop mixture by 1-in. balls onto waxed paper-lined baking sheets. Cover and freeze for 1 hour.
3. Working with a few frozen balls at a time, dip into melted chocolate; allow excess to drip off. Place on waxed paper-lined baking sheets. Let stand until set.
4. Spoon melted candy coating into a heavy-duty resealable plastic bag. Cut a small hole in the corner of bag; drizzle coating over candies. Store in the refrigerator. Remove from the refrigerator just before serving.

QUICK & EASY GUMDROPS

These homemade candies are softer than store-bought versions. They've got that classic fun appeal that people really love.
—**LEAH REKAU** MILWAUKEE, WI

PREP: 25 MIN. + CHILLING
MAKES: 1 POUND (64 PIECES)

- 3 **envelopes unflavored gelatin**
- ½ **cup plus ¾ cup water, divided**
- 1½ **cups sugar**
- ¼ **to ½ teaspoon raspberry extract**
  Red food coloring
  Additional sugar

1. In a small bowl, sprinkle gelatin over ½ cup water; let stand 5 minutes. In a small saucepan, bring sugar and remaining water to a boil over medium heat, stirring constantly. Add gelatin; reduce the heat. Simmer 5 minutes, stirring frequently. Remove from the heat; stir in extract and food coloring as desired.
2. Pour into a greased 8-in.-square pan. Refrigerate, covered, 3 hours or until firm.
3. Loosen edges of candy from pan with a knife; turn onto a sugared work surface. Cut into 1-in squares; roll in sugar. Let stand, uncovered, at room temperature 3-4 hours or until all the sides are dry, turning every hour. Store between layers of waxed paper in an airtight container in the refrigerator.
NOTE *For lemon gumdrops, use lemon extract and yellow food coloring. For orange gumdrops, use orange extract, yellow food coloring and a drop of red food coloring.*

TOP TIP

Candy Making Tips

It's easy to make candy from scratch if you keep these pointers in mind.

- Measure and assemble all ingredients before beginning. Do not substitute or alter basic ingredients.
- Use heavy-gauge saucepans that are deep enough to allow candy mixtures to boil freely without boiling over.
- For best results, use real butter when a recipe calls for it.
- For safe stirring when preparing recipes with boiling sugar, use wooden spoons with long handles.
- Humid weather affects results when preparing candies that are cooked to specific temperatures or that contain egg whites. Make candy on days when the humidity is less than 60%.
- Store homemade candies in tightly covered containers unless otherwise directed. Don't store more than one kind of candy in a single container. Chewy candies like caramels and taffy should be individually wrapped.

COCONUT CREME
CHOCOLATES

COCONUT CREME CHOCOLATES

My marshmallow-filled chocolate confections are a fun way to treat my children and grandchildren when they visit.

—DOLORES WILDER TEXAS CITY, TX

PREP: 15 MIN. + CHILLING • **MAKES:** 2½ DOZEN

- 1 jar (7 ounces) marshmallow creme
- 2⅔ cups flaked coconut, toasted
- 1 teaspoon vanilla extract
  Dash salt
- 1 milk chocolate candy bar (5 ounces), chopped
- 1½ teaspoons shortening

1. In a large bowl, mix marshmallow creme, coconut, vanilla and salt until blended. Refrigerate, covered, at least 1 hour.

2. Shape mixture into 1-in. balls. Place on a waxed paper-lined baking sheet. Refrigerate, covered, at least 3 hours.

3. In a microwave, melt chocolate and shortening; stir until smooth. Dip coconut balls in chocolate; allow excess to drip off. Place on waxed paper; let stand until set.

NOTE *To toast coconut, cook in a skillet over low heat until brown, stirring occasionally, or bake in a shallow pan in a 350° oven for 5-10 minutes.*

HOW-TO

DIPPING IN CHOCOLATE

Dipping candies and confections in chocolate need not be messy work. All you need are a fork and a knife. Drop fillings in melted chocolate, scoop out with a fork and roll off onto to waxed paper with a knife.

CARAMEL PRETZEL BITES

CARAMEL PRETZEL BITES

I created this recipe to put my own twist on a pretzel log dipped in caramel, chocolate and nuts—similar to a version from a popular candy store. We enjoy these homemade treats for Valentine's Day, but they're delightful any time of year.

—MICHILENE KLAVER GRAND RAPIDS, MI

PREP: 45 MIN. + COOLING • **MAKES:** 6 DOZEN

- 2 teaspoons butter, softened
- 4 cups pretzel sticks
- 2½ cups pecan halves, toasted
- 2¼ cups packed brown sugar
- 1 cup butter, cubed
- 1 cup corn syrup
- 1 can (14 ounces) sweetened condensed milk
- ⅛ teaspoon salt
- 1 teaspoon vanilla extract
- 1 package (11½ ounces) milk chocolate chips
- 1 tablespoon plus 1 teaspoon shortening, divided
- ⅓ cup white baking chips

1. Line a 13x9-in. pan with foil; grease foil with softened butter. Spread pretzels and pecans on bottom of prepared pan.

2. In a large heavy saucepan, combine brown sugar, cubed butter, corn syrup, milk and salt; cook and stir over medium heat until a candy thermometer reads 240° (soft-ball stage). Remove from heat. Stir in vanilla. Pour over pretzel mixture.

3. In a microwave, melt chocolate chips and 1 tablespoon shortening; stir until smooth. Spread over caramel layer. In microwave, melt baking chips and remaining shortening; stir until smooth. Drizzle over top. Let stand until set.

4. Using foil, lift candy out of pan; remove foil. Using a buttered knife, cut candy into bite-size pieces.

CREAMY PASTEL MINTS

These mints are easy and versatile. Vary the shapes and colors for each season.
—**JANICE BRADY** SEATTLE, WA

PREP: 40 MIN. • **MAKES:** ABOUT 5 DOZEN

- **3** ounces (6 tablespoons) cream cheese
- **¼ to ½** teaspoon peppermint extract
  Red food coloring
- **3** cups confectioners' sugar

1. Place cream cheese in a bowl; let stand at room temperature to soften slightly. Stir in extract until blended. Tint mixture pink or red. Gradually mix in half of the confectioners' sugar.
2. On a work surface, knead in the remaining confectioners' sugar until smooth. Divide mixture into three portions; roll each to ¼-in. thickness. (Flour or additional confectioners' sugar is not necessary for rolling.)
3. Cut candy with a 1-in. heart-shaped cookie cutter. Store between layers of waxed paper in an airtight container in the refrigerator.

CREAMY ORANGE CARAMELS

Every year I learn a new candy-making technique. One year I started with my basic caramel recipe and added a splash of orange extract for fun. This year I just might try buttered rum extract.
—**SHELLY BEVINGTON** HERMISTON, OR

PREP: 10 MIN. • **COOK:** 30 MIN.+ STANDING
MAKES: ABOUT 2½ POUNDS (80 PIECES)

- **1** teaspoon plus 1 cup butter, divided
- **2** cups sugar
- **1** cup light corn syrup
- **1** can (14 ounces) sweetened condensed milk
- **1** teaspoon orange extract
- **1** teaspoon vanilla extract

1. Line an 11x7-in. dish with foil; grease foil with 1 teaspoon butter.
2. In a large heavy saucepan, combine the sugar, corn syrup and remaining butter. Bring to a boil over medium heat, stirring constantly. Reduce heat to medium-low; boil gently, without stirring, for 4 minutes.
3. Remove from heat; gradually stir in milk. Cook and stir until a candy thermometer reads 244° (firm-ball stage). Remove from the heat; stir in extracts. Immediately pour into the prepared dish (do not scrape the saucepan). Let stand until firm.
4. Using foil, lift out candy; remove foil. Using a buttered knife, cut the caramel into 1x¾-in. pieces. Wrap individually in waxed paper; twist the ends to secure.

VALENTINE'S DAY TREAT BOXES

Transform mini popcorn boxes into adorable Valentine's Day treat holders. Fill them with a single homemade candy to give to someone special. Or set out the emtpy treat boxes on your dessert table and let guests fill their own from your lineup of treats.

MATERIALS
Miniature white or striped popcorn boxes
Red or pink decorative scrapbook paper or card stock
Red or pink ribbon
Heart paper punch or heart template
Craft knife
Glue gun
Decorative shredded paper filler, optional
Desired wrapped treats

DIRECTIONS
1. If using white boxes, trace a folded box twice onto the same scrapbook paper or card stock. Repeat for each remaining white box. Cut out pieces. Glue matching pieces to the front and back of each white box. Let dry.
2. With the template or paper punch, make a heart for each box using contrasting paper or card stock.
3. Using craft knife, cut two small slits about 1¼ in. apart in center of each heart, making the slits long enough so that the desired ribbon can be threaded through the slits.
4. For each box, cut a 16- to 24-in. length of contrasting ribbon.
5. Wrap a ribbon piece once around desired box, then thread each ribbon end from back to front through a slit on desired heart. Tie ribbon ends on front of heart as desired, securing heart on box. In same way, tie a heart to each remaining box.
6. Fill boxes with shredded paper if desired. Add desired treats to each box.

TOP TIP

Candy Thermometers

We recommend that you test your candy thermometer before each use by bringing water to a boil; the thermometer should read 212°. Adjust your recipe temperature up or down based on your test. For accurate temperature readings, your candy thermometer should be attached to the side of the saucepan but should not touch the bottom of the pan.

CREAMY ORANGE CARAMELS
VALENTINE'S DAY TREAT BOXES

Casserole Club

There's no denying it: **Casseroles are comfort food at its best.**
They make the perfect dish to pass when folks gather for a few hours
of laughter and camaraderie, whether it's for book club, ladies'
knitting circle, a monthly dinner party...or any occasion that offers an
opportunity to indulge in a lineup of bubbly, oven-baked goodness.

But these aren't your mother's casseroles. Calling for a mix of unique
flavors and ingredients, this lineup of eclectic hot dishes will delight
the culinary traditionalist and rebel gourmand alike. **Tempt your
taste buds with ethnic flavors and creative spins on classic
family pleasers.** Each one promises to become a new favorite.

It's bring-a-dish-time!

Chicken & Cheddar Biscuit Casserole (p. 190)

"No one will be able to resist the classic trio of ham, Swiss and potatoes in this comforting bake. It was the result of creative experimentation when I wanted to use up ingredients I had on hand. I sometimes replace the ham with turkey ham."

—SARAH WILHAM, ELKHART, IL

HAM AND SWISS POTATO CASSEROLE

HAM AND SWISS POTATO CASSEROLE

PREP: 25 MIN. • **BAKE:** 20 MIN.
MAKES: 8 SERVINGS

- 5 large potatoes (about 4 pounds), peeled and cut into ¾-inch pieces
- ¼ cup butter, cubed
- 1 medium onion, chopped
- 1 garlic clove, minced
- ⅓ cup all-purpose flour
- 2 cups 2% milk
- 1⅓ cups roasted red pepper Alfredo sauce
- 1 teaspoon dried basil
- ¼ teaspoon salt
- ¼ teaspoon dill weed
- ¼ teaspoon pepper
- 2 cups cubed fully cooked ham
- 2 cups (8 ounces) shredded Swiss cheese
- ¼ cup seasoned bread crumbs
- 1 tablespoon butter, melted

1. Preheat oven to 375°. Place potatoes in a large saucepan; add water to cover. Bring to a boil. Reduce heat; simmer, covered, 8-10 minutes or until crisp-tender. Meanwhile, in a large skillet, heat butter over medium-high heat. Add onion; cook and stir 6-8 minutes or until tender. Add garlic; cook and stir 1 minute. Stir in the flour until blended; gradually whisk in milk. Bring to a boil, stirring constantly; cook and stir 1-2 minutes or until thickened. Stir in Alfredo sauce and seasonings; heat through.

2. Drain potatoes; transfer to a greased 13x9-in. baking dish. Layer with ham, cheese and sauce. In a small bowl, combine bread crumbs and butter. Sprinkle over the top. Bake, uncovered, 18-22 minutes or until topping is golden brown and cheese is melted. Let stand 5 minutes before serving.

TO MAKE AHEAD *Can be made a day in advance. Prepare recipe as directed, layering ham, cheese and sauce in baking dish. Cover and refrigerate overnight. Remove from the refrigerator 30 minutes before baking. Prepare crumb topping; sprinkle over top. Bake as directed.*

GREEK CHICKEN BAKE

As soon as the weather turns cold, I know it's time to pull out this go-to recipe. I assemble it in the morning, then put it into the oven before dinner.

—KELLY MAXWELL PLAINFIELD, IL

PREP: 30 MIN. • **BAKE:** 50 MIN.
MAKES: 8 SERVINGS

- 3 tablespoons olive oil, divided
- 1 medium onion, chopped
- 7 garlic cloves, minced
- 2 teaspoons minced fresh thyme or ¾ teaspoon dried thyme
- 2 teaspoons minced fresh rosemary or ¾ teaspoon dried rosemary, crushed
- ¾ teaspoon pepper, divided
- 2 pounds red potatoes, cut into ½-inch cubes
- 2 cans (14½ ounces each) diced tomatoes, undrained
- 2 cups cut fresh green beans (1-inch pieces)
- 2 tablespoons finely chopped ripe olives
- 8 bone-in chicken thighs (about 3 pounds), skin removed
- ½ teaspoon salt
- ½ cup crumbled feta cheese
  Minced fresh parsley
  Hot cooked orzo pasta, optional

1. Preheat oven to 375°. In a large skillet, heat 1 tablespoon oil over medium heat. Add onion; cook and stir 3-4 minutes or until tender. Add garlic, thyme, rosemary and ½ teaspoon pepper; cook 1 minute longer. Remove from pan.

2. In same pan, heat remaining oil over medium heat. Add potatoes; cook and stir until the potatoes are lightly browned. Return onion mixture to pan; stir in tomatoes, green beans and olives. Cook 1 minute longer.

3. Transfer to a greased 13x9-in. baking dish. Sprinkle chicken with salt and remaining pepper; place over top of potato mixture. Bake, covered, 40 minutes. Uncover; bake another 10-15 minutes or until a thermometer reads 170°-175°. Sprinkle with feta and parsley. If desired, serve with orzo.

TO MAKE AHEAD *Can be made a few hours in advance. Cover and refrigerate. Remove from the refrigerator 30 minutes before baking. Bake as directed.*

TURKEY ENCHILADA LASAGNA

Expect folks to devour this layered Southwestern casserole that boasts familiar enchilada flavors in every mouthwatering bite. You can also use ground beef in place of the ground turkey if you like.

—JULIE CACKLER WEST DES MOINES, IA

PREP: 25 MIN. • **BAKE:** 20 MIN. + STANDING
MAKES: 8 SERVINGS

- 1 pound lean ground turkey
- 1 large onion, chopped
- 1 large green pepper, chopped
- 1 small sweet red pepper, chopped
- 1 package (8 ounces) fat-free cream cheese
- 1 teaspoon chili powder
- 1 can (10 ounces) enchilada sauce
- 6 whole wheat flour tortillas (8 inches)
- 1 cup (4 ounces) shredded reduced-fat Mexican cheese blend
  Salsa and sour cream, optional

1. Preheat oven to 400°. In a large skillet, cook turkey, onion and peppers over medium-high heat 5-7 minutes or until turkey is no longer pink, breaking up turkey into crumbles. Stir in cream cheese and chili powder.

2. Pour enchilada sauce into a shallow bowl. Dip tortillas into sauce to coat. Place two tortillas in a 13x9-in. baking dish coated with cooking spray; spread with half of the turkey mixture. Sprinkle with ⅓ cup cheese. Repeat layers. Top with remaining tortillas and cheese.

3. Bake, uncovered, 20-25 minutes or until heated through and cheese is melted. Let stand 10 minutes before serving. If desired, serve with salsa and sour cream.

FREEZE OPTION *Cover and freeze unbaked lasagna. To use, partially thaw in refrigerator overnight. Remove from refrigerator 30 minutes before baking. Preheat oven to 400°. Bake lasagna as directed, increasing time as necessary to heat through and for a thermometer inserted into center to read 165°.*

CHICKEN & CHEDDAR BISCUIT CASSEROLE

I always get rave reviews when I bring this casserole to my son's Cub Scouts meetings. It's also the perfect comfort food to enjoy after a long day.
—SARAH PHILLIPS EAST LANSING, MI

PREP: 40 MIN. • **BAKE:** 35 MIN.
MAKES: 12 SERVINGS

- ⅓ cup butter, cubed
- 1 large onion, chopped
- 2 celery ribs, chopped
- 2 medium carrots, chopped
- 2 garlic cloves, minced
- ½ cup all-purpose flour
- 1 teaspoon salt
- ½ teaspoon pepper
- 4 cups chicken broth or stock
- 5 cups cubed cooked chicken
- 3 cups biscuit/baking mix
- ¾ cup 2% milk
- 1 cup (4 ounces) shredded cheddar cheese
- 1 cup roasted sweet red peppers, drained and chopped

1. Preheat oven to 425°. In a 6-qt. stockpot, heat butter over medium-high heat. Add onion, celery and carrots; cook and stir 3-5 minutes or until tender. Add garlic; cook and stir 1 minute longer. Stir in flour, salt and pepper until blended; gradually whisk in broth. Bring to a boil, stirring constantly; cook and stir over medium heat 4-6 minutes or until thickened. Add chicken.

2. Transfer to a greased 13x9-in. baking dish. Bake, uncovered, for 20 minutes. Meanwhile, in a large bowl, combine biscuit mix and milk just until moistened. Turn onto a lightly floured surface; knead gently 8-10 times. Roll dough into a 12x8-in. rectangle. Sprinkle with cheese and peppers. Roll up dough jelly-roll style, starting with a long side; pinch seam to seal. Cut crosswise into 1-in.-thick slices. Place on top of the hot chicken mixture. Bake casserole, uncovered, 15-20 minutes or until biscuits are golden brown.

FREEZE OPTION *Cool baked casserole; cover and freeze. To use, partially thaw in refrigerator overnight. Remove from refrigerator 30 minutes before baking. Preheat oven to 425°. Bake casserole, covered, 40 minutes or until heated through and a thermometer inserted in center reads 165°.*

MAKE-AHEAD CABBAGE ROLLS

I've relied on this recipe for years, and my cabbage rolls never fail to impress. I host many parties, and my guests have come to expect this main entree.
—NANCY FOUST STONEBORO, PA

PREP: 1 HOUR • **BAKE:** 50 MIN.
MAKES: 12 ROLLS

- 12 cabbage leaves
- 2 pounds ground beef
- ¾ teaspoon salt
- ¼ teaspoon pepper
- 2 cups cooked long grain rice
- 2 large eggs, lightly beaten

SAUCE
- ¼ cup butter, cubed
- 1 large onion, halved and thinly sliced
- 2 celery ribs, chopped
- 2½ cups water
- 2 cans (one 15 ounces, one 8 ounces) tomato sauce
- 2 tablespoons lemon juice
- 2 teaspoons sugar
- 2 teaspoons dried parsley flakes
- 1 teaspoon salt
- ¼ teaspoon pepper

1. In batches, cook cabbage leaves in boiling water 3-5 minutes or until crisp-tender. Drain; cool slightly. Trim the thick vein from the bottom of each cabbage leaf, making a V-shaped cut. Meanwhile, in a large skillet, cook beef, salt and pepper over medium heat 8-10 minutes or until no longer pink, breaking into crumbles; drain. Stir in rice and eggs.

2. In another skillet, heat butter over medium-high heat. Add onion and celery; cook and stir 6-8 minutes or until tender. Stir in the water, tomato sauce, lemon juice, sugar, parsley, salt and pepper. Bring to a boil. Reduce the heat; simmer, uncovered, for 15-20 minutes or until thickened.

3. Spoon about ½ cup meat mixture onto each cabbage leaf. Pull together cut edges of leaf to overlap; fold over filling. Fold in sides and roll up. Transfer to a greased 13x9-in. baking dish. Pour sauce over rolls. Refrigerate, covered, overnight.

4. Remove from the refrigerator 30 minutes before baking. Preheat oven to 350°. Bake, covered, for 50-60 minutes or until cabbage rolls are heated through.

FREEZE OPTION *Cover and freeze unbaked cabbage rolls. To use, partially thaw in refrigerator overnight. Remove from the refrigerator 30 minutes before baking. Preheat oven to 350°. Bake casserole as directed, increasing time as necessary to heat through and for a thermometer inserted into center to read 165°.*

TOP TIP

Peeling Cabbage Leaves Made Easy

It can be tricky to remove the delicate leaves from a head of cabbage without tearing them into pieces. The next time you're making stuffed cabbage rolls, follow these simple steps. Core the cabbage, then immerse the whole head in boiling water until the outer leaves begin to loosen. Remove cabbage from the water and carefully peel away as many outer leaves as will come off easily. If you need more leaves, place the cabbage back in simmering water for a minute or two. Some cabbage leaves have a thick rib, which keeps them from lying flat and being easily rolled up. In that case, trim the end of the leaf (and the thick end of the rib) so you can more easily roll up the leaf with the stuffing.

MAKE-AHEAD
CABBAGE ROLLS

**BAKED NECTARINE
CHICKEN SALAD**

BAKED NECTARINE CHICKEN SALAD

My nectarine chicken casserole is a fun twist on a classic. Folks love the crunchy chow mein noodles on top. I love that I can make it a day in advance and refrigerate until it's time to bake. Serve with hot bread or rolls.

—FAYE ROBINSON PENSACOLA, FL

PREP: 15 MIN. • **BAKE:** 20 MIN.
MAKES: 8 SERVINGS

- 1⅓ cups mayonnaise
- ½ cup shredded Parmesan cheese
- 2 tablespoons lemon juice
- 1 teaspoon salt
- 1 teaspoon onion powder
- 4 cups cubed cooked chicken
- 8 celery ribs, thinly sliced
- 4 medium nectarines, coarsely chopped
- 8 green onions, sliced
- 2 cans (3 ounces each) crispy chow mein noodles

1. Preheat oven to 375°. In a small bowl, mix the first five ingredients. In a large bowl, combine chicken, celery, nectarines, and onions. Add the mayonnaise mixture; toss gently to coat.

2. Transfer to a greased 13x9-in. baking dish. Sprinkle with noodles. Bake, uncovered, 20-25 minutes or until heated through.

TO MAKE AHEAD *Can be made a day in advance. Cover and refrigerate. Remove from the refrigerator 30 minutes before baking. Sprinkle with noodles. Bake as directed.*

SAUSAGE-RICE PHYLLO CASSEROLE

I created this recipe to use up the ingredients I had stocked in my cupboards. You can mix up the herbs and spices to fit any taste. Add rosemary or cayenne to give it a little more kick.

—JENN TIDWELL FAIR OAKS, CA

PREP: 1 HOUR • **BAKE:** 35 MIN.
MAKES: 8 SERVINGS

- 1 pound bulk Italian sausage
- 2 garlic cloves, minced
- 1 teaspoon dried basil
- 1 teaspoon dried oregano
- ⅓ cup chardonnay or chicken broth
- 6 medium tomatoes, peeled and crushed
- 1 medium carrot, peeled and grated
- 4½ teaspoons tomato paste
- 1 bay leaf
- ½ teaspoon salt
- ¼ teaspoon garlic powder
- ¼ teaspoon paprika
- 1½ cups frozen peas
- 3 cups cooked rice
- 2 green onions, sliced
- 1 tablespoon minced fresh parsley
- 1½ cups grated Parmesan cheese
- ¾ cup grated Romano cheese
- 10 sheets phyllo dough (14x9-inch size)
- ¼ cup olive oil

1. In a 6-qt. stockpot, cook sausage over medium heat 6-8 minutes or until no longer pink, breaking into crumbles. Remove with a slotted spoon; drain on paper towels. Add garlic, basil and oregano to skillet; cook and stir for 30 seconds. Add the chardonnay, stirring to loosen browned bits from pan. Cook for 1-2 minutes or until liquid is almost evaporated.

2. Stir in tomatoes, carrot, tomato paste, bay leaf, salt, garlic powder, paprika and sausage. Bring to a boil. Reduce heat; simmer, covered, for 20 minutes. Cool.

3. Preheat oven to 350°. Stir peas into sausage mixture. In a small bowl, combine the rice, green onions and parsley. In a greased 13x9-in. baking dish, layer half of the rice mixture, ½ cup Parmesan cheese, ¼ cup Romano cheese, sausage mixture, ½ cup Parmesan cheese and ¼ cup Romano cheese. Top with remaining rice and cheeses. Unroll phyllo dough. Layer sheets of phyllo in prepared pan, brushing each with oil. Keep the remaining phyllo covered with plastic wrap and a damp towel to prevent it from drying out.

4. Bake 35-40 minutes or until golden and crisp. Let stand 5 minutes before slicing.

TO MAKE AHEAD *Can be made a day in advance. Cover and refrigerate. Remove from the refrigerator 30 minutes before baking. Bake as directed.*

TURKEY STUFFING CASSEROLE

Looking for an all-in-one meal to serve at your next potluck? You'll love this recipe, which includes instruction on how to make an excellent stuffing and gravy. It's a go-to dish in our house and reminds me of one my grandmother used to make.

—SIGNA HUTCHISON WEISER, ID

PREP: 30 MIN. • **BAKE:** 45 MIN.
MAKES: 8 SERVINGS

- ½ cup butter, cubed
- 1 large onion, chopped
- 2 celery ribs, chopped
- 1½ teaspoons salt, divided
- ½ teaspoon rubbed sage
- ½ teaspoon poultry seasoning
- ¼ teaspoon pepper
- 8 cups cubed French bread (8 ounces)
- 3 cups cubed cooked turkey
- 2 large eggs
- 3 tablespoons butter
- 3 tablespoons all-purpose flour
- 1 can (14½ ounces) chicken broth
- ¾ cup water
- 2 tablespoons chopped fresh parsley

1. In a large skillet, melt butter over medium heat. Add onion and celery; cook and stir 4-5 minutes or until tender. Remove from heat; stir in 1 teaspoon salt, sage, poultry seasoning and pepper. In a large bowl, combine the bread cubes, turkey and onion mixture; toss gently to combine. Transfer mixture to a greased 13x9-in. baking dish.

2. In a small bowl, whisk eggs. In a large saucepan, melt butter over medium heat. Stir in the flour and remaining salt until smooth; gradually whisk in broth and water. Bring to a boil, stirring constantly. Cook and stir for 1-2 minutes or until thickened. Gradually whisk broth mixture into eggs; stir in parsley. Pour over turkey mixture. Refrigerate, covered, overnight.

3. Preheat oven to 350°. Remove casserole from refrigerator while oven heats. Bake, covered, 30 minutes. Uncover; bake 15-20 minutes longer or until lightly browned.

CHICKEN-CHILE RELLENO STRATA

This versatile recipe can be an entree, brunch or potluck dish. It's also one of the easiest meals to assemble on a busy night.

—KALLEE KRONG-MCCREERY ESCONDIDO, CA

PREP: 20 MIN. + CHILLING
BAKE: 35 MIN. + STANDING
MAKES: 10 SERVINGS

- 6 cups cubed French bread (about 6 ounces)
- 2 cans (4 ounces each) chopped green chilies
- 2 cups (8 ounces) shredded Monterey Jack cheese
- 2 cups shredded cooked chicken
- 12 large eggs
- 1½ cups 2% milk
- 2 teaspoons baking powder
- 1 teaspoon garlic salt
- 1 cup (4 ounces) shredded cheddar cheese
  Salsa

1. In a greased 13x9-in. baking dish, layer half of each of the following: bread cubes, chilies, Monterey Jack cheese and chicken. Repeat layers.
2. In a large bowl, whisk eggs, milk, baking powder and garlic salt until blended. Pour over layers. Sprinkle with cheddar cheese. Refrigerate, covered, overnight.
3. Preheat oven to 350°. Remove strata from refrigerator while oven heats. Bake, uncovered, 35-40 minutes or until puffed and golden at edges. Let stand 10 minutes before serving. Serve with salsa.

TOP TIP

Shredded Cheese

Shredded cheese always spoiled before I had the chance to use it all. My dad taught me to buy a 5-pound bag of shredded cheddar, put small amounts in resealable freezer bags and freeze individually. Now when I need cheese, I just thaw a bag. It tastes the same, and I no longer worry about wasting it.

—ROSE M. PLANO, TX

TEX-MEX BEAN BAKE WITH CORN BREAD TOPPING

I frequently cooked this dish when I was on the cross-country team in college. We loved this veggie-packed bake so much that I would have to make two! For a meaty version, substitute shredded chicken for half of the potato.

—SAMANTHA WESTVEER KENTWOOD, MI

PREP: 35 MIN. • **BAKE:** 25 MIN.
MAKES: 8 SERVINGS

- 1 tablespoon olive oil
- 1 large sweet potato, peeled and finely chopped
- 1 medium onion, coarsely chopped
- 1 small green pepper, coarsely chopped
- 1 small sweet red pepper, coarsely chopped
- 1 can (15 ounces) black beans, rinsed and drained
- 1 can (15 ounces) pinto beans, rinsed and drained
- 1 cup frozen corn
- 1 can (4 ounces) chopped green chilies
- ½ teaspoon salt
- ½ teaspoon ground cumin
- ½ cup vegetable broth
- 3 ounces cream cheese, softened

TOPPING

- 1 package (8½ ounces) corn bread/muffin mix
- 1 large egg
- ⅓ cup low-fat milk
- ⅓ cup solid-pack pumpkin

1. Preheat oven to 400°. In a large skillet, heat oil over medium-high heat. Add sweet potato, onion and peppers; cook and stir 5-7 minutes or until the potato is cooked halfway through.
2. Stir in beans, corn, chilies, salt and cumin; heat through. Stir in broth and cream cheese until blended. Transfer to a greased 13x9-in. baking dish.
3. In a large bowl, combine corn bread mix, egg, milk and pumpkin. Spoon over bean mixture. Bake, uncovered, 25-30 minutes or until a toothpick inserted into the topping portion comes out clean.

TO MAKE AHEAD *Can be made a day in advance. Prepare as directed, omitting topping. Cover and refrigerate overnight.*

Remove from refrigerator 30 minutes before baking. Prepare topping and bake as directed.

SHRIMP & CRAB CASSEROLE

This is a quick and easy recipe that is truly delicious. The melt-in-your-mouth flavors and different textures are comforting yet elegant. This is a great make-ahead dish, too. Just assemble, cover and refrigerate, than bake when ready.

—JAN BARTLEY EVERGREEN, NC

PREP: 25 MIN. • **BAKE:** 40 MIN.
MAKES: 8 SERVINGS

- 2 packages (8.8 ounces each) ready-to-serve long grain and wild rice
- ¼ cup butter, cubed
- 2 celery ribs, chopped
- 1 medium onion, chopped
- 3 tablespoons all-purpose flour
- 1½ cups half-and-half cream
- 1 teaspoon seafood seasoning
- ¾ teaspoon salt
- ½ teaspoon hot pepper sauce
- ¼ teaspoon pepper
- 1½ pounds uncooked shrimp (31-40 per pound), peeled and deveined
- 2 cans (6 ounces each) lump crabmeat, drained
- 1 cup (4 ounces) shredded Colby-Monterey Jack cheese

1. Preheat oven to 350°. Spread rice into a greased 13x9-in. baking dish. In a large skillet, heat butter over medium-high heat. Add celery and onion; cook and stir 6-8 minutes or until tender. Stir in flour until blended; gradually whisk in cream. Bring to a boil, stirring constantly; cook and stir 1-2 minutes or until thickened.
2. Stir in seafood seasoning, salt, pepper sauce and pepper. Fold in shrimp and crab. Spoon over rice. Sprinkle with cheese. Bake, covered, 40-45 minutes or until shrimp turn pink. Let stand 5 minutes.

TO MAKE AHEAD *Can be made a day in advance. Prepare recipe as directed, cooling sauce slightly before adding shrimp and crab. Cover and refrigerate overnight. Remove from the refrigerator 30 minutes before baking. Bake as directed.*

SHRIMP & CRAB
CASSEROLE

Grandparent's Weekend

The weekend is finally here...and so are the grandkids! That means there are games to play, forts to build, songs to sing and foods to eat. These precious days pass by in a flash, so make them count with kid-approved fare that will bring out the child in everyone.

Here you'll find yummy breakfast specialties, tantalizing appetizers, picnic delights, dreamy cupcakes and other sweet surprises. **Double the good times by inviting your little foodies into the kitchen.** They'll have a blast playing chef, and there's nothing better than savoring the scrumptious results together.

Make tasty meals and happy memories that you and your grandkids will cherish for a lifetime. It's a recipe for fun!

Campfire Pancakes with Peanut Maple Syrup (p. 203)
Fruit Kabobs with Cream Cheese Dip (p. 200) **Favorite Banana Split Smoothies** (p. 204)

PARMESAN SWEET POTATO WEDGES

AVOCADO-RANCH CHICKEN WRAPS

PARMESAN SWEET POTATO WEDGES

I make these sweet potato fries when I want to liven up our meal with a unique side. The Parmesan cheese is the perfect complement. They're also great dipped in garlic aioli.

—AMY GREEN CARROLLTON, TX

PREP: 15 MIN. • **BAKE:** 25 MIN.
MAKES: 6 SERVINGS

- 3 large sweet potatoes (about 2½-3 pounds)
- 4 large egg whites
- ¾ teaspoon salt
- ¼ teaspoon coarsely ground pepper
- 2 cups grated Parmesan cheese Prepared mustard, optional

1. Preheat oven to 425°. Peel and cut sweet potatoes lengthwise into ½-in. wedges. In a shallow bowl, whisk egg whites, salt and pepper until foamy. Place Parmesan cheese in another shallow bowl. Dip potatoes in egg white mixture, then in Parmesan cheese, patting to help coating adhere.
2. Transfer the potatoes to two foil-lined 15x10x1-in. baking pans coated with cooking spray. Roast 25-30 minutes or until potatoes are tender and cheese is golden brown. If desired, serve with mustard.

AVOCADO-RANCH CHICKEN WRAPS

My grandchildren love these wraps. I make them as a snack or a light meal.

—BETTY JO MORTENSEN LAYTON, UT

PREP: 20 MIN. • **BAKE:** 25 MIN. + COOLING
MAKES: 6 SERVINGS

- 1½ pounds boneless skinless chicken breast
- ¼ cup lime juice
- ½ teaspoon garlic salt
- ⅓ cup plus ¼ cup chopped fresh cilantro
- ½ medium onion, chopped
- 1½ cups cherry tomatoes, halved
- 1 medium ripe avocado, peeled and cubed
- ¾ cup shredded cheddar cheese
- 1 cup ranch salad dressing
- 6 flour tortillas (10 inches), warmed

1. Preheat the oven to 350°. Transfer chicken to an 8-in. square baking dish. Drizzle with lime juice. Sprinkle with garlic salt and ⅓ cup cilantro; top with onion. Bake, covered 25-30 minutes or until a thermometer reads 165°. Cool 10 minutes.
2. In a large bowl, combine tomatoes, avocado, cheese and the remaining cilantro. Chop chicken; add to bowl. Drizzle with ranch dressing; toss to coat. Spoon chicken mixture down center of each tortilla. Fold bottom of the tortilla over filling; fold both sides to close. If desired, secure with toothpicks.

HONEY-GLAZED SNAP PEAS & CARROTS

The farmers market is a great place to get all the ingredients called for in this hearty dish. I also include cucumber curls for some added flavor.

—CAROL WITCZAK TINLEY PARK, IL

START TO FINISH: 20 MIN. • **MAKES:** 6 SERVINGS

- 1½ pounds fresh sugar snap peas
- 4 medium carrots
- 3 tablespoons butter
- 3 tablespoons honey

1. Trim sugar snap peas. Cut each carrot crosswise into thirds; cut each lengthwise into quarters.
2. In a large nonstick skillet, heat the butter over medium heat. Add carrots; cook and stir for 4-6 minutes or until crisp-tender. Add snap peas; cook and stir just until the peas and carrots are tender. Add honey; cook and stir until vegetables are glazed.

TOP TIP

Kid-Approved Snacks

Satisfy little tummies and elicit big smiles with these hunger-busting snacks. They're super easy to make, so even the kids can help! For more ideas like these, visit **TasteofHome.com.**

- **S'more-like Sandwiches** Nutella and sliced bananas or mini marshmallows spread over graham crackers.
- **Popcorn Plus** A mix of popcorn, dried cherries and yogurt-covered raisins.
- **Fruit-Filled Cones** An ice cream cone filled with fruit and a dollop of yogurt.
- **Kid-Friendly Kabobs** Fruit skewers served with yogurt for dipping.

- **Peanut Butter Balls** Peanut butter and cornflake balls rolled in crushed graham crackers.
- **Pretzel Kabobs** Fruit and cheese on pretzel skewers.
- **PB&J in a New Way** Peanut butter and jelly spread in between toasted multigrain waffles cut into triangles.
- **Cinnamon Apple Snack** Sliced apple with cinnamon-sprinkled yogurt dip.
- **Chocolate Treat** Chocolate pudding with peanuts, graham crackers and mini marshmallows.
- **Apple Stackers** Chunky peanut butter sprinkled with M&M's or mini chocolate chips and spread between two slices of a cored apple.

**FRUIT KABOBS
WITH CREAM CHEESE DIP**

DEEP-FRIED MAC & CHEESE SHELLS

I created this recipe for my husband, who loves mac and cheese. He describes this recipe as "unbelievably delicious" because of the crispy deep-fried coating and the creamy richness on the inside.

—**SHIRLEY RICKIS** LADY LAKE, FL

PREP: 45 MIN. • **COOK:** 15 MIN.
MAKES: 20 APPETIZERS (2½ CUPS DIPPING SAUCE)

- 2 cups uncooked small pasta shells
- 20 uncooked jumbo pasta shells
- 2 tablespoons butter
- 1 package (16 ounces) process cheese (Velveeta), cubed
- 2 cups (8 ounces) shredded cheddar cheese
- 1 cup heavy whipping cream
- ¾ cup grated Parmesan cheese, divided
- 1¼ cups 2% milk, divided
- 2 large eggs
- 2 cups panko (Japanese) bread crumbs
- ½ cup all-purpose flour
  Oil for deep-fat frying

1. Cook pastas separately according to the package directions for al dente; drain. Meanwhile, in a large saucepan, melt butter over low heat. Add process cheese, cheddar cheese, cream and ¼ cup Parmesan cheese. Cook and stir over low heat until blended. Remove from heat.

2. In another large saucepan, combine the small pasta shells and half of the cheese mixture; set aside. For dipping sauce, stir 1 cup milk into remaining cheese mixture; keep warm.

3. In a shallow bowl, whisk the eggs with remaining milk. In another shallow bowl, mix bread crumbs with remaining Parmesan cheese. Place flour in a third shallow bowl. Fill each large shell with scant ¼ cup pasta mixture. Dip in flour to coat all sides; shake off excess. Dip in egg mixture, then in the bread crumb mixture, patting to help coating adhere.

4. In an electric skillet or deep fryer, heat the oil to 375°. Fry shells, a few at a time, 1-2 minutes on each side or until dark golden brown. Drain on paper towels. Serve with dipping sauce.

FRUIT KABOBS WITH CREAM CHEESE DIP

These fruity kabobs are so refreshing on a hot summer day. They're also a quick and easy side dish for bruches, barbecues and other family get-togethers.

—**KATHLEEN HEDGER** FAIRVIEW HEIGHTS, IL

START TO FINISH: 15 MIN.
MAKES: 6 KABOBS (1¼ CUPS DIP)

- 6 ounces cream cheese, softened
- ⅓ cup confectioners' sugar
- ⅓ cup sour cream
- ¼ teaspoon almond extract
- 12 fresh strawberries, trimmed
- 12 green grapes
- 12 fresh pineapple cubes (1 inch)

In a small bowl, beat cream cheese, confectioners' sugar, sour cream and extract until smooth. Refrigerate until serving. Alternately thread the strawberries, grapes and pineapple onto six wooden skewers. Serve with dip.

MAKE-AHEAD BROCCOLI SALAD

My son-in-law, a professional chef, shared this make-ahead recipe with me. The salad is an excellent medley of fresh vegetables and mixed dried fruit. I even make my own bacon bits to toss in the mix.

—**JANICE STOLTENOW** LEBANON, MO

PREP: 15 MIN. + CHILLING • **MAKES:** 8 SERVINGS

- 2 bunches broccoli, cut into bite-size pieces (about 6 cups)
- ½ cup mixed dried fruit, chopped
- ½ cup chopped sweet onion
- ¾ cup mayonnaise
- ¼ cup honey
  Dash salt
- 4 bacon strips, cooked and crumbled

In a large bowl, combine the broccoli, dried fruit and the onion. In a small bowl, mix mayonnaise, honey and salt. Pour over broccoli mixture; toss to coat. Refrigerate, covered, 2 hours or overnight. Just before serving, top with bacon.

DEEP-FRIED MAC
& CHEESE SHELLS

LOADED
TURKEY SLIDERS

LOADED TURKEY SLIDERS

What these sliders lack in size they make up for in flavor! They're great for little hands, and customize the toppings to suit kids' tastes. Serve as an appetizer or as a main entree paired with sweet potato fries and sliced fresh fruit.

—KATHY DEROUSIE PORT ANGELES, WA

START TO FINISH: 30 MIN. • **MAKES:** 6 SERVINGS

- 1 package (20 ounces) lean ground turkey
- ¼ cup finely chopped red onion
- 2 green onions, thinly sliced
- 1 large egg
- 2 teaspoons hamburger seasoning
- 1½ teaspoons Worcestershire sauce
- ½ teaspoon ground cumin
- 6 slices Muenster cheese, halved
- ½ cup mayonnaise
- ¼ cup Dijon mustard
- 12 potato dinner rolls, split
- 1½ cups shredded lettuce
- ½ medium red onion, thinly sliced

1. In a small bowl, combine turkey, red onion, green onions, egg, hamburger seasoning, Worcestershire sauce and cumin, mixing lightly but thoroughly. Shape into twelve ½-in.-thick patties. Grill burgers, covered, over medium heat or broil 4 in. from the heat for 3-4 minutes on each side or until a thermometer reads 165°.

2. Top with the cheese; grill, covered, 30-60 seconds longer or until cheese is melted. Mix mayonnaise and mustard; spread on roll tops. Layer roll bottoms with burger, lettuce and onion. Replace bun tops.

CAMPFIRE PANCAKES
WITH PEANUT MAPLE SYRUP

TOP TIP

Picnic Coolers

Whether you're camping at the lake, picnicking at the park or soaking up the sun at the beach, there's nothing more fun than dining alfresco. When transporting food from one place to another, load your car with two coolers—one for hot items and one for cold items. You will be amazed at how well the coolers keep your food at their appropriate temperatures.

CAMPFIRE PANCAKES WITH PEANUT MAPLE SYRUP

My family loves eating s'mores around the campfire when we vacation at the lake. Campfire pancakes are my tribute to those happy times.

—CHERYL SNAVELY HAGERSTOWN, MD

START TO FINISH: 20 MIN.
MAKES: 8 PANCAKES (¼ CUP SYRUP)

- 1 package (6½ ounces) chocolate chip muffin mix
- ⅔ cup 2% milk
- 1 large egg, lightly beaten
- ½ cup miniature marshmallows
- ¼ cup butterscotch chips
- ¼ cup maple syrup
- 1 tablespoon chunky peanut butter

1. In a large bowl, combine muffin mix, milk and egg; stir just until moistened. Fold in marshmallows and chips.

2. Lightly grease a griddle; heat over medium heat. Pour batter by ¼ cupfuls onto griddle. Cook until bubbles on top begin to pop and bottoms are brown. Turn; cook until second side is golden brown.

3. Meanwhile, microwave maple syrup and peanut butter in 10- to 20-second intervals until heated through. Serve with pancakes.

PEACH CRISP FREEZER POPS

My little ones love fruit crisps and popsicles. I created a healthy and delicious treat that combines the two. For a sweet addition, use cinnamon sticks in place of the popsicle sticks.

—CARMELL CHILDS FERRON, UT

PREP: 15 MIN. + FREEZING • **MAKES:** 8 SERVINGS

- 2 cartons (5.3 ounces each) fat-free vanilla Greek yogurt
- 2 teaspoons brown sugar
- ¼ teaspoon ground cinnamon
  Pinch ground nutmeg
- 1 cup granola without raisins
- 8 freezer pop molds or paper cups (3 ounces each) and wooden pop sticks
- 1 can (15 ounces) sliced peaches in extra-light syrup or juice, drained and chopped

In a small bowl, combine yogurt, brown sugar, cinnamon and nutmeg; fold in granola. Divide half of yogurt mixture among molds or paper cups. Top with with half of peaches; repeat layers. Top molds with holders. If using cups, top with foil and insert sticks through foil. Freeze until firm.

FAVORITE BANANA SPLIT SMOOTHIES

PEANUT BUTTER & JELLY CUPCAKES

My hubby's love for classic peanut butter and jelly inspired this cupcake recipe.
—**KELLY MCCREA** NORTH KINGSVILLE, OH

PREP: 45 MIN. • **BAKE:** 15 MIN. + COOLING
MAKES: 2 DOZEN

- 1 package yellow cake mix (regular size)
- 3 large eggs
- 1 cup 2% milk
- ½ cup butter, melted
- 1½ teaspoons vanilla extract
- 1 cup peanut butter chips

FROSTING

- 1½ cups butter, softened
- 1½ teaspoons vanilla extract
- 6 cups confectioners' sugar
- 2 to 3 tablespoons heavy whipping cream
- ⅓ cup strawberry spreadable fruit
- ½ cup peanut butter
  Additional peanut butter chips

1. Preheat the oven to 350°. Line 24 muffin cups with paper liners. In a large bowl, combine cake mix, eggs, milk, butter and vanilla; beat on low speed 30 seconds. Beat on medium 2 minutes. Stir in peanut butter chips. Fill prepared cups three-fourths full. Bake 15-18 minutes or until a toothpick inserted in center comes out clean. Cool in pans 10 minutes; remove to wire racks to cool completely.
2. In a large bowl, beat butter and the vanilla until blended. Beat in the confectioners' sugar alternately with enough cream to reach a spreading consistency. Beat on medium-high for 5 minutes until fluffy. Place 1½ cups of the frosting in a small bowl; stir in the spreadable fruit. Add peanut butter to remaining frosting; beat until blended.
3. Cut a small hole in the tip of a pastry bag or in a corner of a food-safe plastic bag; insert a #5 round pastry tip. Transfer strawberry frosting to bag. With a metal or wooden skewer, poke a hole through bottom of paper liner. Insert tip through hole; pipe some of strawberry filling into cupcakes. Using another pastry bag and a #12 round pastry tip, pipe peanut butter frosting over cupcakes. Pipe the remaining strawberry frosting over tops; sprinkle with additional chips.

Banana Basics

When buying bananas, look for those that are plump and evenly yellow-colored. Green bananas are under-ripe, while a flecking of brown spots indicates ripeness. If bananas are too green, place in a paper bag until ripe. Adding an apple to the bag will speed the process. Store ripe bananas at room temperature. To prevent bruises, a banana hook or hanger is a great economical investment. For longer storage, place ripe bananas in a tightly sealed plastic bag and refrigerate. The peel will become brown but the flesh will remain unchanged. One pound of bananas equals about three medium whole bananas or 1⅓ cups mashed.

FAVORITE BANANA SPLIT SMOOTHIES

I try to get lots of fruits and veggies into our diets. A smoothie is a great way to load up on nutrients. Add a maraschino cherry on top for extra fun.
—**TIFFANY VAN ZEE** PELLA, IA

START TO FINISH: 10 MIN. • **MAKES:** 4 SERVINGS

- 2 medium bananas, peeled and quartered
- 1 can (8 ounces) unsweetened crushed pineapple
- 1 cup (8 ounces) vanilla yogurt
- 1 cup crushed ice
- ½ cup orange juice

Place all ingredients in a blender; cover and process until blended. Serve smoothies immediately.

**PEANUT BUTTER &
JELLY CUPCAKES**

Baby Gender Reveal Party

Chubby cheeks, teeny-tiny toes, that first precious coo and big gummy smile. Talk about love at first sight. Mama-to-be is aglow with happiness, and everyone's sharing in the excitement and anticipation. The big question is: **Is it a boy or a girl?**

A tender, fluffy cake and sugar-dusted cookies—tinted pink or blue inside—are two deliciously fun ways to announce if the bundle of joy will be a handsome lad or a pretty little lady. Get inspired with these sweet creations or turn to page 213 for more ideas for the big reveal.

To round out the meal, **treat guests to a menu filled with tasty party favorites:** chicken salad sandwiches, a colorful fruit tart, bacon-wrapped asparagus, chunky layered hummus dip and more.

Gender Reveal Cake (p. 214)

**STRAWBERRY
MIMOSAS**

STRAWBERRY MIMOSAS

Here's a tasty twist on the classic mimosa. To make this beverage friendly for kids or mamas-to-be, substitute the champagne for lemon-lime soda or ginger ale.
—**KELLY MAXWELL** PLAINFIELD, IL

START TO FINISH: 15 MIN.
MAKES: 12 SERVINGS (1 CUP EACH)

- **7 cups sliced fresh strawberries**
- **3 cups orange juice**
- **4½ cups champagne, chilled**
- **GARNISHES**
  - **Fresh strawberries and orange slices, optional**

Place half of the strawberries and orange juice in a blender; cover and process until smooth. Press through a fine mesh strainer. Repeat with remaining strawberries and orange juice. Pour a scant ⅔ cup strawberry mixture into each champagne flute or wine glass. Top with about ⅓ cup champagne. If desired, serve with a strawberry and an orange slice.

BACON-WRAPPED GRILLED ASPARAGUS

I tried this at a friend's house and modified the recipe to appeal to my family's tastes. I recommend cooking it outside on the grill. It's terrific for any celebration.
—**KARYL TOBEL** HELENA, MT

PREP: 15 MIN. • **GRILL:** 20 MIN.
MAKES: 16 APPETIZERS

- **2 tablespoons soy sauce**
- **2 tablespoons olive oil**
- **1 garlic clove, minced**
- **1 pound bacon strips**
- **16 fresh asparagus spears, trimmed**

In a small bowl, mix soy sauce, oil and garlic. Wrap a bacon strip around each asparagus spear. Thread eight spears onto two parallel soaked wooden skewers. Repeat with the remaining asparagus. Grill, covered, over medium-low heat 18-20 minutes or until the bacon is crisp, turning occasionally. Brush spears with soy sauce mixture.

SNOWBALL SURPRISE COOKIES

SNOWBALL SURPRISE COOKIES

Keep the guests guessing until the big cake reveal! Use candy coating disks to tint the inside of these tender cookies pink and blue. Because these disks come in a variety of colors, you also can make the cookies to match any holiday or theme.
—**JAN WHITWORTH** ROEBUCK, SC

PREP: 25 MIN. + CHILLING • **BAKE:** 15 MIN./BATCH
MAKES: ABOUT 3 DOZEN

- **1 cup butter, softened**
- **1½ cups confectioners' sugar, divided**
- **2 teaspoons vanilla extract**
- **2 cups all-purpose flour**
- **¼ teaspoon salt**
- **⅓ cup each finely chopped pecans, walnuts and almonds, toasted**
- **39 pink or blue candy coating disks**

1. In a large bowl, cream butter, ½ cup confectioners' sugar and vanilla until light and fluffy. In another bowl, whisk flour and salt; gradually beat into creamed mixture. Stir in nuts. Refrigerate 1 hour or until firm.

2. Preheat oven to 350°. Shape dough into 1-in. balls; place 1-in. apart on ungreased baking sheets. Insert a candy disk into the center of each cookie, reshaping dough into a ball and covering disk completely.

3. Bake for 12-15 minutes or until bottoms are light brown. Cool on pans 2 minutes. Place the remaining confectioners' sugar in a shallow bowl. Roll warm cookies in confectioners' sugar. Cool cookies on wire racks. Reroll cookies in sugar.

CRUNCHY CHICKEN SALAD CROISSANTS

Folks have come to expect these quick and delicious sandwiches when I host showers or parties. Feel free to add grapes or pineapple to the filling.
—ANGELA LIVELY CONROE, TX

START TO FINISH: 20 MIN. • **MAKES:** 1 DOZEN

- 2½ cups cubed cooked chicken
- 2 celery ribs, finely chopped
- ½ cup sliced almonds, toasted
- ¾ cup mayonnaise
- ½ teaspoon salt
- ¼ teaspoon coarsely ground pepper
- ¼ cup heavy whipping cream
- 1 tablespoon sugar
- 12 miniature croissants, split
  Bibb lettuce leaves, optional

1. In a large bowl, combine chicken, celery and almonds. In a small bowl, mix mayonnaise, salt and pepper. In another bowl, beat cream until it begins to thicken. Add sugar; beat until stiff peaks form. Fold into mayonnaise mixture. Pour over chicken mixture; toss to coat.
2. If desired, line croissant bottoms with lettuce leaves; top each with ⅓ cup chicken salad. Replace tops.

LIME-CILANTRO SHRIMP SKEWERS

My friend gave me this grill-friendly recipe. The combination of lime, cilantro and soy sauce gives these appetizers a memorable taste reminiscent of tropical cuisine. To make it a main dish, serve the skewers with rice or couscous.
—THERESA DIBERT CYNTHIANA, KY

PREP: 10 MIN. + MARINATING • **GRILL:** 10 MIN.
MAKES: 1 DOZEN

- ⅓ cup lime juice
- 3 tablespoons minced fresh cilantro
- 2 tablespoons soy sauce
- 3 garlic cloves, minced
- 2 teaspoons olive oil
- 1¼ pounds uncooked shrimp (26-30 per pound), peeled and deveined
- 1 cup soaked mesquite wood chips, optional

1. In a large bowl, whisk the first five ingredients until blended. Add shrimp; toss to coat. Refrigerate, covered, for 30 minutes.
2. If desired, add wood chips to grill according to manufacturer directions. Moisten a paper towel with cooking oil; using long-handled tongs, rub on grill rack to coat lightly. Drain shrimp, discarding the marinade. On each of 12 soaked wooden appetizer skewers, thread shrimp.
3. Grill, covered, over medium heat 3-4 minutes per side or until shrimp turn pink, turning occasionally.

GRILLED FRUIT PHYLLO TART

This tart was a hit at my friend's baby shower. It reminds me of a fruit salad that my mother used to make with cream cheese and whipped topping. Everyone loves the flaky crust, and the bright colors make it a pretty addition to any spread.
—LAURA MCALLISTER MORGANTON, NC

PREP: 30 MIN. • **GRILL:** 10 MIN.
MAKES: 12 SERVINGS

- 3 tablespoons butter, melted
- 4 teaspoons canola oil
- 8 sheets phyllo dough (14x9-inch size)
- 1 large lemon
- 3 medium peaches, peeled and halved
- 2 cups large fresh strawberries, stems removed
- 4 slices fresh pineapple (½ inch thick)
- ⅓ cup packed brown sugar
- ½ teaspoon salt
- ½ cup heavy whipping cream
- 1 package (8 ounces) cream cheese, softened
- ⅓ cup confectioners' sugar
- 2 tablespoons chopped fresh mint

1. Preheat oven to 400°. In a small bowl, mix the butter and oil. Brush a 15x10x1-in. baking pan with some of the butter mixture. Place one sheet of phyllo dough into prepared pan; brush with butter mixture. Layer with seven additional phyllo sheets, brushing each layer. (Keep remaining phyllo covered with plastic wrap and a damp towel to prevent it from drying out.) Bake 5-7 minutes or until golden brown (phyllo will puff up during baking). Cool completely.
2. Finely grate enough peel from lemon to measure 1 tablespoon. Cut the lemon crosswise in half; squeeze juice from lemon. In a large bowl, toss peaches, strawberries, pineapple, brown sugar, salt, lemon peel and juice. Remove strawberries; thread onto 3 metal or soaked wooden skewers.
3. Moisten a paper towel with cooking oil; using long-handled tongs, rub on grill rack to coat lightly. Place fruit on grill rack. Grill, covered, over medium heat 8-10 minutes for pineapple slices and peaches; 4-5 minutes for strawberries or until fruit is tender, turning once. Remove and set aside.
4. In a small bowl, beat cream until soft peaks form. In another bowl, beat cream cheese and confectioners' sugar until smooth. Fold in whipped cream. Spread over phyllo crust. Slice grilled fruit; arrange over filling. Sprinkle with mint; cut into pieces.

TOP TIP

Phyllo Facts

Phyllo (pronounced FEE-lo) is a tissue-thin pastry that's made by gently stretching the dough into thin fragile sheets. It can be layered, shaped and baked in a variety of sweet and savory ways. Because phyllo is thin, fragile and tears easily, working on a smooth dry surface and handling it quickly is key. Follow the manufacturer's instructions for thawing phyllo in the unopened package. Count out the number of phyllo sheets required for your recipe, place them on a smooth dry surface and immediately cover with plastic wrap and a damp towel. Gently pull sheets from the stack as you need them, keeping the remaining ones covered until needed.

**GRILLED FRUIT
PHYLLO TART**

LAYERED HUMMUS DIP

ARTICHOKE CRESCENT APPETIZERS

This colorful appetizer is sure to please guests at any affair. My family loves it both warm and cold.

—**MARY ANN DELL** PHOENIXVILLE, PA

PREP: 20 MIN. • **BAKE:** 15 MIN.

- 1 tube (8 ounces) refrigerated crescent rolls
- 2 tablespoons grated Parmesan cheese
- 2 packages (3 ounces each) cream cheese, softened
- ½ cup sour cream
- 1 large egg
- ½ teaspoon dill weed
- ¼ teaspoon seasoned salt
- 1 can (14 ounces) water-packed artichoke hearts, rinsed, drained and chopped
- ⅓ cup thinly chopped green onions
- 1 jar (2 ounces) diced pimientos, drained

1. Unroll crescent dough and press onto the bottom and ½ in. up the sides of an ungreased 13x9-in. baking dish; seal seams and perforations. Sprinkle with Parmesan cheese. Bake at 375° for 8-10 minutes or until lightly browned.

2. Meanwhile, in a small bowl, beat the cream cheese, sour cream and egg until smooth. Stir in dill and seasoned salt. Spread over crust. Sprinkle with artichokes, green onions and pimientos.

3. Bake for 15-20 minutes or until edges are golden brown. Cut into squares.

LAYERED HUMMUS DIP

My love for Greece inspired this fast-to-fix Mediterranean dip. It's great for parties and is a delicious way to include garden-fresh veggies on your menu.

—**CHERYL SNAVELY** HAGERSTOWN, MD

PREP: 15 MIN. • **MAKES:** 12 SERVINGS

- 1 carton (10 ounces) hummus
- ¼ cup finely chopped red onion
- ½ cup Greek olives, chopped
- 2 medium tomatoes, seeded and chopped
- 1 large English cucumber, chopped
- 1 cup (4 ounces) crumbled feta cheese
  Baked pita chips

Spread hummus into a shallow 10-in. round dish. Layer with onion, olives, tomatoes, cucumber and cheese. Refrigerate until serving. Serve with pita chips.

BUBBLY CITRUS PUNCH

Puckery lemonade and limeade combined with sweet pineapple juice give this fruity drink its bubbly goodness. It's easy to make and great for large get-togethers.

—**JACKIE FLOOD** GENESEO, NY

START TO FINISH: 15 MIN.
MAKES: 30 SERVINGS (¾ CUP EACH)

- 1 can (46 ounces) unsweetened pineapple juice, chilled
- 2 cans (12 ounces each) frozen lemonade concentrate, thawed
- 1 can (12 ounces) frozen limeade concentrate, thawed
- 4½ cups cold water
- 2 liters lemon-lime soda, chilled

In a punch bowl, mix pineapple juice, concentrates and water. Stir in soda. Serve immediately.

TOP TIP

Creative Gender Reveal Ideas

Try these ideas to share the exciting news of the baby's gender with friends and family. It's even more fun if the parents-to-be are finding out for the first time, too!

THE SECRET'S IN THE CUPCAKE

- Gender reveal cakes are all the rage, so why not try the same concept with cupcakes?

BALLOON LAUNCH

- Place several pink or blue balloons in a large box. When the parents-to-be open the box, the balloons will float out, revealing a boy or a girl.

CONFETTI POPPERS

- Make homemade confetti poppers using toilet paper tubes and a few other simple supplies. Fill the insides of the poppers with gender-hued confetti. When it's time to find out, have guests shoot the poppers into the air. Google "DIY Confetti Popper" to find easy tutorials.

SILLY STRING

- Cover the outsides of cans filled with pink or blue silly string with white or yellow non-transparent paper. When it's time for the big reveal, have guests shake and spray to see baby's gender.

PINATA

- Fill a pinata with pink or blue candies. When it's broken open and the loot spills out, baby's sex is a secret no more!

BABY BLOCKS

- Decorate the outsides of 2-in. white, cube-shaped boxes with letters to resemble blocks. Fill the insides with either pink or blue candies. Pass out when it's time for the big reveal or send them home with guests as a party favor.

GENDER REVEAL CAKE

GENDER REVEAL CAKE

Is it a boy or a girl? Create the perfect reveal with this scrumptious cake tinted with blue or pink frosting on the inside.
—**HEATHER CHAMBERS** LARGO, FL

PREP: 45 MIN. • **BAKE:** 20 MIN. + COOLING
MAKES: 12 SERVINGS

- ½ cup butter, softened
- 1¼ cups sugar
- 3 large eggs
- 1 teaspoon vanilla extract
- 2 cups all-purpose flour
- 2 teaspoons baking powder
- 1 teaspoon salt
- 1 cup 2% milk

FROSTING
- 1 package (8 ounces) cream cheese, softened
- 1 cup confectioners' sugar
- 2 teaspoons vanilla extract
- 2 cups heavy whipping cream
  Blue and pink paste food coloring

1. Preheat oven to 350°. Line bottoms of two greased 8-in. round baking pans with parchment paper; grease and flour paper.
2. In a large bowl, cream butter and sugar until light and fluffy. Add eggs, one at a time, beating well after each addition. Beat in vanilla. In another bowl, whisk flour, baking powder and salt; add to creamed mixture alternately with milk, beating well after each addition.
3. Transfer to prepared pans. Bake 20-25 minutes or until a toothpick inserted in the center comes out clean. Cool in pans 10 minutes before removing to wire racks; remove paper. Cool completely.
4. Place a large bowl and beaters in freezer until cold, about 15 minutes. In chilled bowl, beat cream cheese, confectioners' sugar and vanilla until smooth. Gradually beat in cream until firm peaks form. Based on baby's gender, tint 1¼ cups blue (or pink), ¼ cup pink (or blue) and leave the remaining frosting white.
5. Place one cake layer on a serving plate. Pipe a circle of white frosting around top edge of layer. Spread 1 cup blue or pink frosting inside white frosting. Top with remaining cake layer. Frost top and sides with white frosting. Using a #8 tip and white frosting, pipe pearls around top and bottom edge of cake. Using a #12 tip, pipe blue and pink dots over cake. With a #4 tip and with pink (or blue) frosting, add "It's a..." to top of cake. Refrigerate until serving.

GENDER REVEAL GUESSING GAME

Frame a poem and decorate wood clothespins with ribbon to create a fun "Is it a Boy or a Girl?" guessing game. Guests will select either a pink or blue clothespin and then clip it to their collar or sleeve to reveal their prediction.

MATERIALS
- Standard-size wood spring clothespins (estimate at least two clothespins per guest)
- Grosgrain ribbon of the same width as clothespins—pastel blue and pastel pink
- 8½x11-in. sheet of white card stock
- White 8x10 photo frame
- Craft glue
- Small basket to hold clothespins
- Computer with printer

DIRECTIONS
1. Cut one approximately 4½-in. length of pink ribbon for each of half of the clothespins. Repeat with blue ribbon for the remaining half of the clothespins.
2. Glue a piece of ribbon to one outer side of each clothespin, wrapping the excess ribbon over the ends of clothespin. Let dry.
3. Use computer and printer to type and print the poem shown in photo onto white card stock, centering the poem on the page. Trim card stock as needed so it will fit inside the photo frame, keeping the poem centered.
4. Cut two pieces of pink ribbon so that the length matches the width of card stock. Repeat with blue ribbon.
5. Glue one blue and one pink ribbon across the card stock, positioning them just above the poem. In the same way, glue remaining two ribbons just below the poem. Let dry.
6. Place poem in frame. Place clothespins in basket.
NOTE *To make sure ribbon is secure, use glue to attach it to clothespins even if it has an adhesive backing.*

Baby Boy
or
Baby Girl?

Go ahead,
give it a whirl.

Take a guess,
wear it with zeal...

In due time,
the big reveal!

Welcome Home, Soldier

A great American summer is deserving of a great American picnic. This year, go all out with **a star-spangled feast to welcome home a soldier or honor a veteran.** There's no better way to celebrate life, liberty, the pursuit of happiness—and our love of food!—than with a heartfelt salute to these brave men and women.

Plan your menu around smokin' hot mains like fall-off-the-bone ribs and finger-licking chicken. Don't forget tempting apps, delish salads and sides, and sweet treats. And our firecracker of a napkin idea on page 225 will make your patriotic party go down in family history.

Come on over, wave a flag and grab a plate. It's pure yum when it's piled high with love, gratitude and, of course, great food!

Patriotic Cookie & Cream Cupcakes (p. 224) **Strawberry Watermelon Lemonade** (p. 219)

**SWEET & TANGY
BARBECUED CHICKEN**

SWEET & TANGY BARBECUED CHICKEN

My family loves to grill in the summer, and this is our go-to recipe when hosting friends and family. Every bite is full of flavor, and the chicken is always tender and juicy.

—**JOY YURK** GRAFTON, WI

PREP: 15 MIN. + MARINATING • **GRILL:** 30 MIN.
MAKES: 8 SERVINGS

- 2½ cups white wine
- 2 medium onions, finely chopped (1½ cups)
- ½ cup lemon juice
- 10 garlic cloves, minced
- 16 chicken drumsticks
- 3 bay leaves
- 1 can (15 ounces) tomato puree
- ¼ cup honey
- 1 tablespoon molasses
- 1 teaspoon salt
- ½ teaspoon dried thyme
- ¼ teaspoon cayenne pepper
- ¼ teaspoon pepper
- 2 tablespoons white vinegar

1. For marinade, in a large bowl, combine wine, onions, lemon juice and garlic. Pour 2 cups marinade into a large resealable plastic bag. Add the chicken; seal bag and turn to coat. Refrigerate 4 hours or overnight. Add bay leaves to remaining marinade; cover and refrigerate.
2. Meanwhile, in a large saucepan, combine the tomato puree, honey, molasses, salt, thyme, cayenne, pepper and remaining marinade. Bring to a boil. Reduce heat; simmer, uncovered, for 35-40 minutes or until liquid is reduced by half. Remove from heat. Remove bay leaves; stir in vinegar. Reserve 1 cup sauce for serving; keep warm.
3. Drain the chicken, discarding the marinade in bag. Grill chicken, covered, on an oiled rack over indirect medium heat 15 minutes. Turn; grill 15-20 minutes longer or until a thermometer reads 170°-175°, brushing chicken occasionally with remaining sauce. Serve chicken with reserved sauce.

CAJUN SNACK MIX

Pep up any party with this crunchy, well-seasoned blend of cereal, cheese crackers, pretzels and peanuts. My husband likes his food with a touch of Louisiana spice, so I add Cajun seasoning to give it that extra kick.

—**JAMIE CHAMPAGNE** SOUTHSIDE, AL

START TO FINISH: 20 MIN. • **MAKES:** 2½ QUARTS

- 2 cups Rice Chex
- 2 cups Corn Chex
- 1 cup Wheat Chex
- 1 cup Cheerios
- 2 cups cheddar-flavored snack crackers
- 1 cup miniature cheddar cheese fish-shaped crackers
- 1 cup oyster crackers
- 1 cup corn chips
- 1 cup salted peanuts
- ½ cup butter, cubed
- 3 tablespoons Worcestershire sauce
- 4 teaspoons Cajun seasoning
- 1 teaspoon onion powder
- 1 teaspoon garlic pepper blend

1. In a large microwave-safe bowl, combine cereals, crackers, corn chips and peanuts. In a microwave, melt butter; stir until smooth. Whisk in the Worcestershire sauce, Cajun seasoning, onion powder and garlic pepper blend. Pour over the cereal mixture; toss to coat.
2. Microwave on high 6 minutes, stirring twice. Spread onto baking sheets to cool. Store in an airtight container.

STRAWBERRY WATERMELON LEMONADE

The nutrition department at my local hospital inspired me to create this refreshing summer sipper. I slightly tweaked the recipe to create this drink full of sweet-tart flavor.

—**DAWN E. LOWENSTEIN** HUNTINGDON VALLEY, PA

START TO FINISH: 20 MIN.
MAKES: 12 SERVINGS (1 CUP EACH)

- ¼ cup sugar
- 2 cups boiling water
- ½ pound fresh strawberries, hulled and quartered (about 2 cups)
- 12 cups cubed watermelon (about 1 medium)
- 1 can (12 ounces) frozen lemonade concentrate, thawed
- 3 tablespoons lemon juice
  Ice cubes

Dissolve sugar in boiling water. Place the strawberries and watermelon in a blender in batches; cover and process until blended. Pour blended fruit though a fine mesh strainer; transfer to a large pitcher. Stir in lemonade concentrate, lemon juice and sugar water. Serve over ice.

TOP TIP

Add a Fancy Touch

Add a special touch to lemonade, iced tea or other cold beverages by dipping the rims of the drinking glasses in a little fresh lemon juice. Then twist the glasses slightly in a saucer of sugar. Set trays of glasses in the refrigerator until ready to serve.
—**CHERYL M.** FORT COLLINS, CO

**BACON
HORSERADISH SPREAD**

COCONUT COLESLAW

I guarantee you'll get requests to bring a big batch of this cool, crisp coleslaw to picnics and barbecues.

—**JONI HILTON** ROCKLIN, CA

START TO FINISH: 20 MIN.
MAKES: 16 SERVINGS (¾ CUP EACH)

- 1 **medium head cabbage (about 2 pounds), cut into thin strips**
- 1 **cup dried cranberries**
- 1 **cup flaked coconut**
- ⅓ **cup minced fresh cilantro**
- ¼ **cup sugar**
- 1 **cup coconut milk**
- 1 **cup mayonnaise**
- ½ **cup cider vinegar**
- ½ **cup plain yogurt**
- ½ **teaspoon salt**
- ¼ **teaspoon pepper**

In a bowl, toss cabbage, cranberries, coconut, cilantro and sugar. In a small bowl, mix remaining ingredients. Pour over cabbage mixture; toss to coat. Refrigerate until serving.

HONEY-MELON SALAD WITH BASIL

Loaded with juicy cantaloupe and honeydew melon and glazed with a sweet honey dressing, this salad will be gone in minutes. Watermelon is a great addition.

—**KHURSHID SHAIK** OMAHA, NE

PREP/TOTAL: 20 MIN.
MAKES: 12 SERVINGS (1 CUP EACH)

- 6 **cups cubed cantaloupe (about 1 medium)**
- 6 **cups cubed honeydew melon (about 1 medium)**
- ¼ **cup honey**
- 3 **tablespoons lemon juice**
- ½ **teaspoon paprika**
- ¼ **teaspoon salt**
- ¼ **teaspoon coarsely ground pepper**
- ¼ **cup minced fresh basil or mint**
- ¾ **cup dried cranberries, optional**

In a large bowl, combine cantaloupe and honeydew melon. Refrigerate, covered, until serving. In a small bowl, whisk honey, lemon juice, paprika, salt and pepper. Pour over melons just before serving; toss to coat. Stir in basil and, if desired, dried cranberries. Serve with a slotted spoon.

BACON HORSERADISH SPREAD

This spread is a great choice for any occasion because it's loaded with flavor and comes together in a snap. Start with 1 or 2 teaspoons of horseradish and add more to suit your taste.

—**TERRI PETERSON** SPRING VALLEY, IL

PREP: 15 MIN. + CHILLING • **MAKES:** 2½ CUPS

- 1 **package (8 ounces) cream cheese, softened**
- ½ **cup half-and-half cream**
- 8 **bacon strips, cooked and finely crumbled**
- 1 **cup (4 ounces) finely shredded cheddar cheese**
- 2 **tablespoons prepared horseradish**
- 1 **green onion, finely chopped**
- 1 **teaspoon lemon juice**
- 1 **teaspoon Worcestershire sauce**
- ¼ **teaspoon pepper**
   Assorted crackers, potato chips and baby carrots

In a small bowl, beat the cream cheese and cream until smooth. Beat in bacon, cheddar cheese, horseradish, green onion, lemon juice, Worcestershire sauce and pepper. Refrigerate, covered, 2 hours. Serve with dippers.

SLOW-COOKED BAKED BEANS

My friend suggested this recipe when I needed a new dish to bring to a barbecue. It was an incredible success, and I've been making it ever since.

—**JODI CAPLE** CORTEZ, CO

PREP: 25 MIN. + SOAKING • **COOK:** 9 HOURS
MAKES: 8 SERVINGS

- 1 **pound dried navy beans**
- 2 **cups water**
- ½ **cup dark molasses**
- 5 **slices salt pork belly (about 3 ounces), cut into ½-inch pieces**
- 1 **small onion, finely chopped**
- 3 **tablespoons brown sugar**
- 2 **garlic cloves, minced**
- 1 **teaspoon ground ginger**
- ½ **teaspoon salt**
- ½ **teaspoon ground mustard**
- ½ **teaspoon pepper**

1. Rinse and sort beans; soak according to package directions.
2. Drain and rinse beans, discarding liquid. Transfer beans to a 4-qt. slow cooker. Stir in remaining ingredients. Cook, covered, on low 9-11 hours or until beans are tender.

**HONEY-MELON
SALAD WITH BASIL**

PEACH-CHIPOTLE
BABY BACK RIBS

PEACH-CHIPOTLE BABY BACK RIBS

My son and I collaborated in the kitchen one day to put our own unique twist on baby back ribs. We added a sweet peachy glaze and a little heat with chipotle peppers. It was a great bonding experience, and now we have a keeper recipe for fall-off-the-bone ribs.

—REBECCA SUASO WEAVERVILLE, NC

PREP: 15 MIN. • **BAKE:** 2¾ HOURS
MAKES: 8 SERVINGS (2 CUPS SAUCE)

- 3 **tablespoons brown sugar**
- 2 **tablespoons kosher salt**
- 1 **teaspoon pepper**
- ½ **teaspoon cayenne pepper**
- 8 **pounds pork baby back ribs (about 3 racks)**
- 6 **medium peaches, peeled and sliced**
- 2 **tablespoons olive oil**
- 2 **large sweet onions, finely chopped**
- ⅔ **cup packed brown sugar**
- 4 **finely chopped chipotle peppers in adobo sauce plus 2 tablespoons sauce**
- 3 **tablespoons white vinegar**
- 4 **teaspoons ground mustard**

1. Preheat the oven to 325°. In a bowl, combine brown sugar, salt, pepper and cayenne. If necessary, remove the thin membrane from back ribs; discard. Rub brown sugar mixture over ribs. Transfer to large roasting pans. Add 1 in. hot water. Bake, covered, for 2½-3 hours or until ribs are tender.
2. Meanwhile, place peaches in a blender; cover and process until smooth. In a large saucepan, heat oil over medium heat. Add onions; cook and stir 12-15 minutes or until tender. Add brown sugar, peppers, adobo sauce, vinegar, mustard and peach puree; bring to a boil. Reduce heat; simmer, uncovered, 25-30 minutes or until slightly thickened.
3. Drain ribs. Moisten a paper towel with cooking oil; using long-handled tongs, rub on grill rack to coat lightly. Grill ribs, pork side down, covered, over medium heat 5-7 minutes or until browned. Turn ribs: brush with 2 cups sauce. Cook 5-7 minutes longer or until sauce is thickened. Serve with the remaining sauce.

GREEN BEAN-CHERRY TOMATO SALAD

BLUE CHEESE POTATO SALAD

Try my tasty blue cheese spin on classic potato salad. You can easily double the recipe for large picnics or potlucks.

—JENNIFER LEWIS BRITTON, MI

PREP: 30 MIN. + STANDING
COOK: 20 MIN. + CHILLING • **MAKES:** 10 SERVINGS

- 2½ **pounds red potatoes (about 7 medium), cut into ¾-inch pieces**
- 2 **tablespoons red wine vinegar**
- 1½ **teaspoons hot pepper sauce**
- ½ **teaspoon salt**
- ¼ **teaspoon coarsely ground pepper**
- 2 **hard-cooked large eggs, finely chopped**
- ¼ **cup finely chopped red onion**
- ¼ **cup finely chopped celery**
- ¼ **cup chopped sweet pickles**
- 2 **green onions, finely chopped**
- ¼ **cup sour cream**
- ¼ **cup mayonnaise**
- ¼ **cup blue cheese salad dressing**
- ½ **teaspoon celery seed**

1. Place potatoes in a 6-qt. stockpot; add water to cover. Bring to a boil. Reduce heat; cook, uncovered, for 7-10 minutes or just until tender. Drain; transfer to a large bowl.
2. Add vinegar, pepper sauce, salt and pepper to hot potatoes; let stand 30 minutes at room temperature, stirring gently halfway through standing. Add eggs, onion, celery, pickles and green onions. In a small bowl, mix remaining ingredients; add to potato mixture. Toss gently. Serve immediately or refrigerate until cold.

GREEN BEAN-CHERRY TOMATO SALAD

My grandmother made a cold green bean salad with potatoes for every family barbecue. Now I bring my own version of the recipe to parties. With added color and taste from the cherry tomatoes, this classic favorite is even better.

—ANGELA LEMOINE HOWELL, NJ

PREP: 25 MIN. • **COOK:** 10 MIN.
MAKES: 12 SERVINGS

- 1½ **pounds fresh green beans, trimmed**
- 1 **pint cherry tomatoes, halved**
- 1 **small red onion, halved and thinly sliced**
- 3 **tablespoons red wine vinegar**
- 1½ **teaspoons sugar**
- ¾ **teaspoon dried oregano**
- ¾ **teaspoon salt**
- ¼ **teaspoon garlic powder**
- ¼ **teaspoon pepper**
- ¼ **cup olive oil**

1. In a 6-qt. stockpot, bring 6 cups water to a boil. Add beans in batches; cook, uncovered, 2-3 minutes or just until crisp-tender. Remove beans and immediately drop into ice water. Drain and pat dry.
2. Transfer beans to a large bowl. Add tomatoes and onion; toss to combine. In a small bowl, whisk the vinegar, sugar, oregano, salt, garlic powder and pepper. Gradually whisk in oil until blended. Pour over bean mixture; toss to coat.

PATRIOTIC COOKIE & CREAM CUPCAKES

PATRIOTIC COOKIE & CREAM CUPCAKES

Bring on the red, white and blue with this creative cupcake cake perfect for the Fourth of July, Memorial Day or any favorite occasion. With some delicious and colorful frosting and a careful arrangement, your sweet display will be a patriotic nod to our great American flag.

—REBECCA WETHERBEE MARION, OH

PREP: 40 MIN. • **BAKE:** 20 MIN. + COOLING
MAKES: 2 DOZEN

- ½ cup butter, softened
- 1⅔ cups sugar
- 3 large egg whites
- 2 teaspoons vanilla extract
- 2¼ cups all-purpose flour
- 3 teaspoons baking powder
- ½ teaspoon salt
- 1 cup 2% milk
- 1 cup Oreo cookie crumbs
- **FROSTING**
- ¾ cup butter, softened
- 6 cups confectioners' sugar
- ½ teaspoon clear or regular vanilla extract
- 3 to 4 tablespoons 2% milk
  Blue and red paste food coloring
  Star sprinkles

1. Preheat oven to 350°. Line 24 muffin cups with paper or foil liners.
2. In a bowl, cream butter and sugar until crumbly. Add egg whites, one at a time, beating well after each addition. Beat in vanilla. In another bowl, whisk flour, baking powder and salt; add to creamed mixture alternately with milk, beating well after each addition. Fold in cookie crumbs.
3. Fill prepared cups two-thirds full. Bake cupcakes 20-24 minutes or until a toothpick inserted in center comes out clean. Cool in pans 10 minutes before removing to wire racks to cool completely.
4. In a large bowl, combine butter, confectioners' sugar and vanilla; beat until smooth. Add enough milk to make a stiff frosting. Remove 1 cup frosting to a small bowl; tint with blue food coloring. Divide the remaining frosting in half; tint one portion red and leave remaining portion plain.
5. Cut a small hole in the tip of a pastry bag or in a corner of a food-safe plastic bag; insert a #1M star pastry tip. Fill bag with plain frosting; pipe over nine cupcakes. With red frosting, pipe nine more cupcakes. Pipe the remaining cupcakes blue; add sprinkles. Arrange cupcakes on a platter, forming a flag.

GOOEY PEANUT BUTTER CUP BARS

I wanted a different recipe that could stand out among the numerous trays of desserts served at potlucks and parties. With a marshmallow glaze and rich peanut butter in every bite, these bars are always popular.

—CARLA BENCKERT ALBRIGHTSVILLE, PA

PREP: 15 MIN. • **BAKE:** 25 MIN. + COOLING
MAKES: 2 DOZEN

- 1 cup butter, softened
- 2 cups packed brown sugar
- 2 large eggs
- 2 teaspoons vanilla extract
- 1½ cups all-purpose flour
- 3 teaspoons baking powder
- ¼ teaspoon salt
- 2 cups miniature marshmallows
- 2 cups coarsely chopped peanut butter cups (about 10 ounces)
- 1 cup chopped walnuts or pecans

1. Preheat oven to 350 degrees. In a large bowl, cream butter and brown sugar until light and fluffy. Beat in eggs and vanilla. In a small bowl, whisk the flour, baking powder and salt; gradually add to creamed mixture, mixing well. Fold in marshmallows, chopped candies and walnuts.
2. Spread into a greased 13x9-in. baking pan. Bake 22-28 minutes or until edges begin to pull away from sides of pan and center is almost set. Cool completely in pan on a wire rack. Cut into bars. Store in an airtight container.

TOP TIP

Perfectly Sized Cupcakes

To make cupcakes of the same size, use a solid plastic ice cream scoop to measure out the batter and fill greased or paper-lined muffin cups two-thirds full. This method makes for easy work, and the tops of the cupcakes come out perfectly round. Frost cupcakes as desired or freeze for later use. Note that icing made with confectioners' sugar doesn't stand up well to freezing. For best results, freeze cupcakes and other treats unfrosted and frost them after they have thawed completely.

FIRECRACKER NAPKINS

Have a few minutes to spare before the party? Make your patriotic place settings pop with these sparkling roll-up napkins. They easily stand upright to make fun and colorful accents to your table.

MATERIALS
- **Bandanna**
- **18-in. piece of twine**
- **Firework swizzle stick**

1

FIRST, fold a bandanna in half, and then in half two more times.

2

NEXT, fold the bottom edge of the bandanna to the left.

3

STARTING with that end, roll it all the way up. Then wrap the twine around the bandanna and secure it with a knot. Finally, place a firework swizzle stick in the center.

NOTE *Any square fabric swatch works for these party napkins.*

Pizza Party

If you want to score big with the sports fans in your house, just be the quarterback of a pizza party! We have the secrets to creating fast, simple pies that bake to **cheesy, sauce-filled perfection.**

To defeat hunger in a hurry, turn to this guaranteed-to-please game plan: Start with a winning combination of adventurous pizza, then toss in a bowl brimming with crisp salad greens. And for dessert, you can't go wrong with homemade brownies or ice cream cake.

So roll out the dough, grab a handful of fresh ingredients, crank up the oven and get ready to throw an easy-as-pie party. **It's good no matter how you slice it!**

Reuben-Style Pizza (p. 230)

WHITE PIZZA WITH
ROASTED TOMATOES

WHITE PIZZA WITH ROASTED TOMATOES

I love using fresh, simple ingredients. In this economical recipe, creamy ricotta brings out the sweetness of the tomatoes, all on an onion and herb crust.

—DEBBIE ROPPOLO SAN MARCOS, TX

PREP: 45 MIN. + ROASTING • **BAKE:** 25 MIN.
MAKES: 8 SERVINGS

- 4 plum tomatoes (about 1 pound), cut lengthwise into ½-inch slices and seeded
- ¼ cup olive oil
- 1 teaspoon sugar
- ½ teaspoon salt

CRUST
- 2 tablespoons olive oil
- 1 large onion, finely chopped (about 1 cup)
- 2 teaspoons dried basil
- 2 teaspoons dried thyme
- 1 teaspoon dried rosemary, crushed
- 1 package (¼ ounce) active dry yeast
- 1 cup warm water (110° to 115°)
- 5 tablespoons sugar
- ¼ cup olive oil
- 1½ teaspoons salt
- 3¼ to 3¾ cups all-purpose flour

TOPPING
- 1 cup ricotta cheese
- 3 garlic cloves, minced
- ½ teaspoon salt
- ½ teaspoon Italian seasoning
- 2 cups (8 ounces) shredded part-skim mozzarella cheese

1. Preheat the oven to 250°. In a bowl, toss the tomatoes with oil, sugar and salt. Transfer to a greased 15x10x1-in. baking pan. Roast 2 hours or until the tomatoes are soft and slightly shriveled.

2. For crust, in a large skillet, heat oil over medium-high heat. Add onion; cook and stir 3-4 minutes or until tender. Stir in herbs. Cool slightly.

3. In a small bowl, dissolve yeast in warm water. In a large bowl, combine the sugar, oil, salt, yeast mixture and 1 cup flour; beat on medium speed until smooth. Stir in onion mixture and enough remaining flour to form a soft dough (dough will be sticky).

4. Turn dough onto a floured surface; knead until smooth and elastic, about 6-8 minutes. Place in a greased bowl, turning once to grease the top. Cover dough with plastic wrap and let rise in a warm place until almost doubled, about 1½ hours.

5. Preheat the oven to 400°. Grease a 15x10x1-in. baking pan. Punch down dough; roll to fit bottom and ½-in. up sides of pan. Cover; let rest 10 minutes. Bake 10-12 minutes or until edges are lightly browned.

6. In a small bowl, mix ricotta cheese, garlic, salt and the Italian seasoning. Spread over crust; top with roasted tomatoes and mozzarella cheese. Bake 12-15 minutes or until crust is golden and cheese is melted.

TOSSED GREEN SALAD

A simple green salad is the perfect complement to pizza. I never clutter my table with different bottles of dressing. Everyone who tastes my quick herbed version loves it.

—CAROLE HOLDER NORMAN, OK

START TO FINISH: 5 MIN. • **MAKES:** 8 SERVINGS

- 8 cups torn mixed salad greens
- 1 small cucumber, thinly sliced
- ¾ cup frozen peas, thawed
- 2 green onions, sliced
- 1 celery rib, sliced

DRESSING
- ¼ cup canola oil
- 3 tablespoons white wine vinegar
- 1 tablespoon sugar
- 1 tablespoon dried parsley flakes
- ½ teaspoon salt
- ¼ teaspoon dried oregano
- ⅛ teaspoon pepper

In a large bowl, combine the greens, cucumber, peas, onions and celery. In a bowl, whisk dressing ingredients until blended. Pour over salad; toss to coat.

FUDGY WALNUT BROWNIES

We have many great cooks in our clan, so adding to our collection of family recipes is a tradition. I came up with these moist nut-covered brownies while doing my holiday baking, but we don't need special occasions to enjoy them!

—DIANE TRUVER VALENCIA, PA

PREP: 20 MIN. • **BAKE:** 40 MIN.
MAKES: 1½ DOZEN

- ¾ cup butter, cubed
- 4 ounces unsweetened chocolate, chopped
- 4 large eggs
- 2 cups sugar
- 1 teaspoon vanilla extract
- 1 cup all-purpose flour

WALNUT CRUNCH TOPPING
- ¾ cup packed brown sugar
- ¼ cup butter, cubed
- 2 large eggs, lightly beaten
- 2 tablespoons all-purpose flour
- 1 teaspoon vanilla extract
- 4 cups chopped walnuts

1. In a microwave, melt butter and chocolate; stir until smooth. Cool slightly. In a large bowl, beat eggs and sugar; stir in the vanilla and chocolate mixture. Stir in the flour until well-blended. Pour into greased 13x9-in. baking pan; set aside.

2. For topping, in a small saucepan, combine brown sugar and butter. Cook, stir over low heat until butter is melted. Stir in the eggs, flour and vanilla until well-blended. Stir in nuts.

3. Spread evenly over brownie batter. Bake at 350° for 40-45 minutes or until a toothpick inserted near the center comes out with moist crumbs (do not overbake). Cool completely on a wire rack.

TOP TIP

Pizza Dough

Pressing pizza dough on greased pans can be a challenge. My dough usually shrinks during baking, forming some unusual shapes. I've discovered that if I make sure there's no grease on the outer edges or rim of the pan, the dough stays put and makes a nice round crust.

—MARY G. PORT ST. LUCIE, FL

REUBEN-STYLE PIZZA

I love a good Reuben sandwich and thought, "Why not make it into a pizza?" It has extra cheesy goodness in the sauce, and smells wonderful coming out of the oven.

—TRACY MILLER WAKEMAN, OH

PREP: 20 MIN. • **BAKE:** 15 MIN.
MAKES: 6 SERVINGS

- 1 tube (13.8 ounces) refrigerated pizza crust
- 4 ounces cream cheese, softened
- 1 can (10¾ ounces) condensed cheddar cheese soup, undiluted
- ¼ cup Thousand Island salad dressing
- 2 cups cubed pumpernickel bread
- 2 tablespoons butter, melted
- ½ pound sliced deli corned beef, coarsely chopped
- 2 cups sauerkraut, rinsed and well-drained
- 1½ cups (6 ounces) shredded Swiss cheese

1. Preheat the oven to 425°. Unroll and press the dough onto bottom of a greased 15x10x1-in. baking pan. Bake 6-8 minutes or until edges are lightly browned.
2. Meanwhile, in a small bowl, beat cream cheese, soup and salad dressing until blended. In another bowl, toss bread cubes with melted butter.
3. Spread cream cheese mixture over crust; top with corned beef, sauerkraut and cheese. Sprinkle with bread cubes. Bake 12-15 minutes or until crust is golden and cheese is melted.

ANTIPASTO SPINACH SALAD

A jazzed-up Italian dressing tops off this fresh-tasting medley. This salad pairs well with any pizza!

—ROXANNE CHAN ALBANY, CA

START TO FINISH: 25 MIN. • **MAKES:** 10 SERVINGS

- ⅓ cup Italian salad dressing
- 1 tablespoon dried currants
- 1 tablespoon capers, drained
- ½ teaspoon lemon-pepper seasoning
- ½ teaspoon grated lemon peel
- 6 cups fresh baby spinach
- 2 cups torn radicchio leaves
- 1 can (15 ounces) white kidney or cannellini beans, rinsed and drained
- 1 jar (7½ ounces) marinated quartered artichoke hearts, drained
- 1 small red onion, thinly sliced
- ¼ pound hard salami, finely chopped
- ½ cup cubed part-skim mozzarella cheese
- ½ cup julienned roasted sweet red pepper
- ¼ cup minced fresh parsley
- 2 tablespoons shredded Parmesan cheese

1. In a small microwave-safe bowl, combine the first five ingredients. Microwave, uncovered, on high for 30-45 seconds or until heated through.
2. In a salad bowl, combine the next nine ingredients. Drizzle with the dressing; toss to coat. Sprinkle with Parmesan cheese. Serve immediately.

GARLICKY CHICKEN PIZZA

I like to cook extra chicken for this recipe while making another meal. Just make sure the tomatoes are well-drained to keep the crust nice and crispy.

—TERI OTTE CANNON FALLS, MN

START TO FINISH: 25 MIN. • **MAKES:** 6 SERVINGS

- 1 tube (13.8 ounces) refrigerated pizza crust
- 2 tablespoons olive oil
- 2 garlic cloves, minced
- 1 can (14½ ounces) diced tomatoes, well-drained
- 1 large onion, thinly sliced (about 1 cup)
- ⅓ cup pitted kalamata olives, halved
- 2 cups cubed or shredded cooked chicken
- 1⅓ cups crumbled goat cheese
- 1 teaspoon minced fresh rosemary or ¼ teaspoon dried rosemary, crushed
- ½ teaspoon garlic salt
- ½ teaspoon pepper

1. Preheat oven to 400°. Unroll and press dough onto bottom and ½ in. up sides of a greased 15x10x1-in. baking pan. Bake 8-10 minutes or until edges are lightly browned.
2. Mix oil and garlic; brush over crust. Top with the tomatoes, onion, olives, chicken and goat cheese. Sprinkle with rosemary, garlic salt and pepper. Bake 10-12 minutes or until crust is golden.

TOP TIP

Tasty Pizza Variations

When it comes to pizza, the possibilities are endless. If you're in the mood for a fun twist or simply need a quick-to-fix recipe, give one of these variations a try. For each one, start with a store-bought unbaked pizza.

- For Pizza Joe, add a little leftover sloppy joe meat mixture, Italian seasoning and sliced mushrooms.
- For Taco Pizza, top with shredded Mexican cheese blend. After baking, add shredded lettuce, chopped tomato, sliced olives, sliced jalapeno peppers and chopped green onions. Drizzle with salsa ranch salad dressing.

- For German Sensation, add a sliced plum tomato, fennel seed, dried oregano, sauerkraut and dried basil, a sprinkle of Parmesan cheese, and a little extra mozzarella if desired.
- For Hot & Fresh, add blanched fresh sweet corn kernels and halved cherry tomatoes. After baking, drizzle with hot sauce and sprinkle with fresh basil.

SWEET POTATO
& FONTINA PIZZA

SWEET POTATO & FONTINA PIZZA

The recipe came about mainly thanks to my husband, who's a real pizza fan. And it gets nutrient-rich sweet potatoes, which I love, into a meal.

—LIBBY WALP CHICAGO, IL

PREP: 20 MIN. • **BAKE:** 15 MIN.
MAKES: 6 SERVINGS

- 1 **medium sweet potato (about 10 ounces)**
- 2 **tablespoons water**
- ¼ **teaspoon salt**
- ⅛ **teaspoon coarsely ground pepper**
- 1 **tube (13.8 ounces) refrigerated pizza crust**
- 1 **cup (4 ounces) shredded part-skim mozzarella cheese**
- 1 **cup (4 ounces) shredded fontina cheese**
- 2 **tablespoons olive oil, divided**
- 1 **teaspoon minced fresh rosemary or ¼ teaspoon dried rosemary, crushed**
- 1 **teaspoon minced fresh thyme or ¼ teaspoon dried thyme**
- ¼ **cup grated Parmesan cheese**

1. Preheat oven to 450°. Grease a 12-in. pizza pan. Peel and cut the sweet potato into ¼-in. slices. Cut each slice into ½-in.-wide strips; place in a microwave-safe dish. Add water. Microwave, covered, on high 3-4 minutes or until potato is almost tender. Drain; sprinkle with salt and pepper.

2. Unroll and press dough to fit prepared pan. If desired, pinch edge to form a rim. Sprinkle with mozzarella and fontina cheeses; drizzle with 1 tablespoon oil.

3. Top with sweet potato; sprinkle with herbs. Drizzle with remaining oil; sprinkle with Parmesan cheese. Bake on the lowest oven rack for 12-15 minutes or until crust is golden and cheese is melted.

CHERRY ICE CREAM CAKE

Pizza and ice cream? Yes, please! A friend gave me this recipe, and it's become an all-time favorite. I've substituted different cookies (macaroons or chocolate chip) or ice cream and white chocolate chips with delicious results. It takes 20 minutes to assemble and can be prepped in advance.

—KATHY KITTELL LENEXA, KS

PREP: 20 MIN. + FREEZING
MAKES: 12 SERVINGS (1¼ CUPS SAUCE)

- ⅔ **cup heavy whipping cream**
- 2 **tablespoons butter**
- 1 **package (11 ounces) milk chocolate chips**
- 1 **teaspoon vanilla extract**

ICE CREAM CAKE
- 2 **pints cherry or cherry vanilla ice cream, softened, divided**
- 3 **cups crushed shortbread cookies, divided**
- 1 **pint vanilla ice cream, softened**

1. In a small saucepan, heat cream and butter over low heat until butter is melted; remove from the heat. Add chips; let stand for 1 minute. Whisk until sauce is smooth. Stir in vanilla. Cool for 30 minutes, stirring the mixture occasionally.

2. Meanwhile, line the bottom and sides of a 9x5-in. loaf pan with plastic wrap. Spread 1 pint cherry ice cream into prepared pan; sprinkle with 1 cup cookie crumbs. Top with vanilla ice cream. Freeze 20 minutes or until firm.

3. Spread with ¾ cup chocolate sauce; freeze 20 minutes. Top with remaining cherry ice cream; sprinkle with 1 cup cookie crumbs. Cover and freeze 4 hours. Transfer remaining sauce to a microwave-safe dish; cover and refrigerate.

4. Remove the dessert from freezer 10 minutes before serving. Using plastic wrap, remove dessert from pan; discard plastic wrap. Press the remaining cookie crumbs into sides. Using a serrated knife, cut into 12 slices. Warm reserved sauce in a microwave; serve with ice cream cake.

NOTE *Reader used crisp Italian macaroons instead of shortbread cookies.*

BRAT & BACON APPETIZER PIZZA

Bacon and brats were made for each other. This pizza is slightly sweet and a little smoky, just like a good appetizer should be.

—COLLEEN VROOMAN WAUKESHA, WI

START TO FINISH: 25 MIN. • **MAKES:** 24 SERVINGS

- 1 **tube (11 ounces) refrigerated thin pizza crust**
- 4 **maple-flavored bacon strips, chopped**
- ¼ **cup finely chopped onion**
- 3 **fully cooked beer bratwurst links, finely chopped**
- ⅓ **cup apricot preserves**
- 2 **teaspoons honey mustard**
- 2 **cups (8 ounces) shredded white or yellow cheddar cheese**

1. Preheat oven to 400°. Unroll and press dough onto bottom and ½-in. up sides of a greased 15x10x1-in. baking pan. Bake 8-10 minutes or until edges are lightly browned.

2. Meanwhile, in a large skillet, cook bacon and onion over medium heat until bacon is crisp, stirring occasionally. Remove with a slotted spoon; drain on paper towels. Discard drippings. Add bratwurst to same pan; cook and stir for 2-3 minutes or until browned.

3. In a small bowl, mix preserves and mustard. Spread over crust; top with bratwurst, bacon mixture and cheese. Bake 8-10 minutes or until cheese is melted.

PEPPERONI-SAUSAGE STUFFED PIZZA

For years, friends have been telling me to open a pizzeria using this recipe. It's amazing and freezes well, too.

—ELIZABETH WOLFF CARMEL, IN

PREP: 45 MIN. + RISING
BAKE: 40 MIN. + STANDING • **MAKES:** 12 SERVINGS

- 1 package (¼ ounce) active dry yeast
- 1¼ cups warm water (110° to 115°)
- 2 tablespoons olive oil
- 1½ teaspoons salt
- 1 teaspoon sugar
- 3½ to 4 cups all-purpose flour

FILLING

- 2½ cups (10 ounces) shredded part-skim mozzarella cheese, divided
- 2½ cups (10 ounces) shredded white cheddar cheese, divided
- 2 tablespoons all-purpose flour
- 2 teaspoons dried oregano
- 2 teaspoons dried basil
- ½ teaspoon crushed red pepper flakes
- 1 pound bulk Italian sausage, cooked and crumbled
- ½ pound sliced fresh mushrooms
- 1 package (3½ ounces) sliced pepperoni
- 1 can (15 ounces) pizza sauce
  Grated Parmesan cheese, optional

1. In a small bowl, dissolve yeast in warm water. In a large bowl, combine oil, salt, sugar, yeast mixture and 1 cup of flour; beat on medium speed until smooth. Stir in enough remaining flour to form a stiff dough.

2. Turn dough onto a floured surface; knead until smooth and elastic, about 6-8 minutes. Place in a greased bowl, turning once to grease the top. Cover with plastic wrap and let rise in a warm place until doubled, about 1 hour.

3. Preheat the oven to 425°. Grease a 13x9-in. baking pan. Punch down dough; divide into three portions. On a lightly floured surface, combine two portions of dough and roll into a 15x11-in. rectangle. Transfer to prepared pan, pressing onto bottom and up sides of pan. Top with 2 cups mozzarella cheese and 2 cups cheddar cheese. Sprinkle with the flour, seasonings, sausage, mushrooms and pepperoni.

4. Roll out remaining dough into a 13x9-in. rectangle. Place dough over filling, crimping edges to seal; prick top with a fork. Sprinkle with remaining cheeses. Bake on a lower oven rack 10 minutes.

5. Reduce oven setting to 375°. Spread the pizza sauce over cheese. Bake for 30-35 minutes longer or until edges are lightly browned. Let stand 10 minutes before cutting. If desired, sprinkle with Parmesan cheese.

SALAD-TOPPED FLATBREAD PIZZAS

Put a fresh, new spin on flatbread pizza with crisp salad fixings on top. They're a nice contrast to the heartier meat and cheese ingredients. The red wine vinaigrette lends a nice zing.

—JULIE MERRIMAN SEATTLE, WA

PREP: 45 MIN. • **BAKE:** 10 MIN.
MAKES: 6 SERVINGS

- 1 pound turkey or pork Italian sausage links, casings removed
- 2 tablespoons olive oil, divided
- 2 large onions, halved and sliced
- ¼ teaspoon pepper, divided
- 6 naan flatbreads
- 1 package (8 ounces) reduced-fat cream cheese, softened
- ½ cup reduced-fat red wine vinaigrette, divided
- 1½ cups (6 ounces) shredded part-skim mozzarella cheese
- 3 cups shredded lettuce
- 1 medium cucumber, thinly sliced
- 1 large tomato, seeded and chopped
- ½ medium red onion, thinly sliced

1. In a large skillet, cook sausage over medium heat 6-8 minutes or until no longer pink, breaking into crumbles. Remove sausage with a slotted spoon; drain on paper towels. Remove the drippings from pan.

2. Preheat the oven to 425°. Heat 1 tablespoon oil in same skillet. Add onions and ⅛ teaspoon pepper; cook and stir 4-5 minutes or until softened. Reduce heat to medium-low; cook 15-20 minutes or until golden brown, stirring occasionally. Stir in sausage; remove from heat.

3. Lightly brush remaining oil on both sides of flatbreads. Place on ungreased baking sheets; bake 4-6 minutes on each side or until golden brown.

4. In a small bowl, beat cream cheese and ¼ cup vinaigrette until blended. Spread onto flatbreads; top with sausage mixture. Sprinkle with cheese. Bake 6-9 minutes or until cheese is melted.

5. Meanwhile, in a bowl, combine lettuce, cucumber, tomato and red onion. Add remaining vinaigrette and pepper; toss to coat. Divide salad among pizzas; serve immediately.

TOP TIP

Pizza Par-tay!

Hosting a game day party this year? Your bash will be super by the slice when you serve up your best homemade pie. Make it even more fun when you call your team to the table and dig into any of these trick plays.

Special Delivery. Purchase some plain pizza boxes online at **containerstore.com** (they're amazingly inexpensive), decorate them with your team's name and slide in your homemade pizzas.

Get in the team spirit by topping off your pie with mini NFL-logo helmets. Find them at **partycity.com.** Go team!

Round up the gang for some **halftime team spirit**—paper tablecloth style. Draw outlines of team logos and mascots for the kids to color.

Bowl over your guests with some add-ons. Drizzle slices with their choice of ranch dressing or hot sauce.

It's down to the wire. Time for dessert. Flatten our your favorite cookie dough on a pizza pan and bake a cookie pizza. Cool, and top with frosting and your favorite candies or sliced fruit.

SALAD-TOPPED
FLATBREAD PIZZAS

Halloween Monster Mash

The boogeyman and his monster pals have come out from under the bed to **join in the Halloween fun!** But no need to be scared silly on this night of fright. Our lineup of Frankenstein-friendly foods will please both the young and young of heart.

As guests arrive at your bash, treat them to a cup or two of bone-chilling punch to quench their thirst. Then let them **dig into your "spook-tacular" feast.** Feet-shaped meat loaves, slices of a slithering snake sub, scrumptious sweet treats and more will disappear quickly when hungry creatures' tummies start to grumble.

And there's nothing like a fun game of Pin the Eye on the Monster (page 245) to get the party jumping. **The kids will have a blast!**

Halloween Monster Cookies (p. 240) **Truffle-Filled Cupcakes** (p. 244)

**HALLOWEEN
FEET LOAF**

HALLOWEEN FEET LOAF

If Bigfoot pays a visit this Halloween, treat him to a larger-than-life meal. This "feet loaf" tastes just like your favorite home-style meat loaf. I guarantee it will have enormous appeal with believers and nonbelievers alike.

—**SUSAN SEYMOUR** VALATIE, NY

PREP: 30 MIN. • **BAKE:** 55 MIN.
MAKES: 8 SERVINGS

- 1 tablespoon canola oil
- 1 medium carrot, grated
- 1 small onion, finely chopped
- 1 celery rib, finely chopped
- ½ medium green pepper, finely chopped
- 2 cups soft bread crumbs
- 1 large egg, lightly beaten
- ½ cup 2% milk
- 1 teaspoon garlic powder
- ½ teaspoon seasoned salt
- ½ teaspoon pepper
- 2 pounds ground beef
- 1 medium carrot, cut into 10 thin slices
- ⅔ cup ketchup
- 2 tablespoons balsamic vinegar

Preheat oven to 350°. In a large skillet, heat oil over medium heat. Add carrot, onion, celery and green pepper; cook and stir 3-4 minutes or until tender. Cool slightly. Line a 15x10x1-in. baking pan with foil; grease foil. Place bread crumbs in a large bowl. Stir in egg, milk, seasonings and carrot mixture. Add beef; mix lightly but thoroughly. Shape into two feet with indentations for toes. Transfer to prepared pan. Bake, uncovered, 30 minutes. Position carrot slices on loaves for toenails. In a small bowl, mix the ketchup and the vinegar; brush half over the meat loaf. Bake for 20 minutes longer or until a thermometer reads 160°. Brush with the remaining mixture; bake 5 minutes longer.

TATER TARTS

TATER TARTS

These bite-size potato appetizers combine the tang of sour cream, the sharpness of pepper jack and the distinct flavor of cilantro to make a delectable snack that's easy to prepare.

—**SONA MASSEY** STEPHENS, AR

PREP: 20 MIN. • **BAKE:** 15 MIN.
MAKES: 2 DOZEN

- Pastry for double-crust pie (9 inches)
- 1½ pounds medium potatoes, peeled and cubed (about 4 cups)
- ½ cup sour cream
- 3 ounces cream cheese, softened
- 1 cup (4 ounces) pepper jack cheese
- 2 green onions, finely chopped
- 1 garlic clove, minced
- 1 tablespoon minced fresh cilantro
- ½ teaspoon salt
- ½ teaspoon pepper
- ¼ cup sliced ripe olives, drained

1. Preheat oven to 400°. Divide dough in half. On a lightly floured surface, roll out each pastry to a 12-in. circle. Using a 2½-in. round cookie cutter, cut out 12 circles from each pastry.

Press circles onto the bottoms and up the sides of ungreased mini-muffin cups. Prick bottoms with a fork. Bake 8-10 minutes or until lightly browned. Cool 5 minutes before removing from pans to wire racks.

2. Place potatoes in a large saucepan; add water to cover. Bring to a boil. Reduce heat; cook, uncovered, for 12-15 minutes or until tender. Drain.

3. In a large bowl, beat sour cream and cream cheese until smooth. Add potatoes; beat until light and fluffy. Beat in pepper jack cheese, onions, garlic, cilantro, salt and pepper. Spoon or pipe into tart shells; place on ungreased baking sheets. Broil 4-6 in. from heat 3-5 minutes or until potato is lightly browned. Top each with an olive slice.

PASTRY FOR DOUBLE-CRUST PIE (9 INCHES) *Combine 2½ cups all-purpose flour and ½ tsp. salt; cut in 1 cup cold butter until crumbly. Gradually add ⅓ to ⅔ cup ice water, tossing with a fork until dough holds together when pressed. Divide dough in half. Shape each into a disk; wrap in plastic wrap. Refrigerate 1 hour or overnight.*

HALLOWEEN MONSTER COOKIES

SCARY HAIRY THINGS

This is a cute and tasty version of a caramel apple. Perfect for a kid's Halloween party.
—**SALLY SIBTHORPE** SHELBY TOWNSHIP, MI

PREP: 30 MIN. • **BAKE:** 15 MIN.
MAKES: 10 SERVINGS

- 3 **tablespoons sugar**
- ½ **teaspoon ground cinnamon**
- 2½ **cups crispy chow mein noodles (about 6 ounces)**
- 2 **tablespoons butter, melted**
- 10 **small apples**
- 10 **wooden pop sticks**
- 10 **Nutter Butter cookies, halved crosswise**
- 2 **packages (14 ounces each) caramels, unwrapped**
- ¼ **cup 2% milk**
  Assorted candies and decorations: Mega and milk chocolate M&M's, black shoestring licorice, miniature semisweet chocolate chips

1. Preheat oven to 350°. In a small bowl, mix sugar and cinnamon. Place noodles in a large bowl. Drizzle with butter and sprinkle with the sugar mixture; toss to coat. Spread in a parchment paper-lined 15x10-in. baking pan. Bake 12-15 minutes or until golden brown, stirring once. Cool completely in pan on wire rack.
2. Remove and discard stems from apples; insert pop sticks into tops. Line a baking sheet with parchment paper. For feet, arrange ten pairs of cookie halves on parchment paper.
3. Place the caramels and milk in a microwave-safe bowl. Microwave, covered, on high 3 minutes, stirring once. Cool slightly. Dip each apple in caramel mixture, allowing excess to drip off. Immediately press the chow mein noodles over top and back of the apple; place apple on a pair of cookies. Decorate as desired.

HALLOWEEN MONSTER COOKIES

Don't be surprised if all the monsters come out of hiding when you assemble these fun and easy treats. My children and I made them for their classroom Halloween party one year. Their classmates loved them, and it's now a tradition to make them every year.
—**DINA CROWELL** FREDERICKSBURG, VA

START TO FINISH: 25 MIN.
MAKES: 16 MONSTER COOKIES

- 1 **can (16 ounces) chocolate frosting**
- 1 **package (13 ounces) chocolate chip cookies**
- 8 **large marshmallows**
  Mega buttons or edible candy eyeballs
  Edible black decorating marker
  White baking chips

Spoon about 1 tablespoon frosting on half of a cookie bottom; cover with another cookie, gently press together. Cut the marshmallows crosswise in half. For eyes, decorate Mega Buttons with edible marker; press into cut side of marshmallow. Place a small amount of frosting on bottom of marshmallow; press gently onto cookie. For teeth, press baking chips into frosting. Repeat.

TOP TIP

Secrets for Caramel Apples

Getting the melted caramel to successfully coat an apple can be tricky. To form a nice thick coating, wash and thoroughly dry each apple before dipping. Make sure the caramel is heated until it is melted and smooth. If the caramel "slips" off the apple, it may be too hot. Let the caramel stand a few minutes to cool and thicken before you dip it again.

SCARY HAIRY THINGS

SILLY
SNAKE SUB

SILLY SNAKE SUB

This slithering sub makes a fun and tasty centerpiece. Add your own zany, creative touches and feel free to mix and match the meat and cheeses to suit your family's tastes. You also can add breadsticks to make "legs" if you want the sub to look like a centipede.

—**LINDA OVERMAN** WICHITA, KS

PREP: 15 MIN. + RISING • **BAKE:** 15 MIN. + COOLING
MAKES: 12 SERVINGS

- 12 **frozen bread dough dinner rolls**
- ¼ **cup mayonnaise**
- 10 **slices cheddar cheese**
- ½ **pound thinly sliced deli turkey**
- ½ **pound thinly sliced deli ham**
- 2 **cups shredded lettuce**
- 1 **plum tomato, thinly sliced**
- ¼ **cup yellow mustard**
- 2 **pimiento-stuffed olives**
- 1 **2-inch piece thinly sliced deli ham, optional**

1. Arrange rolls ½ in. apart in an S-shape on a greased baking sheet. Cover with plastic wrap coated with cooking spray and let rise in a warm place until doubled, about 3 hours.
2. Preheat oven to 350°. Bake rolls 15-20 minutes or until golden brown. Cool completely on pan on a wire rack.
3. Using a serrated knife, cut rolls crosswise in half, leaving bottoms intact. Spread bun bottoms with mayonnaise. Reserve 1 cheese slice. Layer bottoms with turkey, ham, lettuce, tomato and remaining cheese. Spread mustard over bun tops; replace tops. Using a frilly toothpick, attach an olive to front of centipede for each eye. Cut remaining cheese into decorative shapes; place on back of centipede. If desired, cut a snake tongue from 2-inch piece of ham; attach to snake. Discard toothpicks before serving.

HARVEST CORN SAUTE

Kids love corn. I discovered this savory combination of flavors while trying to use up some ingredients I had on hand.

—**DIANE SATTLER** ASHEVILLE, NC

START TO FINISH: 30 MIN.
MAKES: 8 SERVINGS

- 6 **ears fresh corn on the cob or 6 cups frozen corn**
- 2 **tablespoons butter**
- 1 **cup chopped sweet onion**
- 1 **small green pepper, chopped**
- 1 **small sweet red pepper, chopped**
- ¾ **teaspoon salt**
- ¼ **teaspoon pepper**

Cut corn off the cobs. In a large skillet, heat butter over medium-high heat. Add corn, onion and peppers; cook and stir 15-20 minutes or until the vegetables are tender. Sprinkle with salt and pepper.

CREEPY CREEK PUNCH

Jeepers creepers! The murky waters in this petrifying punch may give you goosebumps, but it's so tasty and refreshing that guests will be asking for seconds. Toss in some gummy candies—fish or worms—to make it extra eerie.

—**JANNINE FISK** MALDEN, MA

START TO FINISH: 10 MIN.
MAKES: 22 SERVINGS (¾ CUP EACH)

- 4 **cups white grape juice, chilled**
- 3 **cups lemonade**
- 3 **cups prepared limeade**
- 3 **cups lemon-lime soda, chilled**
- 1 **quart lime sherbet**

In a punch bowl, combine grape juice, lemonade and limeade. Stir in soda; spoon small scoops of sherbet over the top. Stir before serving.

TOP TIP

Soggy Sandwich Solution

Spread mustard, mayonnaise, ketchup or ranch salad dressing between slices of meat or cheese instead of directly on the bread. No more soggy sandwiches!
—**SUE M.** LYONS, GA

TRUFFLE-FILLED
CUPCAKES

3. Fill prepared cups three-fourths full. Top with 2 teaspoons chocolate mixture. Bake 18-22 minutes or until the top springs back when lightly touched. Cool in pans for 10 minutes before removing to wire racks to cool completely.

4. For frosting, in a small bowl, beat butter, confectioners' sugar, vanilla and salt until smooth. Beat in melted chocolate and enough milk to reach desired consistency. Frost cupcakes. Decorate as desired.

SESAME-GARLIC PUMPKIN SEEDS

These are real nail biters! This "everything" mix of pumpkin seeds tossed with other seeds and seasonings is a fun treat for the spookiest time of the year.

—DANIELLE ULAM HOOKSTOWN, PA

PREP: 10 MIN. • **BAKE:** 35 MIN.
MAKES: 2 CUPS

- 1 large egg white
- 1 tablespoon canola oil
- 2 cups fresh pumpkin seeds
- 1 teaspoon sesame seeds
- 1 teaspoon poppy seeds
- 1 teaspoon dried minced onion
- 1 teaspoon dried minced garlic
- ¾ teaspoon kosher salt
- ½ teaspoon caraway seeds

1. Preheat oven to 325°. In a small bowl, whisk egg white and oil until frothy. Add pumpkin seeds and toss to coat. Stir in sesame seeds, poppy seeds, onion, garlic, salt and the caraway seeds. Spread in a single layer in a parchment paper-lined 15x10x1-in. baking pan.

2. Bake 35-40 minutes or until dry and golden brown, stirring every 10 minutes.

TRUFFLE-FILLED CUPCAKES

All creatures of All Hallows' Eve are sure to delight in this treat that has an unexpected surprise. These are delicious served warm. You also can use store-bought canned frosting to keep prep simple.

—BEVERLY NOWLING BRISTOL, FL

PREP: 1 HOUR + CHILLING
BAKE: 20 MIN. + COOLING
MAKES: 1½ DOZEN

- ¾ cup dark chocolate chips
- ⅓ cup heavy whipping cream
- 1 package white cake mix (regular size)
- 1¼ cups water
- 3 large egg whites
- ⅓ cup canola oil
- ½ teaspoon orange paste food coloring

FROSTING
- ½ cup butter, softened
- 3¾ cups confectioners' sugar
- 1 teaspoon vanilla extract
- ¼ teaspoon salt
- 2 ounces unsweetened chocolate, melted
- 4 to 5 tablespoons evaporated milk
   Assorted decorations: regular and Mega M&M's, Laffy Taffy, Candy Corn, Mega Buttons, Oreo Cookies, sprinkles, pretzels, marshmallows and edible pens

1. Place the chocolate chips in a small bowl. In a small saucepan, bring cream just to a boil. Pour over chocolate; let stand for 5 minutes. Cool to room temperature, stirring occasionally. Refrigerate, covered, until firm.

2. Preheat the oven to 350°. Line 18 muffin cups with paper liners. In a large bowl, combine cake mix, water, egg whites, oil and food coloring; beat on low speed 30 seconds. Beat on medium 2 minutes.

PIN THE EYE ON
THE MONSTER

DIRECTIONS

1. Cut two large circles, one slightly bigger than the other, from card stock for the body and head. Cut several smaller dots for decoration, rectangular strips for the arms and legs, a jagged piece for a mouth and a contrasting rounded rectangle for a tongue. Glue all pieces on a poster board, using photo above as a guide. Hang on a wall at a height children can reach.

2. Make one eye for each child at the party: Cut a 2½-in. white circle for the base and a 2-in. black circle for the center. Cut eyelashes from various colors of card stock. Glue all pieces together as shown. Attach a large Glue Dot on the back of each eye. To take a turn, a player is spun around, blindfolded, then tries to stick the eye on the monster. The player who gets closest to the center of the monster's head wins.

Alphabetical Index

A complete listing of all recipes in this book.